THE CAMPAIGNS OF
ALEXANDER OF TUNIS
1940–1945

THE CAMPAIGNS OF ALEXANDER OF TUNIS 1940–1945

by

Adrian Stewart

Pen & Sword
MILITARY

First published in Great Britain in 2008
and republished in this format in 2022 by
Pen & Sword Military
an imprint of
Pen & Sword Books Ltd
Yorkshire – Philadelphia

ISBN 978 1 39907 465 0

Typeset in Sabon by Phoenix Typesetting, Auldgirth, Dumfriesshire

Printed and bound in the UK by CPI Group (UK) Ltd, Croydon, CR0 4YY.

Pen & Sword Books Limited incorporates the imprints of Atlas, Archaeology,
Aviation, Discovery, Family History, Fiction, History, Maritime, Military,
Military Classics, Politics, Select, Transport, True Crime, Air World,
Frontline Publishing, Leo Cooper, Remember When, Seaforth Publishing, The
Praetorian Press, Wharncliffe Local History, Wharncliffe Transport,
Wharncliffe True Crime, White Owl and After the Battle.

For a complete list of Pen & Sword titles please contact

PEN & SWORD BOOKS LIMITED
47 Church Street, Barnsley, South Yorkshire, S70 2AS, England
E-mail: enquiries@pen-and-sword.co.uk
Website: www.pen-and-sword.co.uk
or
PEN AND SWORD BOOKS
1950 Lawrence Rd, Havertown, PA 19083, USA
E-mail: Uspen-and-sword@casematepublishers.com
Website: www.penandswordbooks.com

To the memory of Brigadier Bryan Watkins
and in recognition of his help and encouragement.

Contents

List of Maps   vii
Acknowledgements   viii
Introduction   1

Part 1 – The Saviour of Armies
1   The Corps Commander: Dunkirk   7
2   The Army Commander: Burma   24
3   The Theatre Commander: Middle East   49
4   The Army Group Commander: North Africa   74

Part 2 – The Liberator of Italy
5   Success in Sicily   105
6   Success in the South   128
7   Deadlock   154
8   Diadem   182
9   The Road from Rome   215

Conclusion   242
Bibliography   253
Index   257

Maps

1. The German Offensive, May 1940   8
2. Burma   27
3. The Desert Battleground   50
4. French North Africa   75
5. Tunisia   77
6. Sicily   106
7. Southern Italy   130
8. The Anzio Beachhead   161
9. The Battles of Cassino   167
10. Operation DIADEM –The First Stages   187
11. Operation DIADEM – The Breakout from Anzio   204
12. Northern Italy   216
13. Alexander's Final Offensive   234

Acknowledgements

My grateful thanks to: Bryan Watkins, my guide and adviser throughout; Bobby Gainher, my editor; Brigadier Henry Wilson and his team at my publishers, Pen & Sword Books Ltd.; Andrew Hewson and his team at my agents, Johnson & Alcock Ltd.; Sylvia Menzies-Earl for her help with the manuscript; Philip Fisher and the staff at the Birmingham Institute & Library and the staff of the Taylor Library for their help with the photographs. My thanks and my appreciation.

Every effort has been made to trace copyright holders but where this has proved unseccessful, sincere apologies are offered.

Introduction

Nothing ever disturbed or rattled him, and duty was a full satisfaction
in itself, especially if it seemed perilous and hard. But all this was
combined with so gay and easy a manner that the pleasure and
honour of his friendship were prized by all those who enjoyed it,
among whom I could count myself.

The officer to whom Winston Churchill was referring in that quota-
tion from *The Second World War*, was the then Lieutenant General
Sir Harold Alexander who, in the fullness of time, would become
Field Marshal the Earl Alexander of Tunis. To have gained the
friendship and respect of the man who was Britain's Prime Minister
throughout most of the greatest war in human history might seem
advantageous for a serving soldier, particularly since Churchill's
high opinion of him was shared by the majority of Alexander's
military equals and superiors. In reality it might almost be said that
the reverse was the case, for whilst it did not save Alexander from
being the recipient of harsh, unrealistic criticism from the Prime
Minister, it did ensure that he was entrusted with a whole succession of difficult tasks. Indeed few, if any, generals throughout
history can have been thrust deliberately into so many potentially
disastrous situations or emerged from them all with such credit.

That this achievement is recognized all too rarely may also be
due, in part at least, to Churchill's admiring attitude. It was perhaps
inevitable that Harold Rupert Leofric George Alexander, son of the
Earl of Caledon, married to a daughter of the Earl of Lucan,
educated at Harrow and commissioned into the Irish Guards,
should appear different and remote from the majority of his brother
officers. He never presumed upon his position, being a model of

1

courtesy and quiet good manners. Nonetheless, his instinctive air of authority, increased by striking good looks and an invariably immaculate turnout, often overawed those who did not know him well, and caused them to mistake his natural modesty and a reluctance to push himself forward for haughtiness and aloofness. When the regard and friendship of Churchill was added, there were plenty of unkind critics to imply that he owed his advancement to his connections rather than to his ability. The unfairness of that suggestion will, it is hoped, become abundantly clear in the chapters which follow.

Alexander had many interests besides his career as a soldier. In private life he was a devoted husband and father. He was an exceptional athlete, a fine cricketer and possessed a natural gift as a landscape painter which he would seek to exercise wherever he went. None of these interests, however, were allowed to interfere with his military duties. During the Italian campaign, Churchill once invited his friend to join him for a short painting holiday in Morocco, promising that if he accepted, his wife would be flown out to join them. Alexander, gently but firmly, declined to leave his post.

Even before the Second World War broke out in September 1939, Alexander's record as a fighting soldier and battlefield commander was a remarkable one. In the First World War he had commanded at every level from platoon to brigade. Twice wounded, he had won the French Legion of Honour when still a subaltern and later the DSO and MC. In 1919 he volunteered to lead a polyglot force of almost divisional size, known as the Baltic 'Landeswehr', with which he fought alongside the White Russians, inflicting a resounding defeat upon part of the Bolshevik Red Army which many years later was wryly acknowledged by Stalin.

Later Alexander commanded the Noshera Brigade of the Indian Army in operations on the North-West Frontier. This was an unusual appointment for a British service officer but Alexander proved a conspicuous success, earning the deep respect and affection of his Indian and Gurkha troops, not least because he took the trouble to master both Hindi and Urdu. At the end of his tour of duty he was appointed a Commander of the Star of India, but he gained far greater pleasure from his invitation to become Honorary Colonel of the 3rd Battalion of the 2nd Punjab Regiment.

Yet just as Churchill would feel that all his past life had been 'but a preparation' for his appointment as Premier, so Alexander's previous career seems in retrospect little more than a prelude to the campaigns which he would fight as Churchill's favourite general. The saga of those campaigns – on the beaches of Dunkirk, in the disease-infested jungles of Burma, across the deserts and mountains of North Africa, over the whole length of the rugged terrain of Italy – is one of endless problems and difficulties, political as well as military, of frequent set-backs and disappointments, but also of continuous courage and determination and, ultimately, of victory.

PART 1

The Saviour of Armies

Chapter 1

The Corps Commander: Dunkirk

It was all most peculiar. On 10 May 1940, the day that Churchill became Prime Minister, Germany's Army Group B under General Fedor von Bock had burst into the Low Countries. The Allied armies in the north of France, including Lieutenant General Lord Gort's British Expeditionary Force (BEF), had wheeled into Belgium to oppose it. They intended to advance to the River Dyle which runs northward from the neighbourhood of Namur to join the Scheldt just south of Antwerp. Here, with the river providing a natural anti-tank obstacle, backed by strong supporting positions, which the Belgians assured them had been prepared, they should be able to hold the enemy attack. By so doing, they could save northern France from invasion, protect Brussels, shorten their defensive line and incorporate the Belgian Army into their Order of Battle.

It appeared self-evident that this movement would attract the unwelcome attentions of General Albert Kesselring's Luftflotte (Air Fleet) 2, which was already actively supporting von Bock. German parachutists seized the vital Veldwezelt and Vroenhoven bridges over the Albert Canal, and German troop-carrying gliders captured Fort Eben-Emael by landing literally on top of it. German bombers pounded towns, airfields and railway junctions – though not road bridges, for the last thing they would have wanted to do was to impede the advance of their fast-moving armoured formations. No attacks, however, were made on the troops moving up to the Dyle. To some, this was not just peculiar, it was sinister. It looked almost as if their enemies welcomed the Allied advance.

They certainly did. The German attack in the west, code-named Operation SICHELSCHNITT (SICKLE CUT), had originally been conceived as, in effect, a second Schlieffen Plan, but with modern weapons, and including the occupation of Holland as well as

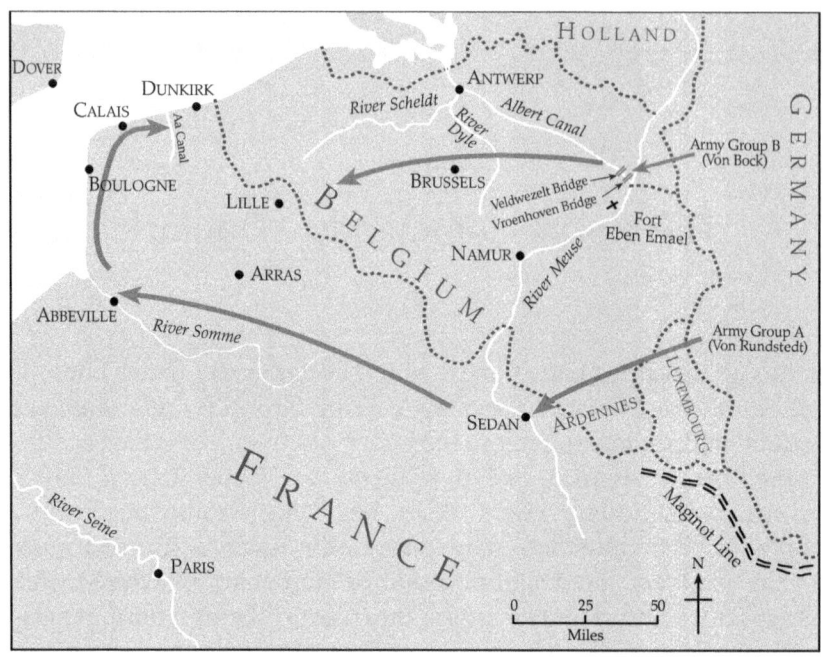

Map 1: The German Offensives May 1940

Belgium. The main assault would be delivered by Army Group B while Army Group A, under General Gerd von Rundstedt, backed by General Hugo Sperrle's Luftflotte 3, covered von Bock's southern flank. Meanwhile, Army Group C, under General von Leeb, would watch the Maginot Line. It was rather an obvious plan – so much so that the Allies had anticipated it. Years before the war, the French had envisaged just such a move, and the consequent need to counter it by an advance to the Dyle – one reason why the Maginot Line had not been extended along their frontier with Belgium. The German dictator Adolf Hitler, whose famous intuition was by no means always wrong, was uneasily aware that this might be the case. As early as 11 November 1939, he ordered the strengthening of von Rundstedt's motorized units with a view to their delivering a secondary strike across the Meuse in support of von Bock's main offensive.

General Erich von Manstein, von Rundstedt's Chief of Staff, was convinced that the existing plan would not achieve surprise, and agreed that von Bock should invade Holland and Belgium, but only as a diversion. The main blow, he urged, should be struck by Army Group A which should move through the Ardennes – difficult country, so unlikely to be well defended – cross the Meuse near Sedan, then head northward towards the sea, for which purpose it should be given the bulk of the German armour. If any Allied troops had pushed into Belgium to engage von Bock, as von Manstein was sure they would do, they must automatically be cut off by von Rundstedt's advance.

The 'Manstein Plan' received the eager approval of both von Rundstedt and the Panzer expert General Heinz Guderian, but not that of the German Commander-in-Chief, General von Brauchitsch, his Chief of Staff, General Halder, or the Army High Command – Oberkommando des Heeres (OKH) – as a whole. OKH not only rejected it but did not bother to forward it for consideration by the Supreme Command of all the German armed forces – Oberkommando der Wehrmacht (OKW) – which meant, in practice, Hitler.

Though von Manstein reiterated his views at every possible opportunity, he had made no impression on OKH when, in early January 1940, a German aeroplane, losing its way in bad weather, force-landed in Belgium. Documents seized by Belgian Intelligence revealed the details of the planned assault on the Low Countries and confirmed the Allies' forecasts.

In his book *Dunkirk: Anatomy of Disaster*, Patrick Turnbull puts forward the fascinating suggestion that the crash-landing was secretly ordered by Hitler to force a change of strategy, thereby achieving 'one of the most brilliant, and certainly one of the most successful examples of deception in the annals of warfare'. Hitler was a past master in the art of deception and undoubtedly already had anxieties about the transparency of the existing plan. Yet if the incident had been a ruse, surely Hermann Göring, as head of the Luftwaffe, must have known this and would not have been concerned by it. In fact, he reacted with fury to the breach of security involved – so much so that he dismissed the commander of Luftflotte 2, General Felmy, replacing him with the redoubtable Albert Kesselring. Guderian knew nothing of the supposed ruse either; he would later record that 'an aeroplane accident compelled our masters to abandon the Schlieffen Plan'.

Then on 27 January, Halder, increasingly exasperated by von Manstein's importunities, attempted to get him out of the way by promoting him to a command in eastern Germany. Before taking up his new appointment, however, on 10 February von Manstein called to pay his respects to his Führer, as was customary in such cases. He seized this opportunity to put forward his ideas and, to his delight, Hitler adopted them with enthusiasm so that when the BEF moved forward to the Dyle, it was marching into a carefully prepared trap.

Among the formations at risk was the (British) 1st Division, commanded by the youngest major general in the Army, Harold Alexander. He, like most of his men, was delighted to be taking positive action after a very severe French winter, spent constructing fortifications which everyone knew would be abandoned on the outbreak of active hostilities. As the units of the BEF moved up, they were greeted with grateful enthusiasm by the Belgian people and showered with flowers.

On reaching the Dyle, however, Alexander's satisfaction swiftly evaporated, though he took care not to make this apparent to those under his command. The Belgians had been so anxious to offer no provocation to Hitler that they had not even allowed the British or French to study their planned defence line. When the Dyle was reached, it was found to be much less of an obstacle than had been believed and its far bank could easily be approached undetected through thickly wooded country. As for the defensive positions supposed to guard the river, these were a figment of the Belgians' optimistic imagination.

It very soon became clear that the Germans' brutally efficient onslaught, understandably enough, was already proving too much for the Dutch and Belgian Armies. The former capitulated on 15 May, while the latter was thrown back in considerable disarray, allowing von Bock to reach the Dyle much sooner than had been anticipated. At the same time, the First French Army on the right of the BEF came under heavy pressure. It is now known that the Germans had planned to deliver a major attack on the 17th, of which the principal target would have been Alexander's 1st Division. That Alexander was at least spared that ordeal was solely due to the fact that the second part of the 'Manstein Plan' was already proceeding apace.

By the afternoon of 13 May the infantry units of Army Group

A, having successfully pushed through the 'impassable' Ardennes, were preparing to cross the Meuse under the gaze of von Rundstedt in person. Although he had been unable to bring up his heavy artillery, the attack was preceded by a tremendous barrage from the Germans' 'flying field guns', some 200 of the hideous Junkers Ju 87 Stuka dive-bombers, which were fitted with screaming sirens to heighten their already terrifying effect. These inflicted surprisingly little material damage but morally they proved decisive, breaking the defenders' will to resist and ensuring that no counter-attack was ever attempted.

By nightfall on the 15th, all von Rundstedt's tanks were across the Meuse as well – General von Kleist's Panzer Group which contained three Panzer divisions under Guderian, and two under General Reinhardt, and a separate Panzer Corps of two more divisions led by General Hoth. With the Luftwaffe ranging ahead of them to pounce on any opposition, all the armour raced north-westward for the Channel coast, which they reached near Abbeville on the 21st; they then turned due north to capture the ports in the area. Cut off from the main French forces and under increasing pressure from Army Group B, the BEF, like the rest of the northern Allied armies, fell back from the Dyle on the night of 16/17 May. The retreat to Dunkirk had begun.

At this time Alexander's 1st Division formed part of I Corps, commanded by Lieutenant General Michael Barker who was not a superior in whom Alexander placed a great deal of confidence. Neither did Lieutenant General Alan Brooke, who was then commanding II Corps. He considered Barker a gallant officer but lacking the physical strength and mental resilience needed to cope with such a critical situation. Indeed, the strain soon robbed Barker of the ability to sleep, leaving him so exhausted that he was unable to issue clear orders or even follow an agreed line of action without constant changes of mind.[1]

Realizing that his fellow Corps Commander had problems, Brooke, with the connivance of Alexander's senior staff officer, Brigadier William Morgan, relieved him of part of his burden by taking 1st Division under his command on 18 May. It remained under Brooke's direction until the early hours of the 24th when it reverted to I Corps. 'I was very sorry to lose Alex,' Brooke noted in his diary.

It was during this brief but dramatic period that Brooke formed an appreciation of Alexander which appears in Sir Arthur Bryant's *The Turn of the Tide 1939–1943*. This is made the more interesting by Brooke's comparison of Alexander with Major General Bernard Law Montgomery, then in command of the 3rd Division, which was also part of II Corps. It has been quoted frequently, though not always to Alexander's advantage:

> In taking over the 1st Division I was for the first time having the experience of having Alexander working under me. It was a great opportunity . . . to see what he was made of, and what an admirable commander he was when in a tight place. It was intensely interesting watching him and Monty during those trying days, both of them completely imperturbable and efficiency itself, and yet two totally different characters. Monty with his quick brain for appreciating military situations was well aware of the very critical situation that he was in, and the very dangers and difficulties that faced us acted as a stimulus on him; they thrilled him and put the sharpest of edges on his military ability. Alex, on the other hand, gave me the impression of never fully realising all the very unpleasant potentialities of our predicament. He remained entirely unaffected by it, completely composed, and appeared never to have the slightest doubt that all would come right in the end.

As regards Montgomery, that assessment was correct. From the moment that he brought his men to the Dyle with such swift efficiency that the Belgians opened fire on them, thinking they must be a German parachute unit,[2] until the time when he succeeded Brooke in command of II Corps, Montgomery justified the note made by his superior in his diary: 'I thanked heaven to have a commander of his calibre.'

This comment was made on 27 May, at which time the Belgian Army was rapidly disintegrating – it capitulated next day – as a result of which a gap was opening on the left of the British front. To fill this Brooke had to withdraw Montgomery's 3rd Division from an exposed position; it then had to cross behind a sector where fierce fighting was taking place to new positions on the BEF's left – all this, moreover, during the hours of darkness. Brooke for once was unable to conceal his anxiety from his staff, but next morning 'with a feeling of intense relief' he found that Montgomery 'had, as usual, accomplished almost the impossible'.

Neither Alexander nor anyone else could match this achievement during the retreat, but the commander of 1st Division was certainly not found wanting. On 18 May, for instance, a premature withdrawal by I Corps made the right flank of II Corps dangerously vulnerable, but Alexander immediately took action to counter the threat and was able to retire in good order, although with the loss of a considerable amount of materiel. Similarly, the crucial 27 May saw Major General Harold Franklyn's 5th Division being heavily attacked by superior numbers, and Brooke was eager to stiffen its resistance with three of Alexander's battalions, including 3rd Battalion, Grenadier Guards, which had been withdrawn into reserve. The 1st Division was back in I Corps by this time, but Brooke, with Barker's consent, drove to Alexander's Headquarters near Lille to request the immediate move forward of these units.

'Alexander, as I expected, cooperated at once, and these three battalions played a great part in restoring the situation on the right of the 5th Division front.'

Nor was the suggestion that Alexander was not fully aware of the 'unpleasant potentialities of our predicament', in any way well founded. The contrast between him and Montgomery arose not from a different appreciation of the situation but from a different reaction to it, arising from different temperaments. All accounts confirm Brooke's belief that the extroverted, self-confident Montgomery was exhilarated by the experience. Captain George Stevens-Guile, who commanded HMS *Codrington*, the destroyer that carried Montgomery to England, would later state that his passenger was 'the coolest customer' he had ever met; he appeared to be 'in his seventh heaven', showing intense interest in the Luftwaffe's tactics, on which he kept up a running commentary.

Alexander possessed a quieter, more restrained self-confidence. His great strength was his ability to radiate calm serenity. Perhaps he was not really certain that 'all would come right in the end', but he was sure it was his duty to give such an impression with complete conviction. By adopting this pose, he automatically checked any tendency to panic, reassured the doubters, confirmed the optimism of the resolute – and thereby increased the possibility that every-thing might indeed 'come right' after all.

Gort's staff had first drawn up a plan for the withdrawal of the BEF to Dunkirk on 18 May. Two days later, orders were given for the evacuation by sea of line of communications troops, personnel of the Royal Army Pay Corps and soldiers who were sick or had been wounded. By the 26th, nearly 28,000 men had left – a fore-taste of the greater achievement still to come.

The French High Command, to which Gort was officially subor-dinate, had no objection to this action, but they certainly never intended that the entire BEF should be evacuated. Their initial anticipation was that the BEF, together with the French formations in the north, would strike southwards against the outflanking German units, while the main French forces thrust northwards to meet them. The two parts of the Allied command would thus be reunited and the panzers in their turn cut off and isolated.

Orders on these lines were issued on 20 May by General Weygand, once the Chief of Staff to Marshal Foch, who had replaced General Gamelin as the French Supreme Commander on the previous day. Unhappily the chances of success for the 'Weygand Plan' as it was called, were already very doubtful and in practice the efforts of the French in the south were never properly coordinated and had little effect.

In the north, the British mounted a thrust south of Arras on 21 May. It was delivered by only three battalions of infantry supported by seventy-four infantry (or 'I') tanks of the 4th and 7th Battalions, Royal Tank Regiment, the commanding officers of both of which were killed in the battle. The attack, under the overall control of Major General Franklyn, achieved complete surprise and advanced some 10 miles, inflicting considerable casualties and causing a great deal of confusion. Sadly, though, so small a force could not hope to do more than check the German advance, and by early evening, Franklyn had wisely ordered his men back to their start line. Two days later, Gort withdrew all his troops from Arras, by then in imminent danger of encirclement.

Yet Franklyn's limited success would have momentous conse-quences. His blow had fallen mainly on 7th Panzer Division, and its commander, a certain Major General Erwin Rommel, who was always apt to exaggerate when attacked resolutely, estimated that he was opposed by five infantry divisions, together with 'hundreds' of tanks!

Rommel's reports naturally alarmed von Rundstedt, who had already received warnings from other subordinates, notably von Kleist and the commander of the German Fourth Army, General von Kluge, that the armour was getting dangerously far ahead of its supporting infantry. Accordingly, on the evening of 23 May, he issued instructions that the tanks should halt on the line of the Aa Canal while the infantry closed up. That this halt was intended only to be temporary is shown by the fact that both Guderian and Reinhardt later resumed their march, gaining bridgeheads across the canal.

However, in the mid-morning of the 24th, Hitler visited von Rundstedt's headquarters where he stated emphatically that the armour should be conserved for future operations. That evening he instructed OKH to forbid the armour to advance beyond the Aa Canal. Although undoubtedly influenced by the caution prevailing in Army Group A, the decision was entirely Hitler's, and it is significant that he did not once attempt to answer protests at OKH by claiming the support of the highly respected von Rundstedt.

There were, in fact, perfectly adequate military reasons for the Führer's decision. It must not be forgotten that the destruction of the northern Allied armies was only the first part of the German plan of conquest. The next stage would be a thrust over the Somme towards Paris, leading to the ultimate surrender of France – which, in turn, Hitler fondly believed, would cause Britain to abandon the struggle as well. For this move, tanks would be vital; so it is hardly surprising that Hitler was much concerned over mounting losses which by 26 May had put 50 per cent of von Rundstedt's panzers out of action. Tanks were also having to be diverted to deal with garrisons in Boulogne and Calais which, though isolated, were still resisting valiantly, while the area around Dunkirk was, in any case, unsuitable for armoured warfare since it was criss-crossed with canals.

Hitler had therefore concluded that it would be best to preserve his tanks for future use, leaving the destruction of the encircled Allies to von Bock's infantrymen – and, as Halder noted in his diary, to the Luftwaffe. On the evening before Hitler visited von Rundstedt – the timing is surely important – Göring had telephoned to 'guarantee unconditionally' that he would prevent the escape of a single British soldier. A note in Army Group A's War Diary confirms that pressure in the Dunkirk area would, it was considered, only restrict 'the activity of the Luftwaffe'. It was by no means the last time that Hitler would have reason to regret having relied on the promises of the man whom he would shortly promote to the unique rank of Reichsmarschall, with a special king-sized baton to prove it.

While the triumphant Germans debated over the best way to complete their victory, the defeated British were taking action. On 26 May, despite French protests, Gort, on his own initiative – though prompt approval was forthcoming from London – decided that the 'Weygand Plan' was no longer practicable. His only proper course, he was certain, was to withdraw to Dunkirk, the one remaining port available to him, form a defensive perimeter and get as many troops as possible away over the Channel.

The BEF's retirement was hampered by thousands of refugees, aerial bombing, the surrender of the Belgian Army and pressure from Army Group B. Fortunately, as already described, sturdy resistance and fine generalship, particularly by Brooke, Alexander and Montgomery, ensured that von Bock was unable to break through on one flank. On the other, the Royal Navy had rescued the bulk of the defenders of Boulogne by the early hours of 24 May. The Calais garrison surrendered on the 26th but only after gaining vital time for the Dunkirk defences to be strengthened. As a result, when Guderian toured the forward positions two days later, he considered that 'further tank attacks would involve useless sacrifice of our best troops', that infantry were 'more suitable than tanks for fighting in this kind of country', and that his armoured divisions should be withdrawn to refit. Since he was then only 8 miles from Dunkirk harbour, his decision suggests that Hitler's earlier appreciation had not been as far wide of the mark as is usually believed.

In the south of the Allied salient, where the terrain was favourable for tanks, the Germans pressed on to Lille, cutting off part of the French First Army on 28 May. This fought on until the evening of the 31st when, short of food and with ammunition exhausted, it was compelled to surrender. Yet, by containing large numbers of German troops, its gallant resistance had finally ensured that the remainder of the northern Allied forces were able to make good their retreat to the Dunkirk perimeter.

Alexander personally entered the perimeter late on the 28th. Unlike many of the fugitives who had reached Dunkirk earlier or many of the stragglers who came in later, his 1st Division was still an organized fighting unit, its Grenadier Guards battalion, as might have been expected, setting a splendid example – as for that matter did the Divisional Commander.

Such an example was urgently needed. It must be recorded with regret that the early days of the evacuation witnessed many shameful cases of a complete breakdown of military discipline: of troops looting stores of alcohol; of men screaming, weeping, howling dementedly; and of officers being threatened by groups of armed soldiers who no longer recognized their authority. The first task of all the senior British commanders was to re-establish firm control.

Happily, they succeeded. Even after the main body of the BEF had come to Dunkirk, some individuals inevitably broke under the strain but they were the exceptions to a general rule. Order was restored, defences organized to keep the enemy at bay and plans for the withdrawal by sea put in hand.

Alexander's poise made him the ideal man to restore shattered morale, and it was reinforced by his immaculate appearance which in itself helped to build confidence.[3] He had been forced to abandon his car with most of his personal equipment some way from the perimeter because all roads were hopelessly congested. His 'sole remaining possessions' he would afterwards claim, were 'my revolver, my field glasses and my brief case'. Others have added a spare uniform to that list.

This impressive appearance gave added weight to Alexander's orders which were clear, firm, always sensible, occasionally inspired. It was Alexander who directed that vehicles which were blocking the roads to the front line and which in any case would have to be left behind, should be pushed into the ditches. It was also Alexander who found a more constructive use for the abandoned lorries. The beaches at Dunkirk sloped very gradually down to the sea and small boats from the vessels offshore could only reach the troops after these had waded out for long distances; it then took a considerable time to get them on board. Alexander's solution was to arrange for trucks to be driven into the water as far as possible, nose to tail. Planks were then lashed to their roofs to form a continuous pier, from the end of which the soldiers were able to pass directly into the ships' whalers.

With discipline restored, the Royal Navy, supported by the French Navy, the Merchant Navy and the civilian volunteers – the famous 'little ships' – was able to conduct the evacuation more successfully than anyone had dared to hope. Nonetheless, it was clear that the perimeter could not be held indefinitely and a time would come when the troops not yet embarked would have to surrender. Not wishing the enemy to capture the BEF's commander, and well aware that Gort would not leave voluntarily while a single one of his men remained on the beaches, Churchill sent express orders on 30 May that once Gort's effective fighting strength had been reduced to three divisions, he should hand over responsibility to a corps commander and return to England.

Churchill clearly envisaged that the corps commander selected would in due course be forced to capitulate. The War Diary of Gort's General Headquarters confirms that Gort also considered surrender 'the more probable contingency'. Since I Corps was scheduled as the last to be evacuated, Gort nominated Barker to take his place 'and if and when the time came, to arrange . . . the terms of capitulation'.

This was not a step which appealed to Montgomery, who had been present at the conference where the decision was made, having taken over II Corps after Brooke had been recalled home. When the meeting broke up, he asked Gort for a word in private and, with typical effrontery, gave his own opinion of the correct action needed. As he describes it in his *Memoirs*:

> I then said it was my view that Barker was in an unfit state to be left in final command; what was needed was a calm and clear brain, and that given reasonable luck such a man might well get I Corps away, with no need for *anyone* to surrender. He had such a man in Alexander, who was commanding the 1st Division in Barker's corps. He should send Barker back to England at once and put Alexander in command of the I Corps. I knew Gort very well; so I spoke very plainly and insisted that this was the right course to take.

Gort, to his credit, accepted the advice. He must have had some qualms, for he considered Alexander his most able subordinate and had already told Barker, according to the GHQ War Diary, that he 'was very anxious that General Alexander should be sent home if possible', so as to avoid any risk of his capture. Nonetheless, on the morning of 31 May, Alexander received orders to take over I Corps.

Montgomery's recommendation, coming from the most ruthlessly realistic officer at Dunkirk, was a considerable compliment – but no one could have blamed Alexander if it was a far from welcome one. The longer the evacuation lasted, the more dangerous the situation in the perimeter would inevitably become – but quite apart from that, Alexander's appointment coincided with an improvement in tactics on the part of his enemies and an increase in problems in his dealings with his allies.

Göring's belief that he could destroy the trapped Allied armies was not shared by his own subordinates. Even Kesselring, an incorrigible optimist, whose nickname was 'Smiling Albert', considered the task was impossible. Yet the Luftwaffe would almost certainly have caused far greater damage than it did, had it not been for two main factors.

The Royal Air Force was not popular with its sister services during or immediately following the Dunkirk evacuation. In an attempt to provide continuous protection, Fighter Command flew standing patrols, some of which encountered no enemy at all, while others found overwhelming numbers of German aircraft, by now mustered on nearby French airfields, bursting past them to assault the beaches.[4] These clashes also cost the Command 106 machines and although 132 German warplanes failed to return – some of them the victims of AA fire – the much larger Luftwaffe was better able to afford such casualties. But even so, the achievements of the defending fighters had been considerable. Time and again they had forced the enemy raiders to turn back or to jettison their bombs at random in hurried evasive action: in short, they had prevented the Germans from concentrating on their objective.

In addition though, the Luftwaffe directed far too much effort for far too long against the men on the beaches, only to find that the soft sand deadened the effects of the bomb blasts to a surprising extent. Unhappily, its leaders realized their error just at the moment when Alexander took command of the BEF. On 1 June the Germans delivered an all-out assault on the rescuing vessels, sinking eleven ships, including four British or French destroyers, and forcing Admiral Ramsay, in charge of the operation, to prohibit future evacuation in daylight.

Even this failed to daunt Alexander. He anticipated that many of the wounded could not be rescued, taking the hard decision to detail the numbers of medical personnel, both officers and other ranks, who were to stay with them, but he never, for an instant, accepted a general surrender as a probable, or indeed possible contingency. When Captain William Tennant, Ramsay's liaison officer, wondered aloud how a capitulation was conducted, Alexander coldly observed that he had never had to capitulate in the past and left no one in any doubt that he had not the slightest intention of doing so in the future either.

Gort's written orders had told Alexander to 'assist our French allies in the defence of Dunkirk', and to 'occupy yourself with arrangements for the evacuation of the Force under your command'. In the performance of these duties he was to act in collaboration with and under the instructions of Admiral Jean Abrial, the supreme French commander at Dunkirk (to whom the French military leaders were subordinate), but 'should any orders which he may issue to you be likely, in your opinion, to imperil the safety of the Force under your command, you should make an immediate appeal to His Majesty's Government, through the Secretary of State for War' (Mr Anthony Eden).

These directions clearly envisaged that Dunkirk should be defended solely for the purpose of allowing as many soldiers as possible to escape – French as well as British, for Alexander was advised that it was 'important that the troops of the French Army should share in such facilities for evacuation as may be provided by HM Government.' Alexander also spoke on the telephone to the War Office before leaving Gort's Headquarters and, as he would later state, was notified that 'my duty was to hold the Dunkirk area as long as possible provided the safety of the BEF was not imperilled'. And finally, Captain Tennant would report that 'General Alexander . . . was told by Lord Gort in my hearing that he was to do nothing to imperil his army and was ultimately responsible for their safety and evacuation.'

In contrast, the French High Command still hoped to hold Dunkirk not as an evacuation port but as a permanent, if besieged, fortress on the flank of the German advance southwards, which might have a crippling effect, just as a besieged Tobruk would later do on Rommel's advance in North Africa. Abrial, it appears, was never sent any instructions to the contrary, with the result that the French Navy's contribution to the rescue work was belated, the retirement of French forces to Dunkirk was slow and, as should not be forgotten, it was French soldiers who defended the perimeter. To complicate matters still further, Tennant confirms that Gort, before his departure, had assured Abrial that Alexander 'would assist in holding the perimeter for the French to embark'. Meanwhile, in Paris, Churchill was uttering wild promises that the rearguard covering the evacuation would be provided by the three remaining British divisions.

On reporting to Abrial therefore, Alexander soon realized that he had been placed in 'a terrible position'. The Admiral insisted that he understood that 'only specialists, technicians etc. were being evacuated, and the troops were to remain'. Alexander could only repeat that he had had no such orders; his understanding was that he must get his men away as soon as possible, though he would provide every facility to help the French to escape with them. Since his attitude appeared so different from that of Gort and Churchill, it is perhaps not surprising, though it is most unfair, that in many French accounts Alexander has been bitterly criticized and his actions widely resented.

It seemed to Alexander that Abrial's requirements did 'imperil the safety' of the Force under his command and he therefore had no alternative but to contact London as envisaged by Gort's directions. He was able to talk to Eden just before all communications were cut. Eden, who had heard nothing from Churchill in Paris, ordered him to withdraw 'as rapidly as possible on a 50–50 basis with the French Army' – which Alexander took to mean 'equal numbers of French and British soldiers from that time on'.

When Alexander advised Abrial of his instructions, his nominal superior accepted with commendable dignity that 'no other plan was possible', but Alexander now had to take another agonizing decision. Because the bulk of the troops embarked hitherto had been from the BEF, there were now six times more French than

British in the perimeter. Gort's promises had led Abrial to believe that, with evacuation now inevitable, it would proceed on a proportional basis: out of every seven men taken off in future, six would be French. This had not been the sense of Eden's message, however, and Alexander concluded that his duty to his country must take priority. He would save as many Frenchmen as possible but not one unwounded British soldier would be left behind if he could prevent it.

By the night of 2/3 June, Alexander had gone far towards achieving both his aims. During his period of command, 98,000 Frenchmen had been carried to safety, and now the BEF's last soldiers, the men of 1st Battalion, King's Shropshire Light Infantry, were taken onto the waiting destroyers or personnel ships. Alexander, Tennant and a small party then entered a motorboat in which they patrolled the beaches and harbour to make certain that no British troops had been left behind. Only when he was convinced that all had been embarked, did Alexander condescend to board a destroyer himself at 0200, reaching Dover safely at daybreak.

The First French Army kept up its gallant resistance all through 3 June. That night, the Royal Navy rescued over 26,000 more men, including Admiral Abrial, before shells falling on the harbour compelled the last vessel to withdraw at 0340 on the 4th. The Germans finally pushed into Dunkirk next morning. At 1030 the rearguard surrendered and over 30,000 French troops passed into captivity.

It will have become clear that the bulk of the BEF was saved from a similar fate by a combination of many factors and that many people could claim a share of the credit for what Churchill would call 'The Deliverance of Dunkirk'. Even so, Alexander must be entitled to particular praise. His actions and his attitude during the retreat to the perimeter and in the early days of the evacuation were valuable enough, but he rose to his greatest height in the appallingly difficult and dangerous period when he commanded I Corps. 'The last minute decision to replace Barker by Alexander,' declares Patrick Turnbull – who served throughout the Dunkirk campaign, being awarded a Military Cross – 'saved a very considerable number of lives.' 'Alex got everyone away in his own calm and confident manner,' was Montgomery's verdict.

'Alex' had made his reputation and won the admiration and respect of Churchill and Eden – but had he been able to foresee the future, he would have known that his troubles had only just begun.

Notes:
1. It is worth recalling that the accumulated tension of the retreat was such that Brooke himself, though renowned as a reserved, hard, self-controlled man, broke down and burst into tears just before leaving for England aboard the destroyer HMS *Worcester*.
2. Fortunately, the misunderstanding was quickly resolved at the cost of one unlucky soldier badly wounded.
3. Richard Collier, in his anecdotal *The Sands of Dunkirk*, tells a delightful if probably exaggerated story of an exasperated soldier storming up to Alexander to say, 'You look like a big brass hat – perhaps you can tell me where we get a boat for England?' Other officers present were not amused but Alexander gave calm directions, to be rewarded with the grateful assurance that he was the 'best pal' the soldier had ever had.
4. It did not help to improve relations that every aeroplane sighted was automatically considered hostile. When Flight Lieutenant Sir Archibald Hope of 601 Squadron, who was making his way home via Dunkirk after being shot down, assured a high-ranking army officer that the aircraft the soldiers were reviling were in fact RAF Hurricanes, he was simply disbelieved. 'But we've seen lots of those,' the officer protested indignantly.

Chapter 2

The Army Commander: Burma

The fires of war spread relentlessly across the globe. In 1940, the Italian dictator, Benito Mussolini, entered the conflict and North Africa, East Africa and the Middle East were added to the combat zones. In 1941, so was Russia. By early 1942, there was fighting in the Pacific, Indian, Arctic and Southern Oceans, and the Atlantic as far west as the Caribbean and the eastern seaboard of the United States; while in South-East Asia, the British faced the onslaught of a new and formidable foe.

When hostilities with Japan exploded, in December 1941, the armed services, which Britain had so neglected in the years before 1939, had been fighting both Germany and Italy for some eighteen months, single-handedly for most of the time. It was perhaps inevitable, therefore, that British possessions in the Far East should have remained totally unprepared to receive the blows which were now rained upon them. The Japanese attack on Pearl Harbour, by bringing the United States into the war, would ensure the Allies' ultimate triumph, but it could do nothing to alter a catastrophic sequence of events that would result in the destruction of the British Empire.

By mid-February 1942, the Japanese had taken Hong Kong, Malaya, Singapore and the long southern 'tail' of Burma, and Lieutenant General Thomas Hutton, commanding the Burma Army, believed that the loss of the Burmese capital, Rangoon, was a distinct possibility. As early as 22 January, his chief administrative officer, Major General Goddard, had begun to transfer three-quarters of all reserve stocks of fuel and petrol northward to depots in the vicinity of Mandalay. Though Hutton's pessimistic attitude did not find favour with the Commander-in-Chief, India, General Sir Archibald Wavell, whose Chief of Staff Hutton had previously been, the movement, which was completed in early March, would later help to save the Burma Army from total destruction.

It would not, however, save Hutton. On 19 February, Alexander was informed by General Sir Alan Brooke, now Chief of the Imperial General Staff, that he had been appointed to command the Burma Army with the local rank of full general in place of the luckless Hutton who, to his own distress, would remain in Burma for another month as his successor's chief staff officer. Brooke made it very clear to Alexander that the situation in Burma was extremely serious. Vice Admiral Lord Louis Mountbatten, Chief of Combined Operations, went so far as to warn Alexander that there was no possibility of holding Burma, let alone Rangoon. Churchill for his part considered that he had never 'taken the responsibility for sending a general on a more forlorn hope'. When he dined with the new leader of the Burma Army, shortly before the latter's departure to the Far East, Churchill wrote that 'Alexander was, as usual, calm and good-humoured', saying he was 'delighted to go', but the Prime Minister confessed that he 'found it difficult to emulate' his guest's 'composure'.

Alexander's difficulties and dangers began before he ever reached Burma. We are accustomed from reading about Churchill's wartime journeys to visualize important personages travelling in some comfort on warships, great liners or luxurious flying boats. Admittedly, Churchill's historic flight to Cairo and on to Moscow in August 1942 was made in a converted Liberator bomber which lacked heating, but at least he had plenty of blankets and a shelf on which he could sleep. He also had an escort of four Beaufighters during the most dangerous part of the trip. How different the experience of Churchill's general was is revealed in *With Alex at War* by Major Sir Rupert Clarke, Alexander's Australian ADC.

The first part of the journey was also made in a Liberator but, since this one had not been converted, Alexander and Clarke had to travel in its bomb-bay. Their aircraft was unescorted, so flew at a height of some 20,000 feet, where the cold was so intense that icicles formed on the mouth pieces of the oxygen masks they were forced to wear. A wide detour was made over the Bay of Biscay to avoid German interceptors; Spanish AA guns fired at them, happily without effect; and they then made for Cairo, this time at very low level to prevent detection. At Cairo they transferred to a Dakota which had been converted, but only so as to carry an enormous extra fuel tank which all but filled the fuselage. This most reliable of aeroplanes then suffered engine trouble which compelled it to land on a beach in the Persian Gulf. Fortunately the Dakota's two pilots were accompanied by a mechanic who, after some anxious hours, rectified the fault, enabling Alexander to proceed to Delhi and thence to Calcutta which he reached on 3 March.

Neither the discouragement that had preceded his new appointment, nor the difficulties that had accompanied his flight, appear to have affected Alexander's remarkable mental resilience in any way. This, though, was to be tested still further on his arrival in India, as the chilling responsibilities with which he was faced became increasingly obvious.

Alexander, in fact, had hardly been notified of his appointment to command the Burma Army before a critical situation became an impossible one. First, the Australian Government, fearful that their country would be subjected to a Japanese invasion – which in reality had not been and never would be planned – ignored Churchill's pleas to divert 7th Australian Division, then being shipped home from the Middle East, to Rangoon. Next, in Burma, a typical battlefield misunderstanding – for which the Divisional Commander, who took full responsibility, was dismissed – resulted in the destruction of a vital bridge over the Sittang River on 23 February, cutting off the retreat of 17th Indian Division, which was so mauled in consequence that it temporarily ceased to be an effective fighting force.

It was fortunate that Lieutenant General Shojiro Iida, commanding Japan's Fifteenth Army, was compelled to pause at this stage: his men who had advanced more than 200 miles in just over a month along rough jungle tracks without proper supply facilities simply had to be rested and his stocks of ammunition which had fallen dangerously low had to be replaced. Nonetheless it was clear that it was only a matter of time before the Japanese poured over the Sittang. The river flows into the Gulf of Martaban, which bites deeply into the south coast of Burma, and

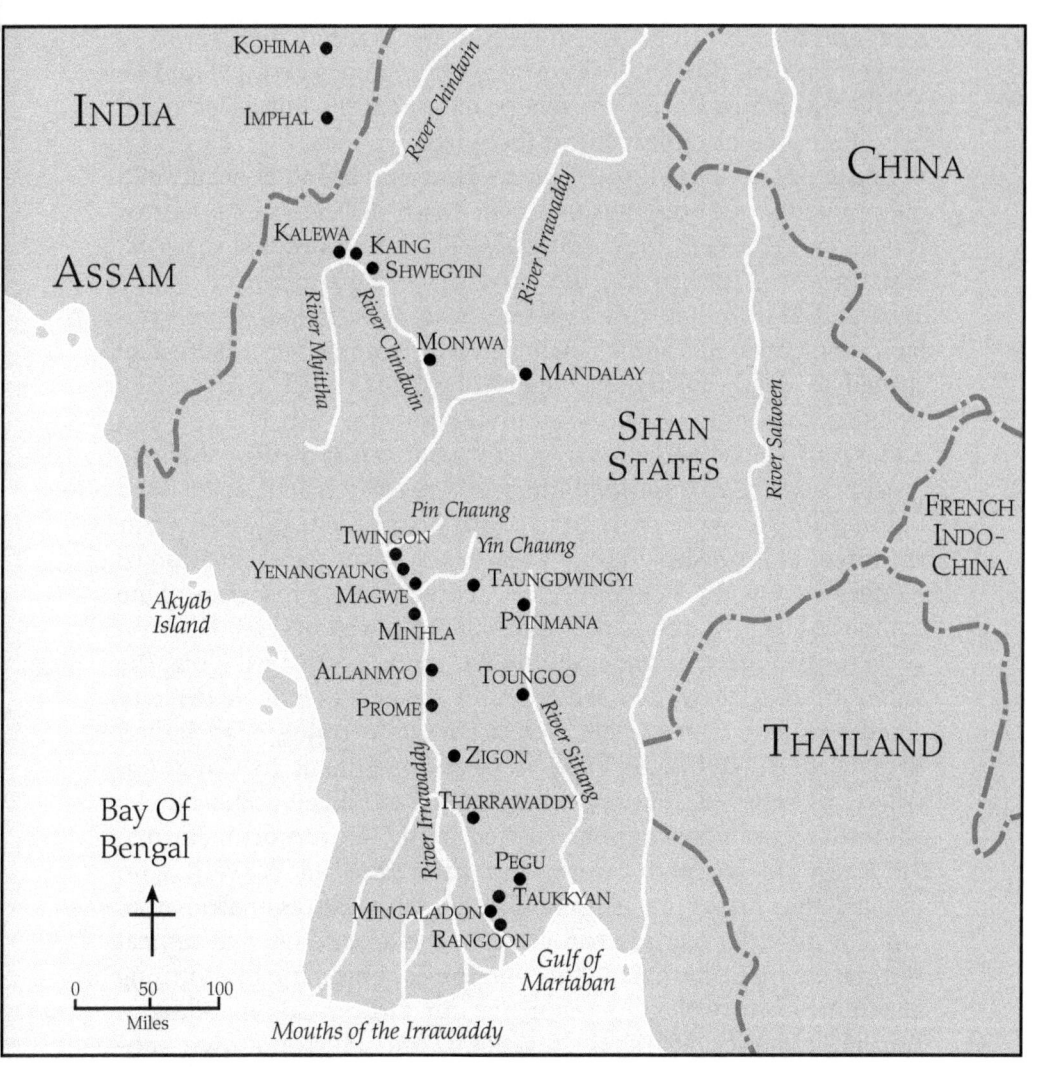

Map 2: Burma

Rangoon lies well to the south-west of its mouth. Having crossed it, therefore, all Iida had to do was advance due westward and he would automatically bar any troops in or near the Burmese capital from their line of retirement to the north.

This scenario was all too clear to Hutton. He had concentrated the remnants of 17th Division at the town of Pegu, north-east of Rangoon. Here 46th Indian Brigade, which had suffered the most casualties was broken up, the survivors being transferred to the 16th and 48th Indian Brigades, and several battalions were similarly amalgamated.[1] Some newly arrived reinforcements were also rushed to Pegu, chiefly Brigadier John Anstice's 7th Armoured Brigade, consisting of two armoured regiments, 7th Hussars and 2nd Royal Tanks, and a most welcome battery of the Royal Horse Artillery with 25-pounder guns, all of which had seen hard fighting in the Western Desert. Hutton intended, however, that the forces at Pegu should do no more than cover the evacuation of Rangoon. On 27 February, he decreed that this should be completed by 1 March and its garrison, followed by 17th Division and 7th Armoured Brigade, should withdraw northward along the valley of the Irrawaddy River, on a branch of which the city stands. Hutton also turned back a convoy carrying 63rd Indian Brigade and 1st Indian Field Artillery Regiment to Rangoon, where, he believed, they would merely be sacrificed uselessly.

Hutton's opinions were supported by the Governor of Burma, Sir Reginald Dorman-Smith, but they enraged Wavell, who insisted that no action be taken without his express permission. On 1 March, he met Hutton at the airfield of Magwe in central Burma, where he humiliated his unhappy subordinate by storming at him in front of the Governor, the Air Officer Commanding in Burma, Air-Vice Marshal Stevenson, and Hutton's own subordinates. Hutton, who had already been informed of his replacement, did not deign to reply. Wavell then ordered that Rangoon be held and the troop convoy resume its course. It reached the capital on 5 March.

The basic problem was that Wavell had fatally underestimated his enemy. After the war, he would honestly accept that: 'I was mistaken about the Japs. I didn't appreciate what fine, brave and ruthless soldiers they were.' During the war, however, he was convinced that resolute counter-attacks would solve all his difficulties and that 'a battle as aggressive as our resources will permit' could still save Rangoon.

Consequently, when Alexander arrived at Calcutta, Wavell made his wishes very clear. In his biography, *Alex*, Nigel Nicolson sets out the orders that the new leader of Burma Army now received:

> The retention of Rangoon is a matter of vital importance to our position in the Far East and every effort must be made to hold it. If, however, that is not possible, the British force must not be allowed to be cut off and destroyed, but must be withdrawn from the Rangoon area for the defence of Upper Burma. This must be held as long as possible in order to safeguard the oil fields at Yenangyaung, keep contact with the Chinese[2] and protect the construction of the road from Assam to Burma.

Armed with these requirements, Alexander flew on to Magwe and thence to Rangoon, landing at noon on 5 March in the last Allied aircraft to reach the city. By now, he must have become only too used to receiving bad news, so perhaps he was not surprised when he was informed by Hutton and Governor Dorman-Smith that since his meeting with Wavell, his position had become still less promising. On the evening of 2 March, the first Japanese soldiers had crossed the Sittang. Iida had then directed Lieutenant General Yutaka Takeuchi's 55th Division against the remnants of 17th Division at Pegu, while Lieutenant General Shozo Sakurai's 33rd Division, a unit with a distinguished record in the fighting in China, made a huge sweep westward, passing north of Takeuchi before turning south to race directly for Rangoon.

Faced with this threat and with 55th Division already menacing his position at Pegu, Hutton had again given preliminary orders for the evacuation of Rangoon. He pleaded with Alexander to be allowed to carry this out forthwith and there is no doubt that his views were both wise and correct. Yet Alexander, with reinforcements still arriving at Rangoon, with Wavell's clear instructions before him, and with no personal knowledge of the situation or the terrain, had no alternative but to disregard them. Instead of withdrawing, he mounted a counter-offensive from Pegu by 48

Brigade and 7th Armoured Brigade, with 16 Brigade being kept in reserve.

During 6 March, Alexander's push enjoyed some success against 55th Division, though not without one dreadful tragedy: Brigadier Wickham, commanding the newly arrived 63 Brigade, and all three of his battalion commanders, who had come up to the front with the praiseworthy intention of assessing the position for themselves, were killed in an ambush. By late afternoon though, the Japanese, having received reinforcements, were employing their favourite tactic of infiltrating behind the British lines, then setting up road blocks to cut off their retreat. Alexander had done everything possible to obey Wavell's orders, as the C-in-C, India would later acknowledge. It was now clear to him that Rangoon was doomed and he must concentrate on saving as much of his army as he could.

Rangoon, indeed, had already been abandoned during the previous fortnight by most of its civilian population, including the staffs of prisons and lunatic asylums, whose occupants had been released onto the streets, thereby completing the breakdown of public order. Now the Governor and his remaining officials were taken out by sea. They were followed by the demolition squads who had been entrusted with the grim task of denying everything of value to the enemy – they had destroyed transport, harbour facilities, the power station and the great Burma Oil Company's refining and storage tanks at Syriam, the smoke from which continued to pour upwards to a height of 23,000 feet for another six weeks.

Part of the Rangoon garrison had also evacuated the capital on 6 March, to head up the valley of the Irrawaddy. Early next morning the remaining troops – chiefly 63 Brigade, elements of 7th Armoured Brigade and a mass of administrative personnel – left as well. Passing through the village of Taukyan, where the road from Pegu joined the main route to the north, they set off after their advance guard. At the same time, the few remaining RAF Hurricanes and the Tomahawks of an American Volunteer Group commanded by Colonel Chennault – the famous 'Flying Tigers' – retired to a rough landing ground cut out of paddy fields at Zigon, 120 miles north of Rangoon, from which they could cover the retreat.

Further protection was given by the troops under Alexander's direct control. On the morning of 7 March, 48th Indian and 7th Armoured Brigades fought their way back past the road blocks to rejoin 16 Brigade. This then acted as the rearguard while the whole force retired to Taukkyan, whence it followed the Rangoon garrison northward.

This move was unhampered by the Japanese 55th Division, which was reforming after the actions around Pegu, but their 33rd Division was still moving rapidly. At about 0400 on that fateful day it crossed the main road northward just beyond Taukyan. Here Sakurai detached the 3rd Battalion of his 214th Regiment to act as a flank guard. Its commander, Major Takonubu, promptly set up a road block. Dense jungle on both sides prevented any manoeuvre in strength off the road. Alexander and the bulk of his Burma Army had been trapped.

First to encounter the road block were the troops from Rangoon. A company of 1st Battalion, the Gloucestershire Regiment, supported by tanks, made a most gallant attack on it but without success. Then the advance guard which had now reached Tharrawaddy, well to the north, hearing the news, turned back to strike at Takonubu from the rear. Then 2nd Battalion, 13th Frontier Force Rifles, again aided by tanks, attacked once more from the south. Takonubu was wounded but his men, backed by artillery, held their ground with that stubborn tenacity for which their army had already become renowned.

By this time 17th Division and the rest of 7th Armoured Brigade, from Pegu, had reached Taukyan. Unable to move off the road or to get at the enemy because of the forces in front of them, their vehicles milled about in a state of chaos. Alexander ordered that the whole of 63 Brigade, supported by every available tank and gun, should be ready to resume the assault on the road block at dawn next day. He accepted that, should this fail, he would have to 'order units, groups and individuals to save themselves' by dispersing through the jungle, which, even if successful, would entail the loss of all their transport and heavy equipment.

Had Sakurai reinforced his subordinate, this attack would almost certainly have failed and the ruin of the Burma Army would have been completed. Mercifully, the one great weakness of Japanese commanders was their tendency to adhere too rigidly to their plans; on occasions they were even disconcerted when those plans matured more swiftly than anticipated. It never occurred to the leader of 33rd Division that the British would abandon Rangoon or that he had Alexander's entire command at his mercy. On the contrary, he regarded the fighting at Taukkyan as an irritating distraction which might delay his attainment of the great prize, the capture of the Burmese capital.

Accordingly, at 2030 on 7 March, Takonubu's warriors were ordered to break off their defence and move westward to rejoin their division. Daylight on the 8th revealed the amazing sight of the two sides' main formations racing parallel to each other but in different directions. While Sakurai stormed on to the charnel house that had once been Rangoon, Alexander, astonished by, but duly grateful for the turn of events, was hurrying out of danger. Two days later he had reorganized his command at Tharrawaddy.

That Alexander's deliverance had been remarkable is obvious, but to label him a 'lucky general' as many have done seems an exaggerated reaction. It might indeed be argued that since he had had the ill luck to be placed in such a perilous situation by Churchill and Wavell, it was only poetic justice that he should enjoy a dramatic spin of fortune's wheel. Nor did that fickle goddess continue to smile on him, for he was now to be deluged by a whole sequence of unpalatable problems.

For a start, the Japanese followed their capture of Rangoon by pouring reinforcements into its harbour. 33rd Division, which had previously controlled only two infantry regiments, was brought up to strength by the arrival of a third. Two regiments of the 56th Division came in on 25 March and three regiments of the 18th Division on 7 April. By 19 April, 56th Division's third regiment, two tank regiments and two heavy field artillery regiments had also arrived, more than doubling Iida's strength. The only British reinforcement was 1st Battalion, the Royal Inniskilling Fusiliers which was ferried to Magwe between 8 and 13 March by American bombers acting in the role of aerial transports.

During the latter half of March, Iida's supporting V Air Group also almost doubled its numbers, and was now able to complete the Allied misery by obtaining total command of the air. The Allied fighters had left Zigon by 12 March, some retiring to Akyab, an island off Burma's north-western coast, while the remainder went to Magwe, where they joined nine Blenheim bombers from 45 Squadron. On 21 March, the Blenheims blasted the installations at the former RAF base at Mingaladon near Rangoon while ten escorting Hurricanes strafed Japanese aircraft on the ground, claiming to have destroyed sixteen of them. When enemy fighters attempted to intervene, they were engaged as they climbed, the Hurricane pilots and Blenheim gunners claiming eleven more between them.

This assault roused the Japanese to savage retaliation. That same afternoon they began a series of raids on Magwe which destroyed two Hurricanes in the air, eight Hurricanes, six Tomahawks and three Blenheims on the ground, and most of the airfield. The survivors struggled off to Akyab where further attacks destroyed seven more Hurricanes on the ground. There was no alternative but to withdraw the remaining Allied warplanes to India.

Curiously enough, the Japanese airmen struck at the British and Commonwealth soldiers comparatively rarely, though the absence of any friendly aircraft had a most depressing effect on morale. The Burmese cities, however, were subjected to devastating raids, which added to the flood of terrified fugitives, whose presence further hampered the fighting troops. In addition, of course, Japanese commanders were kept fully informed of their enemies' dispositions by their reconnaissance machines, while Alexander and his subordinates had to fight 'blind'.

Then there was the problem of the Chinese. The Fifth Chinese Army had now moved into the valley of the Sittang, the Sixth Chinese Army had entered the Shan States in the east of Burma, and the Sixty-Sixth Chinese Army had taken up station on Burma's northern frontier to act as a reserve. It might seem that these reinforcements would be an advantage not a problem, but unhappily this was not the case. A Chinese 'army' was at best equivalent to a British corps in manpower and vastly weaker in equipment, transport and supporting units. A Chinese division was scarcely more powerful than a normal British brigade. And the attitude of most of the inhabitants of Burma – at best indifference, at worst hostility – was hardly improved by the Chinese propensity for looting, stealing and burning.

Worst of all, the arrival of the Chinese masked the full

seriousness of the situation. With their command of the air and their ability to send in reinforcements at will, the Japanese must now win the campaign. Alexander had the clarity of vision to realize this and was quite capable of ignoring Wavell's orders to hold Upper Burma 'as long as possible' had he believed that this was not the best course of action. Without the Chinese complication, the British retreat might have been an orderly one, carried out as rapidly as was consistent with destroying such strategic prizes as the Yenangyaung oil fields before the Japanese could seize them.

Unfortunately, the Chinese intervention not only entitled Alexander to feel that he could now 'impose the maximum delay on the enemy and make him expend resources which he might have employed elsewhere', but made a rapid British retreat impossible in any case for political reasons. China's leader, Chiang Kai-shek, had been most unhappy to learn that his soldiers would not receive the Allied air protection that had been promised, hinting that his country might 'be forced to reconsider her position'; he would clearly never tolerate a British retirement which would leave Chinese troops 'out on a limb'. Alexander would thus have to ensure that the movements of his own command were coordinated with those of his difficult allies, a necessity which would cripple his freedom of movement throughout the remainder of the fighting.

Nor was Alexander helped by Chiang's wish that all the forces in Burma – British, Commonwealth and Chinese alike – should come under the control of Major General Stilwell, an American officer who had served in China for many years and spoke the language fluently, and whom Chiang had appointed as his representative. Later Chiang changed his mind but still suggested that Alexander should lead the British troops and Stilwell the Chinese, and that there should be no overall commander. This, Alexander believed, would render his position 'impossible from the start'.

It was therefore very important that Alexander should rectify the situation, but his early meetings with Stilwell on 13 and 14 March were far from successful. In the eyes of 'Vinegar Joe', as his fellow Americans called him, Alexander had two fatal flaws: he was British and he was an aristocrat. Feeling that Alexander was 'looking down' on him, which was certainly untrue, Stilwell took offence at Alexander's immaculate turnout, his cool poise and even his 'Limey' accent. Alexander, who would become increasingly accustomed to dealing with difficult personalities, remained unruffled, but though his quiet good nature gradually softened Stilwell's hostility, the deadlock regarding the command set-up remained unbroken.

So on 24 March, Alexander flew to Chiang's capital, Chungking, where he remained for three days of discussions. He found the Generalissimo 'most friendly and cooperative', and no doubt his own natural charm had its effect. Chiang agreed that 'in order to ensure unity of command', all Chinese forces, while remaining under the immediate direction of Stilwell, should be brought under Alexander's ultimate control.

Stilwell, to his credit, took the decision very well. It seems clear that, though he could never really bring himself to like Alexander, he had begun to realize that Alexander was a brave and experienced soldier. As Rupert Clarke tells us: 'relations became almost cordial and the mutual respect established was very evident, greatly improving the command situation.' In his diary, Stilwell even unbent sufficiently to refer to his new superior as 'Alex'. Unfortunately, this by no means solved the Chinese problem, for while Stilwell personally gave his full cooperation, in his own words: 'A reluctance to attack seemed to drench the spirit of the Chinese command beyond any measure of encouragement I could give.'

This reluctance had already had ill-effects. Prior to Chiang's decision, Alexander and Stilwell had at least correctly predicted that the Japanese advance into Upper Burma would follow the valleys of the Irrawaddy and Sittang rivers. It was provisionally decided that the British would defend the former route and the Chinese the latter, as well as protecting the Shan States against a possible attack from northern Thailand. Sadly, the leading Chinese troops would not advance further south than the town of Toungoo on the Sittang. This meant that 1st and 2nd Burma Brigades from 1st Burma Division, which had previously been detailed to block the Sittang route and were stationed further south, had to fall back to Toungoo on 19 March, thereby abandoning one of Burma's best rice-production areas, much to the dismay of the Burmese soldiers. The Burma Brigades then retired to Allanmyo on the Irrawaddy, where they were joined by their division's third brigade, 13th Indian. At the same time, 17th Division and 7th Armoured Brigade retreated to Prome, some 50 miles south of Allanmyo, again in order to conform to the Chinese dispositions.

On 19 March also, Alexander's direct control of his fighting troops came to an end – in future his role would be a strategic and political one. Tactical command would be exercised by Lieutenant General William Slim, to whom were entrusted all the British and Commonwealth units, combined as Burma Corps.

In *Springboard to Victory* (which deals principally with the siege of Kohima in April 1944), Brigadier C.E. Lucas Phillips says of 'Bill' Slim:

> He was perhaps not a tactician of great genius, except as displayed in his ultimate great battle in the plains of Mandalay and Meiktila, but he had other splendid qualities that were to bring him out as the greatest military figure of the Burma war . . . First and foremost he was a great leader. His bulldog face and jutting chin were an index of the tenacity and drive that were his mainsprings. His presence gave men confidence that here indeed was a fighter . . . Slim's instincts were all for aggression.

Yet with the perverse fate that always seemed to dog Alexander's footsteps, in the particular circumstances of the retreat from Burma, his Corps Commander's aggressive instincts proved a positive disadvantage. Nigel Nicolson suggests that Slim's appointment was a stroke of luck for Alexander. If anything it was a stroke of ill luck, not only at the time but for the future as well.

Dealing with the latter point first, Slim would later tell Lieutenant General Sir Ian Jacob, Military Assistant Secretary to Churchill's War Cabinet, that during the retreat Alexander had not had 'the faintest idea of what was going on'. It was an extra-ordinary remark for a man of Slim's calibre and experience to have made about a soldier whose reputation as a fighting commander was almost unrivalled, but it was far from being the only one. In his memoirs, *Defeat into Victory*, Slim mentions Alexander only slightly and slightingly, criticizes his decisions and, while accepting that Alexander had been called on to carry out an impossible task, considers that he was 'out-generalled' and that 'the most distressing aspect of the whole disastrous campaign had been the contrast between our generalship and the enemy's.'

Alexander, indeed, has rarely received the credit he deserves for his achievements, and a major reason for this is that he has been subjected to this sort of comment from colourful, outspoken subordinates. Slim was not the only such critic but, whereas the views of others – Stilwell for example – have at least been challenged, *Defeat into Victory* tends to be regarded with a reverence bordering on idolatry, with the result that most denigrations of Alexander commence with the Slim voice of authority. Even General Sir William Jackson, in his *Alexander of Tunis as Military Commander*, thinks that Slim's complaints were 'probably true'.

So it seems only fair to Alexander, to examine *Defeat into Victory* less unquestioningly in order to assess how reliable it really is. Sadly, the answer, in many respects, must be: it isn't! There are some curious omissions: for example, Slim makes no reference to the period in July 1944 during which he had had to hand over command of the Fourteenth Army to Lieutenant General Sir Geoffrey Scoones while he recovered from a prostate operation. There are a number of errors of fact. Those relating to events outside Burma may, perhaps, be put down to lapses of memory, but inaccuracies, both general and particular, on aspects of the later Burma campaigns, are a very different matter.

Thus Slim claims that, throughout his time in Burma, he received poor Intelligence. This was certainly the case during the retreat, but we learn from Michael Smith's *The Emperor's Codes*, that in later campaigns the 'Ultra' Intelligence was 'providing Slim with a wealth of information' including 'a complete order of battle of the Japanese forces', Army and Army Air Force. This was particularly valuable during the decisive actions at Kohima and Imphal, as Slim would accept – but only in private. Admittedly Slim could not refer specifically to 'Ultra' in *Defeat into Victory* as it was then still a closely guarded secret, but it was surely grossly unjust of him to have complained: 'I had not at my disposal the sources of information of the enemy's intentions that some more fortunate commanders in other theatres were able to invoke. We depended almost entirely on the Intelligence gathered by our fighting patrols.'

As an example of a particular error, Slim constantly refers to the activities of Japanese Mitsubishi Zero fighters in various Burma campaigns. No Zeros fought in any Burma campaigns, nor was it likely that they would. The Zero was an Imperial Navy aircraft; the fighters encountered in Burma were less efficient Japanese Army Air Force machines, Nakajima Ki 27 'Nates' or Ki 43 'Oscars'.

Slim's disinformation becomes most noticeable in his references to those whom he resented for any reason, especially that admittedly awkward character Major General Orde Wingate. In October 1944, Slim had described him as a 'great leader' who had several attributes of 'genius' and was 'really irreplaceable'. Unhappily, Slim had a very human concern for his own reputation and, although by the time that he brought out *Defeat into Victory*, his triumphant leadership of the Fourteenth Army had made him a public and military hero, he had apparently come to dislike the amount of praise that had been heaped on Wingate for his part in turning the tide in Burma.

Consequently Slim dismisses the first raid behind enemy lines carried out by Wingate's Chindits in February 1943 as 'an expensive failure'. He does concede that the raid was justified but only because, as a result of 'somewhat phoney propaganda', it seemed the beginning of a change of fortune. Yet it was not propaganda but fact that, albeit at high cost, British and Indian troops had for the first time outfought and outwitted the Japanese in the Burma jungles – with all that that meant in the field of morale – and that their experiences had also encouraged the British to transfer their lines of communication to the air in future, thereby enabling them to neutralize the dangers of the Japanese outflanking manoeuvres.

Nor does Slim refrain from slighting personal comments about the man he had earlier praised so highly. He tells us, for instance, how just before the second Chindit expedition of March 1944 was about to take off, aerial photographs revealed that one of the proposed landing grounds for its gliders had been blocked with tree trunks. Wingate, according to Slim, got into a very emotional state and wished to call off the whole operation, which Slim refused to do. Wingate in an official report written straight after the event states, on the contrary, that he urged the operation should continue and this was accepted by Slim. By now it will perhaps cause no surprise to reveal that the accounts of at least five other witnesses who were present, two of them RAF officers, who may be considered reasonably impartial, all support Wingate's version and believe Slim's to be 'decidedly inaccurate'.[3]

And just as Slim resented Wingate, so he resented Alexander – possibly for similar reasons. At the time that *Defeat into Victory* appeared, little had been written about the First Burma Campaign, but it was generally understood that Alexander, having been saddled with a terrifyingly difficult task, had performed little short of a miracle in saving the Burma Army. That belief was perfectly correct, but it would seem that Slim was not happy that so much credit had been given elsewhere, while his own part in the retreat remained almost unknown. His discontent would deeply influence his account of that campaign.

Thus Slim's conclusion that Alexander was 'out-generalled' was simply not true. It must not be forgotten that Slim's tactical control of his Corps was only one aspect of an extremely complex situation over which Alexander had had to exercise strategic and operational control. Nothing, for instance, could have been more worrying or frustrating than the involvement and the often poor performance of the Chinese armies. Nothing could have been more of a handicap than the complete absence of tactical air support. That Alexander, in such circumstances, managed to retain his control and prevent the total destruction of the Burma Army would seem to call for wonder and admiration, not ill-considered censure.

In addition, Slim completely failed to appreciate Alexander's sterling qualities, perhaps partly as a consequence of the latter's conduct during an air strike against a divisional headquarters which they were visiting together. Slim, who had had unpleasant experiences with strafing aircraft in the past, had hastily taken refuge in a slit trench, and it is easy to understand his feelings when he discovered that his example had not been followed. Alexander had preferred, Slim reports, 'to stand upright behind a tree. I was very annoyed with him for this, not only because it was a foolhardy thing to do, but because we had been trying to stop the men doing it. We had lost a number in this way.'

It is true that Slim adds that 'I found the Army Commander's courage above my standard', but the circumstances in which this comment is made give it the appearance of being less of a compliment than a quiet sneer. In the only other such incident recorded by Slim, he advised Alexander that they should enter a tank in which to cross a bridge under shellfire, leaving the driver of Alexander's car to 'take his chance' unprotected. Had Slim had the remotest understanding of Alexander's character, he would never have made such a suggestion. Alexander politely rejected it and eventually both of them went in the car.

Finally, it may be added that *Defeat into Victory* alone among first-hand accounts of the retreat largely ignores Alexander's immense contribution to the maintenance of morale, which, Slim suggests, was less than that of the divisional commanders. Enough then has surely been said to indicate that any criticisms made by Slim about Alexander should be treated with scepticism at the very least.

If any criticism has to be directed against Alexander, it must lie in Nigel Nicolson's comment that 'Alexander rarely interfered with Slim's dispositions' – for which, incidentally, Slim showed no gratitude either at the time or later. Alexander's good nature did lead him to give his subordinates considerable latitude; sometimes, it may be felt, too much latitude. We shall soon see an example of this when Alexander failed to prevent his Corps Commander from adopting a course of action which subjected their men to a whole series of ordeals from which the survivors only escaped with the utmost difficulty.

Alexander clearly recognized that, even with Chinese help, he could do no more than delay Japan's inevitable conquest of Burma. As was shown earlier, he therefore planned to withdraw slowly but steadily, coordinating his movements with those of his allies. Unfortunately, Slim had a very different agenda in view, probably because at this time he, like Wavell, badly underestimated the Japanese, though unlike Wavell, he would never admit it. Major General James Lunt, in his account of the campaign, *A Hell of a Licking*, describes how Brigadier John Bourke, Commander of 2nd Burma Brigade, returned from a conference with Slim shortly after the latter's appointment to inform his officers (of whom Lunt was one) that 'it was the Corps

Commander's intention to recapture Rangoon before the monsoon broke in mid-May.'

It was an intention which can only be seen as absolute folly in the light of the strength and condition of the formations then making up Burma Corps and the fact that such an operation would have to be launched without any air support. Slim's memoirs discreetly omit any mention of it, but they do tell us that he desired 'to concentrate our two divisions with a view to counter-attacking at the earliest possible opportunity'; also, that he felt 'we were fast approaching the dangerous state when our solutions to all problems threatened to be retreat.'

In view of their very different attitudes, it is ironical that Slim's first counter-attack, by 17th Division and 7th Armoured Brigade from Prome on 28 March, was made on the orders of Alexander, despite Slim's own complaints, then and later, that his Corps had not yet been concentrated. It was an action, however, which the Army Commander was compelled to take because of that other great cross he had to bear – the Chinese forces in Toungoo were under heavy attack and Stilwell was unable to persuade other Chinese units to intervene. He therefore sent a desperate appeal for a British diversionary move. Alexander, for the sake of Allied solidarity, had no option but to comply.

The resultant action would provide a vivid illustration of how impossible the Allied situation had become. The British attack failed to assist the Chinese who, on 30 March, escaped from Toungoo only at the cost of all their vehicles, all their guns, most of their equipment and over 3,000 casualties. Meanwhile, a Japanese flanking movement had not only brought Slim's advance to a halt on the very first day, but had cut off the vanguard of the attackers. On 29 March this fought its way out of the trap, retiring to Prome with the loss of ten tanks – six of which, captured more or less intact, were later used against their former owners – two guns, most of their vehicles, twenty-one officers and 290 men.

At a conference on 1 April, Wavell, Alexander and Slim were for once united in their belief that Prome had become dangerously exposed and should be abandoned. It would have made no difference if they had decided otherwise for that night, before an orderly retirement could be organized, the Japanese 33rd Division attacked. The defenders were driven out of the town, leaving behind large quantities of valuable supplies, and withdrew to Allanmyo where 1st Burma Division was already stationed. Slim's Corps was now concentrated and he felt at first that he had a good chance of 'staging a counter-offensive' – only to find he was again in danger of being outflanked as a result of the continued Chinese retirement to the east. He therefore fell back again to the Yin Chaung[4] where he took up a new defensive position.

At least this affair should have convinced Slim of the futility of his counter-attack policy. Iida was putting maximum pressure on the Chinese. His 55th Division and all his later reinforcements, as these arrived, were sent against them, leaving only 33rd Division for use against the British in the Irrawaddy Valley. Since Sakurai proved quite capable of throwing back the British on his own, it was hardly reasonable to expect the Chinese to withstand the assaults of an enemy whose strength would eventually reach three divisions. But if the Chinese could not hold the Allied left flank, then the further south Slim's counter-attacks progressed, the more chance there was that the men who carried them out would be isolated when that flank gave way; and the greater the numbers of the counter-attackers, the more who would be so endangered. That Slim never did learn this lesson would suggest that it was he rather than Alexander who should be accused of not having 'the faintest idea of what was going on'.

All Alexander's problems – Slim's faulty tactics, Stilwell's inability to hold back the main Japanese forces and his own need to coordinate his movements with those of the Chinese – now came together to bring about another disaster. The official explanation for the British stand on or, strictly speaking, just south of the Yin Chaung, was the need to guard the great oilfields around Yenangyaung, with their 5,000 wells and their straggling forest of derricks, until these could be blown up to prevent their use by the enemy. Yet since all preparations for their demolition had been completed by 9 April and the British were still in position when the Japanese attacked two nights later, it may be permissible to doubt this.

In reality the explanation seems to have been twofold. Any further retirement would have severed all contact with the Chinese, then stationed some way to the south-east at Pyinmana.

And Slim hoped that the retreat to the Yin Chaung 'would be the last' he would have to make and that his new defensive line might instead form a base from which he could 'stage a counter-blow'.

It was a totally unrealistic hope. Slim's defences stretched from Minhla on the Irrawaddy in the west to Taungdwingyi at the foot of the jungle-covered hills separating the valleys of the Irrawaddy and the Sittang in the east, a distance of 40 miles. Moreover 17th Division was told to stand firm in Taungdwingyi, which meant that most of the front was held only by 1st Burma Division. As this order came directly from Alexander, Slim is loud in his complaints, though he does acknowledge that Alexander's action resulted from the pressure put on him by Chiang and Stilwell to protect the Chinese right flank. Had Taungdwingyi fallen, the Japanese could have assaulted Pyinmana from the west – and incidentally 1st Burma Division from the east. Once more, the political issue of Allied solidarity which Alexander, unlike his subordinates, had always to consider, exerted its baleful influence on military events.

Not that Alexander did not realize the danger. On 6 April, he had met with Chiang from whom he had obtained a promise to send a Chinese division to Taungdwingyi, from which it could reinforce 1st Burma Division. Unfortunately, it had not yet appeared when the Japanese assault began on the night of 11/12 April; nor on 14 April when 1st Burma Division, harried by enemy soldiers and enemy airmen, was driven back over the Yin Chaung with heavy casualties. On the 15th, the demolition squads did their work and Yenangyaung was covered by a vast pall of smoke, through which vivid orange flames rose to a height of 500 feet, as buildings, machinery and millions of gallons of crude oil burned.

Since there was no point in 1st Burma Division defending a blackened ruin, it should have moved forthwith north of Yenangyaung to the next source of water, the Pin Chaung. In fact Slim had ordered the Divisional Commander, Major General Bruce Scott, to retire slowly in order that the Japanese forces engaging him could be attacked on the flank by the Chinese division which Slim had now been told would arrive on 16 April.

The result was depressingly predictable. The Chinese still did not appear and Scott, fiercely attacked on the ground and from the air, suffered severe casualties. He then found that his delay had enabled the enemy to outflank him to the east. Scott had sent all his unwanted transport in advance, guarded by a few tanks. They had just crossed the Pin Chaung when the Japanese severed the road in front of them. The tanks finally broke through early on the 17th but many of Scott's vehicles had already been wrecked by enemy air attacks during their enforced halt.

Meanwhile, on the 16th, the Japanese had also seized the ford over the Pin Chaung and the village of Twingon to the south of this, thereby trapping the bulk of 1st Burma Division. Counter-attacks by the British from Taungdwingyi on the 17th failed to ease the pressure. At dawn on the 18th the Chinese 38th Division from their Sixty-Sixth Army, commanded by Lieutenant General Sun Li-jen, a graduate of the Virginia Military Academy, at last reached the scene. Sun then attacked from the north while Scott attempted to fight his way through Twingon. Both assaults failed.

By 1630, 1st Burma Division was completely surrounded in an area where there was no water. Scott reported that his command, in particular the Burmese units, was on the point of disintegration and asked permission to abandon all his remaining transport before breaking out that night. Instead Slim instructed him to hold his ground, assuring him that the Chinese would renew their offensive at dawn on the 19th. They in fact renewed it at 1500 hours.

By that time Scott's men were beginning to die or go mad from exhaustion in the intense heat. At 1400, a last desperate bid to escape was made and Scott's tanks finally forced their way over the Pin Chaung, followed by the infantrymen who, regardless of Japanese bullets, flung themselves down to drink the precious water. The Chinese, it should be added, did valuable work in covering Scott's subsequent retreat, but 1st Burma Division was now temporarily unfit for combat. It had suffered a 20 per cent casualty list, and most of its guns and all its remaining transport had been left behind south of the Pin Chaung, including ambu-lances filled with wounded soldiers whom the Japanese, with a brutality that equalled yet shamed their bravery, slaughtered to a man.

While it is impossible not to admire Slim's resilience, it is astonishing to learn that he believed even now that 'we might turn the tables on the Japanese and thus avoid abandoning Burma'. He wanted another two Chinese divisions to reinforce Sun's 38th. With these he would engage 33rd Division, which he thought was in an 'exposed position' at Yenangyaung, from the north, while 17th Division from Taungdwingyi attacked it from the rear. Having routed Sakurai, his whole strength would cross the hills into the Sittang Valley to strike at the Japanese opposing Fifth and Sixth Chinese Armies. He admitted that his plans were 'a little ambitious'.

It would swiftly become obvious that they were also more than a little ridiculous. At the same time as the British were suffering defeat at Yenangyaung, their allies were meeting with total disaster. On 18 April, Japan's 56th Division all but annihilated the Chinese Sixth Army's 55th Division, only 1,000 of its men surviving. Three days later, Sixth Army's other two divisions fled back to China. Soon afterwards the three divisions of Fifth Army and two from Sixty-Sixth Army followed them. Sun's 38th Division, though badly mauled, escaped to India instead. The indomitable Stilwell, his command having disintegrated, also made for India on foot with his staff and a number of refugees. He reached Imphal on 15 May after a gruelling march of 140 miles over some of the worst terrain in Burma.

Alexander now showed both his clear-sightedness and his ability to make harsh judgements. On 25 April he advised Slim and Stilwell that Burma was to be abandoned forthwith. Two days earlier he had notified Wavell that 'owing to the supply situation', it was impossible for even part of Burma Corps to retire to China, as Churchill had suggested for political reasons. It was high time that such decisions were reached and by doing so, says Major General Lunt, Alexander 'certainly saved the Burma Army'. His intention was that all British forces, except 2nd Burma Brigade, which had been stationed west of the Irrawaddy earlier, should cross that river, then retreat along the line of its tributary the Chindwin into India. By the late evening of 30 March, the last troops had left the once-beautiful city of Mandalay, now reduced to ruin and ashes by Japanese bombers. The sappers then blew up the two centre spans of the great Ava Bridge, which collapsed into the Irrawaddy.

On 28 April, Alexander had issued orders that, after leaving

Mandalay, Burma Corps should have as its ultimate destination Kalewa, on the west bank on the Chindwin, whence a rough track led to Imphal. 2nd Burma Brigade having crossed the Irrawaddy south of its junction with the Chindwin, was already west of the latter river; it would reach its destination via the valley of the wide, sluggish Myittha, which flows northward to the west of, but parallel to, the southward-flowing Chindwin, joining it near Kalewa. Meanwhile, 16, 48 and 7th Armoured Brigades would proceed to the little river port of Shwegyin on the east bank of the Chindwin; from there they would travel the last 6 miles to Kalewa in river steamers. At the same time, 13, 63 and 1st Burma Brigades would go to Monywa, another river port on the Chindwin some 150 miles to the south, from which they too would be ferried to Kalewa.

Alexander had expressly stated that 'a strong detachment' should be left in the Myittha Valley to cover the south-western approaches to Monywa, but Slim who, quite wrongly, believed that 2nd Burma Brigade was in danger of being cut off in this area, ordered it to retire without delay. Alexander, who always gave his subordinates loyal support, did later confirm that order, but it was 'Slim's costly miscalculation', as Lunt calls it, which ensured that Monywa was temporarily guarded by only 150 men of the 1st Gloucesters.

On 1 May, an enemy force approached from the south-west, crossed the Chindwin in small boats and broke into Monywa. Next day, desperate attempts to recapture the town were made by the brigades scheduled to be withdrawn from it. These were on the brink of success – albeit at a cost of 790 casualties, 403 prisoners, 2 tanks, 2 bren-gun carriers, 6 anti-tank guns and 158 lorries – when a message was received cancelling the attacks and ordering a withdrawal northward. It seems that this was a Japanese trick: no such commands were ever issued by either Alexander or Slim.

The whole of Alexander's command, apart from 2nd Burma Brigade, was now compelled to make for Shwegyin, hampered by a shortage of supplies, by the need to take care of some 2,000 wounded, and by thousands of refugees. Moreover, there were only six river steamers at Shwegyin on which the men could be embarked. Even so, by the morning of 10 May, all except 48

Brigade and 7th Armoured Brigade had been evacuated, though since the steamers could carry no more than four vehicles at a time, a mass of guns and transport was still left on the Chindwin's east bank.

At about 0530 on the 10th, the Japanese opened fire with mortars and machine guns from the cliffs that overlooked Shwegyin from the south and south-east. All attempts to drive them back failed. With bullets raking the jetty, orders were given to destroy tanks, lorries and other equipment. At about 1700 all guns started to fire off their ammunition. The barrage reached its greatest intensity at 1955 and ceased twenty minutes later. Then the guns were wrecked and the men moved northward up a difficult track to Kaing, from which they crossed the river to Kalewa. Behind them enormous flames from the burning vehicles lit up the gathering darkness. The whole of Burma Corps now possessed only fifty lorries, thirty jeeps, twenty-eight guns and one solitary tank. Mercifully though, its ordeal was almost over. On 12 May, as it staggered along the track towards Imphal, the monsoon broke in full fury, finally bringing the Japanese advance to a halt.

The last men of the Burma Army reached Imphal on 20 May and Alexander's command came to an end. At a press conference he and Wavell referred to past events as 'a glorious retreat'. Neither can really have believed it. Stilwell was more blunt, declaring there was no such thing: 'All retreats are as ignominious as hell.' Alexander himself would later state, equally honestly, that 'Burma was a complete military defeat.'

Nonetheless, it was not an unmitigated defeat. The Japanese victory, though impressive, was only a partial one. They had conquered Burma but the Burma Army had survived. Furthermore, it had survived as an army in being. As Slim, whose empathy with his soldiers was his most attractive feature, reports: 'They were still recognisable fighting units. They might look like scarecrows, but they looked like soldiers too.' They could therefore provide the basis on which the forces required for operations in the future could be built.

This survival owed a tremendous amount to Alexander, and his achievement was all the greater because it was attained despite Wavell's near-fatal belief that it was possible to save Rangoon, Slim's near-fatal persistence in counter-attacking, the political and military restrictions that had been imposed by the presence of the Chinese, the lack of almost any support from the air, the hostility or at best indifference of the local population, and, it must be said, the redoubtable qualities of the enemy soldiers. Churchill could well boast that he had been unable to send an army to the aid of the troops in Burma, but he had sent them quite a man.

Notes:
1. It should be mentioned that it was the general practice in the Indian Army for one battalion in every brigade to be British, while the other two were manned by Indians or Gurkhas.
2. The Chinese Fifth and Sixth Armies were at this time moving southwards to participate in the fighting.
3. Further details and a full consideration of Slim's change of outlook may be found in *Wingate and the Chindits: Redressing the Balance* by David Rooney, a former senior lecturer at Sandhurst. That most of Wingate's subordinates felt that the Chindits had been very badly handled after their leader's death, for which Slim bore the ultimate responsibility, probably did nothing to soften that officer's asperity.
4. 'Chaungs' are minor watercourses that only become real obstacles at the time of the monsoon.

Chapter 3

The Theatre Commander: Middle East

After his ordeals in Burma, which had caused him to lose several pounds in weight, Alexander was more than ready for the brief spell of leave which was granted to him on his return to England in July 1942. A fortnight at home with his beloved family must have seemed all too brief, but at least it gave him a chance to rest and regain his strength. This was just as well, since Churchill and Brooke had already determined to entrust him with new and important duties.

On his arrival at Gibraltar during his flight back from Burma, Alexander had been notified that he had been designated Commander of the British First Army, which was to provide the main striking force in a planned joint British and American seaborne invasion of Vichy French North Africa. The Supreme Allied Commander for this operation, to which Churchill had given the inspiring code name of TORCH, was to be an American, Lieutenant General Dwight Eisenhower, and on 4 August, Alexander met him for the first time in London.

It was a moment of considerable historical importance, though probably neither man appreciated this at the time. Eisenhower must have felt some apprehension, for he was junior to Alexander in rank, and, not having previously commanded in war, he was somewhat embarrassed to have so distinguished and experienced an officer appointed as his subordinate. Fortunately, Alexander's charm, courtesy and eagerness to cooperate quickly allayed all anxieties. By the time they parted, the two men were firm friends and Eisenhower was sure that he had gained an ally whose value to him would be beyond all price.

This would, indeed, be the case – but not in the immediate future. Hardly had Alexander returned to the War Office than

Map 3: The Desert Battleground

fresh instructions necessitated a quick farewell to his family and a hasty packing of his kit. On 7 August, he and the faithful Rupert Clarke were on their way to Cairo. Two days later, they arrived in time for breakfast, and Alexander was promptly advised by Churchill and Brooke of his new responsibilities – which were far wider and far more vital than any he would have had in Operation TORCH.

The struggle that was being fought out in the Western Desert of Egypt and Libya was always a matter of great concern to the Prime Minister. Indeed, the reason why he could provide Alexander in Burma with so little in the way of material support was that, in defiance of his military advisers, he had poured troops and aircraft, originally destined for the Far East, into North Africa instead. Thus strengthened, on 18 November 1941, the British Eighth Army had attacked the German and Italian forces under General Rommel and, after a series of savage, confused encounters, had driven them out of the Libyan province of Cyrenaica and relieved the British garrison in Tobruk, which had been under siege since the previous April.

Sadly though, this victory, like that of the Japanese in Burma, was incomplete. Rommel, like Alexander, had saved his army, which remained a fighting force capable of immediate action. As Churchill signalled to General Sir Claude Auchinleck, his Commander-in-Chief, Middle East, on 11 January 1942, the bulk of the enemy divisions had 'got away'. He was not impressed by Auchinleck's assurance that these were 'divisions only in name'.

To make matters worse, Hitler had come to realize that, paradoxically, the most important position in the North African war lay outside North Africa. While Allied supplies were compelled to travel the weary miles round the Cape of Good Hope, Axis convoys had only to cross some 350 miles of sea from the port of Messina in northern Sicily to Libya's capital, Tripoli. Yet this passage was far more perilous, for 60 miles south of Sicily lay the island fortress of Malta, from which aircraft, submarines and surface warships could decimate the Axis shipping – and did. In September 1941, 28 per cent of all cargoes sent to Rommel was lost. In October, the proportion was 21 per cent. In November, it reached a staggering 63 per cent.

Malta's activities had thus played a vital part in Eighth Army's recent success, but, by a rather horrible irony, the one person on either side who failed to appreciate this, was its principal beneficiary. As early as August 1941, Churchill had written delightedly to his C-in-C, Middle East, of the way in which Malta could disrupt the effective maintenance of Rommel's army. As late as August 1942, General Auchinleck could state that the retention of the island was not absolutely necessary for his plans.

Auchinleck's lack of gratitude, to say nothing of lack of strategic insight, was now deservedly repaid. At the cost of weakening his air force on the Moscow front, Hitler, on 2 December 1941, had transferred Fliegerkorps II to Sicily. This was added to Fliegerkorps X in the Balkans to form Luftflotte 2, the leader of which, Field Marshal Kesselring, was appointed C-in-C, South, giving him authority over Luftwaffe units in Libya as well. His orders were to 'ensure safe lines of communication' with North Africa, in which connection, Hitler told him, it was 'particularly important' that he achieve 'the suppression of Malta'.

Kesselring did his level best and from 22 December onwards, Malta reeled under an ever-increasing weight of bombs. With the island forced to look to its own defence, sizeable reinforcements were at last able to reach Rommel. On 21 January 1942, his men, now known as 'Panzerarmee Afrika', launched a counter-offensive, completely fooling Auchinleck who had believed they would be 'hard-pressed' to hold their ground. By 5 February, the British had lost most of the gains made in their previous offensive, including the vital Martuba airfield complex, the capture of which tightened the Axis grip on Malta. Then on 26 May, Rommel resumed his advance and, after much fierce fighting, completed his victory on 21 June by capturing Tobruk together with 32,000 prisoners. It was a British disaster second only to that of Singapore, but there was one hidden compensation – in order to provide warplanes to assist Rommel, Kesselring had been forced to discontinue his sustained raids on Malta.

Not that the island-fortress was out of danger. As convoys making for it were sunk or forced to turn back, its garrison and civilian population alike began to suffer greatly from a lack of food and fuel. Moreover, the bulk of the Axis airmen now returned to Sicily, where they renewed their assaults on Malta, in preparation for the final elimination of its threat to Rommel's supply lines by combined seaborne and airborne landings. Pending these, it had been agreed that Panzerarmee Afrika should pause temporarily on the Egyptian frontier. Mercifully, however, Rommel was intoxicated by his triumph and the award of a field marshal's baton. Ignoring the protests of Kesselring, he persuaded that other great gambler, Hitler, to let him dash for the Suez Canal without waiting for Malta to be subdued.

It was an amazing decision. Rommel's soldiers were already weary from weeks of combat, and every mile that he advanced into Egypt made his supply lines more vulnerable. His Italian troops fell ever further behind the Germans. So did his supporting air groups. Eighth Army, which even after the fall of Tobruk already contained many more men, tanks, guns and supplies than Panzerarmee Afrika, was, by contrast, now receiving massive reinforcements. By the time Rommel reached the 40-mile 'gap' at El Alamein between the Mediterranean and the huge, impassable quicksand known as the Qattara Depression, his men and his momentum alike were totally exhausted and his advance ground to a halt.

Auckinleck, who had taken direct command of Eighth Army, then went onto the offensive, proclaiming his intention to 'destroy the enemy as far east as possible'. Certainly he could never have a better opportunity of doing so. Eighth Army was greatly superior in manpower, was backed by a dominant air force and enjoyed the benefits of a short, easily defended supply line. By 10 July, it had over 200 tanks, by the 20th, almost 400; the number of German tanks at this time ranged from under thirty to about fifty. But despite all these advantages, five successive attempts by Eighth Army did not destroy their enemies, or even drive them back. The disgusted troops dubbed these depressing failures 'the nonsenses of July'.

Their feelings were shared by Brooke, whose responsibilities as professional head of the British Army sharpened his anxiety. In early August, Panzerarmee Afrika, in its turn, received reinforcements of men and materiel. They included new Mark IV Specials, tanks which, for the first time, were superior to any the British possessed in North Africa, then or later, anti-tank guns, in which the Germans had always been superior, and fighter aircraft. In consequence, as Captain B.H. Liddell Hart points out in *The Second World War*, 'the strength of the two sides was nearer to an even balance than it was either before or later', and the 'Ultra' code-breakers confirmed that Rommel was planning to renew his advance before the end of the month.

It was therefore essential, Brooke felt, that he should visit the Middle East to assess the situation in person. On 3 August, he arrived in Cairo, where he was soon joined by Churchill. The Prime Minister had decided at short notice that he too would fly to Cairo and that thereafter he and Brooke would both proceed to Moscow for consultations with Stalin.

The series of interviews and discussions which followed have been covered in numerous accounts, most notably perhaps in Field Marshal Lord Carver's *El Alamein* and General Sir David Fraser's biography *Alanbrooke*. It is only necessary therefore, to record the decisions reached – and to rejoice that they were such good ones.

By 6 August, Brooke was ready, says General Fraser, 'to agree with any solution which took Auchinleck from Cairo'. Churchill was in full agreement, and both have been strongly criticized by Auchinleck's admirers ever since. It need only be pointed out, however, that Auchinleck's own official biographer, John Connell, after venting a great deal of abuse on the Prime Minister in particular, ends by weakly admitting that 'It is not to be disputed that a change of command was desirable.'

At least there could be little argument about Auchinleck's successor. Alexander had been the first choice of both Churchill and Brooke, though for somewhat different reasons. The former, according to Fraser, looked on Alexander as 'the ideal general, a man of panache, a figure to whom a certain natural aura of romance attached itself, harmonious with the Prime Minister's own character.' Brooke, on the other hand, valued Alexander because he was 'imperturbable and a man who would trust subordinates and keep a fair balance between interests – and later, Allies: and who would, in turn, be trusted by all.'

Brooke next set about providing the new C-in-C, Middle East with reliable lieutenants. It had been decided to replace not only Auchinleck but also his senior staff officer, Lieutenant General Thomas Corbett. 'I at once thought of Dick McCreery,' says Brooke, and when Alexander arrived in Cairo early on 9 August, Brooke promptly recommended McCreery to him.

Major General Richard McCreery, whom Brooke believed to be 'one of our best armoured divisional commanders', had been sent to the Middle East in early 1942 to be the tank expert at Auchinleck's Headquarters. Unfortunately, the forceful, outspoken, independently minded McCreery was not appreciated by Auchinleck who rarely welcomed advice which did not coincide with his own ideas. As Brooke indignantly reflects, McCreery was 'practically ignored and never referred to by the Auk on the employment of armoured forces'. Their unsatisfactory relationship came to an end on 29 July when Auchinleck dismissed his subordinate, telling him that he was valueless if he was not prepared to 'fall in with his Commander-in-Chief's intentions'.

Alexander, by contrast, welcomed McCreery as the Middle East's new Chief of Staff. He would henceforth perform his difficult duties most efficiently, never flinching from taking severe, sometimes harsh action if he deemed this necessary. He thereby compensated for Alexander's one real weakness: a reluctance to cause hurt or offence to anyone.

Such reluctance would rarely be shown by the officer whom Brooke selected as Alexander's tactical commander. This was a less easy task, since Churchill at first insisted that Lieutenant General William 'Strafer' Gott, the distinguished leader of Eighth Army's XIII Corps, should be promoted to Army Commander – but tragically, Gott was killed on 7 August, when the transport aircraft in which he was flying to Cairo was shot down by enemy fighters. Even then, Brooke had some trouble persuading the Prime Minister to accept the brilliant but already notoriously 'difficult' Lieutenant General Bernard Montgomery.

Subsequent events must not be allowed to mask the fact that Alexander had once more been placed in a far from pleasant position. He personally was well aware of this almost from the moment he reached Cairo. His faithful aide, Rupert Clarke, tells us that, 'Nothing could have been clearer to Alex as he listened to Brooke than that his whole command, and the Eighth Army in particular, was in urgent need of drastic change and firm hands to apply it.' When Alexander 'emerged from his talk with Winston and Brooke', his first words to Clarke were: ' "Bargo" again Rupert!' – 'Bargo' being a code word between them to denote a chaotically confused situation.

Just how big a 'Bargo' becomes clear from an examination of the problems that had to be put right. The most comprehensive summary of these has been given by Ian Jacob, then a colonel, who accompanied Churchill to Egypt as Military Assistant Secretary to the War Cabinet. On 6 August, he inserted in his diary a detailed account of why, as he put it, 'the Army in the Middle East' was 'in a rather bewildered state'.[1]

Jacob's conclusions are clear and damning – so damning that those determined to believe otherwise are forced to belittle him. This they do by stating that Jacob, though a brilliant staff officer, had had no personal experience of modern armoured warfare; he had only just come to the desert; and his was only one man's opinion anyway. The first two points are correct, but they are irrelevant because the third one is entirely inaccurate. Indeed it is difficult to see how anyone who has actually read Jacob's diary entry could possibly make such a statement, for he prefaces his summary by saying that he had talked with a number of officers of his own or similar rank, who did have a wide experience of armoured warfare and warfare in the desert generally, and while these held many different viewpoints, there were 'certain things, however, on which all agree'.

For a start, 'all are agreed,' reports Jacob, 'that faulty leadership and bad tactics were the principal causes of our defeat.' With regard to the latter, he singles out three matters in particular: the breaking-up of divisions into brigade groups, or the even smaller battle groups, which were frequently defeated in detail at heavy cost; the failure to concentrate the artillery, which was Eighth Army's most effective arm; and a lack of cooperation between the infantry and the armour. This last was a polite way of saying that, in several cases, particularly during the 'nonsenses of July', the infantry had simply been left unsupported at the mercy of Axis tanks. Nor is this the only way in which Jacob's summary is generous, since he does not mention at least two other major problems which bedevilled Eighth Army as a result of Auchinleck's mistaken tactics.

In his Official Despatch, Auchinleck states, not as an opinion but as a fact, that his tanks were inferior to those of the Germans. His judgement has been widely accepted, yet, if the *British Official History* is consulted,[2] it will be seen that Eighth Army's tanks, in both gun power and armour, were slightly superior to their rivals even before the American Grants arrived in time to participate in the fighting which preceded the loss of Tobruk. Thereafter, they were considerably superior. Major General 'Pip' Roberts relates in his memoirs, *From the Desert to the Baltic*, that during this fighting, his own Grant was hit eight times without a shell penetrating it, while another Grant resisted twenty-five hits successfully. The presence of the Grant, he reports, gave Eighth Army 'a magnificent opportunity of inflicting a heavy defeat on the Germans'.

It was not taken. The German tanks sought out weaker targets such as supply echelons or unprotected infantry, and when attacked themselves were protected by anti-tank guns, especially the 88mm anti-aircraft gun, which also made a deadly effective tank-destroyer. The British tanks, on the contrary, did not coordinate their actions with the Eighth Army's own artillery or anti-tank guns, scorned standing on the defensive, and delighted in making gallant but costly 'charges' on the enemy armour. The problem was not inferior Allied equipment but, as Roberts tells us, 'a failure to understand tank warfare' on the part of the Higher Command.

Then again, when Auchinleck had taken personal control of Eighth Army, he had unwisely set up his Headquarters in an isolated piece of desert, over 40 miles away from that of the Western Desert Air Force which remained on the coast. Major General Sir Francis de Guingand, then Eighth Army's Brigadier General Staff, declares in his *Operation Victory* that this separation, which had never previously occurred in the North African campaigns, 'produced great difficulties in the laying on of the best air support'. The result was that, at a time when Allied supremacy in the air was overwhelming, it was the Luftwaffe which intervened more effectively in the fighting on land. The airmen became increasingly discontented, and in due course would make this very clear to Churchill.

It was therefore not surprising that Eighth Army was 'in a rather bewildered state', that its men were 'brave but baffled' as Churchill described them, that there was ill feeling between the various arms, a tendency to lay the blame on others and a loss of confidence in the Higher Command. Even a majority of Eighth Army's staff officers, as one of their number, General Sir Charles Richardson, confirms in his memoirs, *Flashback: A Soldier's Story*, 'felt that the removal of Auchinleck was essential'.

With regard to the charge of 'faulty leadership', the officers to whom Jacob spoke united in putting this squarely on the shoulders of three men: Auchinleck, who was respected but 'has not created a coherent Army'; Corbett, whom Auchinleck had selected, against the advice of Brooke, although he had never held a senior staff appointment at such a high level before, and under whom GHQ, Middle East resembled a 'rudderless ship'; and Major General Eric Dorman-Smith, Deputy Chief of the General Staff, who had become Auchinleck's personal adviser and was considered 'a menace of the first order and responsible for many of the evil theories which have led to such mistakes in the handling of the Army'. This was not surprising either, for Field Marshal Carver, then a staff officer with Eighth Army's XXX Corps, tells us in his autobiography, *Out of Step*, that Dorman-Smith's 'principal motive seemed to be to suggest some startlingly novel solution, regardless of whether or not it had a hope of working'.

Mistakes in wartime are inevitable and normally can readily be forgiven, but there can surely be no excuse for the refusal of Auchinleck and his adviser to learn from their errors. That they had every intention of repeating them when Rommel renewed his attacks is shown conclusively by a number of documents that appeared at the time. These are an 'Appreciation of the Situation in the Western Desert' prepared by Dorman-Smith on 27 July, which was approved without qualification by his chief, and the mass of records – summaries, orders, reports, messages – which together make up the War Diaries of GHQ, Middle East, Eighth Army, and XIII and XXX Corps.[3]

They make disheartening reading. Dorman-Smith's Appreciation and the Operation Orders of the two corps all envisage that when Rommel attacked, Eighth Army's infantry divisions would retire from their existing forward areas to strong points some way to the rear. Here they would be split up, part holding the strongpoints, part forming 'mobile battle groups' which would manoeuvre between these, falling back into them if necessary. The bulk of the artillery would be divided among the battle groups, thereby, as de Guingand remarks, creating 'a great danger of the guns being driven hither and thither and confusion setting in'.

Similarly, Dorman-Smith makes no mention of how cooperation between infantry and armour could be improved, or even suggests that this might be desirable. He does proclaim that 'it is necessary to husband our armour carefully', but since this had been one of Auchinleck's declared aims during the July actions, his comment must have aroused grim reflections in the minds of any infantry commanders who read it. He makes no comment on the problems posed by the enemy's anti-tank guns, nor does he consider how to ensure effective support from the Desert Air Force, though he glibly acknowledges that air superiority is 'a very considerable, if somewhat indefinable asset'.

Mercifully, Auchinleck's 'evil genius' fell with his master – to the great relief of almost every single person in the Middle East[4] – but Alexander and his subordinates still had the task of detecting the follies in the existing plans and rectifying them in the short time that remained before Rommel attacked. And even if they did, they had to face the disheartening prospect that the attitude of Eighth Army hardly seemed to encourage hopes of a determined defence.

Auchinleck's most recent actions might have been designed to reduce confidence still further. After the war, he would claim that he had never contemplated a retirement from the Alamein position once Rommel had been checked in early July. He must have forgotten that he had written to Brooke on the 25th of that month, warning that 'we may yet have to face a withdrawal from our present positions'; he was therefore creating a system of reserve defences protecting Alexandria and Cairo. He must also have forgotten that thereafter the progress of those defences was the main, almost the only concern of General Headquarters, Middle East, as is shown by Dorman-Smith's Appreciation, its own War Diary, and the fact that as late as 14 August, Auchinleck would still be enquiring about them himself.

For all the attention paid to reserve defences, however, it was felt by many that there was no real hope of holding them. For example, Field Marshal Lord Harding, then a staff officer at GHQ, Middle East, would inform Alexander's biographer, Nigel Nicolson, that:

> If Rommel had broken through at Alamein the time factor, the topography, and the effect on the general political and social situation in the Delta would have been such that nothing could have stopped him from entering Cairo . . . If you were realistic, you had to admit to yourself that if the Alamein position became untenable through penetration and subsequent exploitation by Rommel, there was no other place in which you could fight an effective battle.

Moreover, Harding believed that Auchinleck was aware of this, and had the enemy triumphed at Alamein, he only 'intended to impose delay on Rommel in the Delta'. This would give him time to 'extricate the bulk of his force south of Cairo, and then over the Suez Canal into Palestine'. Harding could speak with considerable authority on this point since it was he who was instructed to draw up the necessary plans for such a move.

Nor is Harding's statement the only such evidence. General Richardson relates that he also was ordered to prepare 'a plan for the possible withdrawal of Eighth Army to Khartoum'. Major General Sir Miles Graham, then Eighth Army's Deputy Chief Administrative Officer, would confirm (in a BBC radio broadcast of 24 September 1958) that he too was made responsible for 'arrangements to evacuate Eighth Army' should this prove necessary. De Guingand reports that already 'a new site for the Headquarters had been selected on the Nile, sixty miles south of Cairo.' The Operation Orders at this time deal constantly with the need to deny vital supplies or equipment to the enemy in the event of an Eighth Army defeat; one on 7 August discusses the destruction of oil supplies in Palestine, Syria, Trans-Jordan, the Sudan, Iraq, Persia, Saudi Arabia, Bahrein and Aden – which clearly envisages a fairly total collapse!

No wonder then, that even the good-natured Alexander included in his Official Despatch the definite statement that 'it was fairly well known' that Eighth Army 'would retreat again, in accordance with the theory that it must be kept in being'. Alexander added that this would be 'in the last resort' but since news of all the plans had become common knowledge, it seemed very probable that this qualification would have had little practical effect. 'I don't say that it is not prudent to be prepared for the worst,' declares de Guingand, 'but on the other hand, if there is too much of this sort of thing it is most unlikely that the troops will fight their best in their existing positions.' It was an opinion with which Alexander entirely agreed. 'Anyone,' he would later observe, 'can be forgiven for "looking over his shoulder" if he is aware that preparations have been made for a possible retreat.'

Happily, by a strange turn of fate, the very factor which had caused so much discouragement would ultimately provide the basis for redemption. As Harding explained to Nicolson: 'Monty and Alex (Monty primarily, but Alex in full support) said that there would be no retreat. In any circumstances . . . This had a tremendous moral effect on the army.'

'Monty and Alex', 'Monty primarily', be it noted. As these two very different but very fine soldiers agreed on what problems had to be rectified and the best ways of doing so, and as Alexander was not only the senior but, at that time, enjoyed the greater reputation, it might have seemed certain that credit for this effect would have been given to 'Alex and Monty'. That it was not was the fault of Alexander's own kindness and his consideration for others.

Before leaving for Moscow via Teheran in the early hours of 11 August, Churchill had signalled to London that 'the transfer of responsibility' to the new commanders 'will be effected in three days from the 9th unless General Alexander asks for a few more days which is unlikely'. It has never been suggested that Alexander made any such request; as Clarke relates, he believed the need for action was urgent. Unfortunately, his predecessor had other ideas.

Auchinleck had been outraged by the loss of his high position. He received an embarrassed Colonel Jacob, carrying Churchill's letter of dismissal, with calm dignity, earning the admiring tribute: 'A great man and a fighter'.[5] A meeting between Auchinleck and Churchill was, says the latter, 'at once bleak and impeccable'. But to Brooke, who, as he knew, was ultimately responsible for his removal, Auchinleck revealed his true feelings. 'I tried to soften the blow as much as I possibly could,' Brooke would recall. 'In the end, I had no alternative but to turn on him and put him in his place; he left me no alternative. I had to bite him back as he was apt to snarl; that kept him quiet.'

Perhaps therefore it was wounded vanity that persuaded Auchinleck to take a step for which no reasonable explanation has ever been offered. The Prime Minister's party had hardly left before Auchinleck expressed a desire that his leadership of both the Middle East and Eighth Army should continue until 15 August. Montgomery might go to Eighth Army Headquarters before that date, to 'get the feel of his responsibilities and his opportunities' according to Connell, but he was not to take over command. Alexander, presumably, would remain similarly inactive in Cairo.

It was an astonishing suggestion and an appallingly dangerous one. Auchinleck was well aware from 'Ultra' interceptions that Rommel was planning a fresh offensive with his strongly reinforced army, probably on 26 August at the period of the full moon. As it happened, Rommel's assault, which would later be known as the Battle of Alam Halfa, was postponed until the night of the 30/31st, but that was still well before Eighth Army could receive any reinforcements of its own, and so close in point of time that the new C-in-C, Middle East and the new Eighth Army

Commander could scarcely afford to waste a single moment acting as mere observers.

Even ignoring Churchill's clearly stated wishes therefore, Alexander would have been justified in rejecting Auchinleck's request. It appears from his action on a subsequent occasion that he may have come to realize this. At the time though, his sympathy for his unhappy predecessor prompted his heart to overrule his head.

Montgomery arrived on 12 August, bursting with eager enthusiasm, full of ideas, delighted to have a command in the field again under a superior whom he, along with everyone else, respected and liked. His euphoria did not last long. He found Alexander 'calm, confident and charming – as always', but when he explained his proposals for the future, he learned that, while Alexander was in almost complete agreement with these, he felt that they should not be put into effect until after the changeover on 15 August.

It was still surely permissible to make preliminary preparations, so Major General Harding was summoned to join the conference and asked to explore the possibilities of forming a mobile reserve corps. Harding's account confirms that, inevitably perhaps, Montgomery did most of the talking, but that Alexander, whom Harding had not met before, was 'in full support'. Moreover, when Harding returned that evening to confirm that the force required was feasible, he again saw Alexander as well as Montgomery, and the latter states in his *Memoirs* that 'We' – that is both Alexander and himself – 'told him [Harding] to go ahead.' Harding's creation would in due course become X Corps and though its role was not really very different from that of XXX Corps at the time of the relief of Tobruk, this certainly marked a change from Harding's previous task of planning possible withdrawals for General Auchinleck.

Harding had also been asked for his views on the current situation. His replies were forthright and far from reassuring and, perhaps because he had been so closely involved with the plans for retreat, he impressed both his listeners with the damage to morale that these had caused. Montgomery was particularly concerned. He had had an interview with Auchinleck which had proved short and difficult – the two men disliked each other, having clashed when Montgomery was serving under Auchinleck in England. In this, Auchinleck apparently made no distinction between the tactical retreats to the rear strongpoints which were definitely intended and the major retirements which would only be carried out if they became necessary. As a result, Montgomery had formed the mistaken impression that the Alamein position would be abandoned automatically when Rommel attacked.

Next day Montgomery was driven to Eighth Army Headquarters. He was accompanied by de Guingand, who had spent the previous day drawing up a list of those maladies affecting Eighth Army which he thought required the most urgent attention. The first of them was: 'The dangerous "looking over the shoulder" defensive policy'. His report thus confirmed the observations of Harding and must have caused Montgomery more disquiet. A professional soldier to his fingertips, no one understood better than he how urgent was the need for reorganization and for the creation of a new sense of confidence throughout the Army, if he was to have any hope of dealing successfully with Rommel's imminent assault. He therefore quickly concluded that it would be absurd to waste a further two days before making any attempt to achieve those aims.

Accordingly, at 1400 on 13 August, Montgomery took over command of Eighth Army, cancelled all existing plans for retreat, whether to the rear strongpoints, to the reserve defences, or to further afield, and made arrangements for the return of his Headquarters to the coast so as to restore the previous close and cordial relationship between the Eighth Army and the Desert Air Force. To his assembled staff he announced curtly: 'I do not like the general atmosphere I find here. It is an atmosphere of doubt, of looking back to select the next place to which to withdraw, of loss of confidence in our ability to defeat Rommel, of desperate defence measures by reserves in preparing positions in Cairo and the Delta.' Those measures he dismissed as 'quite useless; if we lose this position we lose Egypt'. He proclaimed that 'there will be no further withdrawal' and concluded: 'If we can't stay here alive, then let us stay here dead.'

This message spread like wildfire, and would quickly be repeated in visits to units and in specific written instructions.[6] With one gesture, Montgomery had ended the uncertainties, silenced the grumblers, and united all branches of the army behind him in relieved approval. When Major General Leslie Morshead, stern commander of 9th Australian Division, heard the news, he exclaimed simply: 'Thank God!'

Montgomery had also unintentionally 'stolen a march' on Alexander. Previously the most important figure in the Middle East had always been its Commander-in-Chief. From now onwards, it would be the head of an Eighth Army which would come to give him an increasingly personal loyalty; he would take the lead in deciding courses of action and Alexander would quietly and unostentatiously approve and confirm.

Since their present aims and beliefs were almost identical, this situation caused no difficulty for a long time. It is therefore most unfortunate that Nigel Nicolson, who also disliked Montgomery, having been on the receiving end of a regrettably not untypical display of ill manners, should have assured us that 'Montgomery's version of their relationship, for all its outward sweetness, was intended to indicate that he had no rival in the desert.' It is difficult to accept that it was intended to do anything of the kind. On the contrary, in his *Memoirs*, Montgomery unhesitatingly declares that he 'always kept Alexander fully informed' of his intentions and that Alexander in turn 'supported us magnificently from behind; he never refused any request; without that generous and unfailing support we could never have done our part.'

Indeed, if anything, it was Alexander's own self-effacing attitude that has served to disguise the part he played in restoring Allied fortunes in the Middle East – which is a great pity, since it was a vital one. Whilst Montgomery, for all the importance of his role, was essentially a field commander, in operational and tactical control of a large Army, Alexander, as the Theatre Commander, had far wider responsibilities. The Eighth Army was obviously the most vitally important of these, as he was well aware, but it was by no means the only one. For a start, he automatically became a member of the Middle East Defence Committee, coordinating the strategic needs of that area with his fellow Cs-in-C – Admiral Harwood, the victor of the Battle of the River Plate, and Air Chief Marshal Tedder. He dealt with its political-military problems in happy cooperation with the Minister of State, Middle East, Mr Richard Casey. He prepared the way for future Allied unity by fostering good relationships with American officers, in particular

Major General Lewis Brereton, who commanded the American Air Forces in the Middle East, the men and machines of which were now beginning to arrive in the war zone.

Nor were Alexander's duties confined to Egypt. On the contrary, he now carried the responsibility for a vast territory and for the garrisons, depots, workshops and training schools of various sizes scattered throughout it. In pursuance of those duties, he visited, at different times, the Sudan, Eritrea, Cyprus, Palestine, Syria and Trans-Jordan, in the last named of which, reports Rupert Clarke, he delighted his host, the Emir Abdullah, by signing his name in the visitors' book as 'Iskander', its Arab equivalent. On 17 August, on the return of Churchill and Brooke from Moscow, he took part in a conference which discussed the future of a new Persia-Iraq Command which Churchill intended to form, and the delivery of equipment through those countries to Russia. He supervised the construction of a rail link through Syria to the frontier of Turkey as part of the political pressure designed to ensure that country's continued neutrality, personally hammering in the final spike and greatly enjoying the opportunity of driving a railway engine.

Nor, again, has much credit been given to Alexander's role in transforming GHQ, Middle East from a 'rudderless ship' into an efficient, smooth-running organization, dedicated to providing every possible assistance to Eighth Army. The title of saviour of the army may this time have gone to 'Monty primarily' but he had 'Alex in full support'.

That support was moral as well as material. Almost the first action taken by Alexander on his assuming formal command on 15 August was to give emphatic approval to Montgomery's 'no withdrawal' policy, demanding that all talk, and if possible all thought of retreat, should cease forthwith. Since Montgomery had already made this clear enough, Alexander's order might seem somewhat redundant. In fact, coming as it did from the Commander-in-Chief, it emphasized still more the importance of the Alamein position – one for which men could worthily risk their lives.

Alexander also hastened to confirm the organizational changes that his Army Commander had initiated. For example, Montgomery had determined to end the costly obsession with battle groups, so favoured by Auchinleck and Dorman-Smith in defiance of the principle of concentration. According to de

Guingand, he ordered that 'the expression ceased to exist. Divisions would fight as divisions and be allowed to develop their great strength.' The Official History confirms that Alexander made it equally clear that 'the basic formation would be the division, which was not to be split up into detachments except temporarily for a definite task.'

Alexander agreed with Mongtomery that it would be futile to try to hold Cairo or Alexandria if the Alamein position was lost. He was therefore eager to strengthen it as much as possible. Indeed, he had begun to do so even before his official assumption of command. Among the forces intended to hold the reserve defences had been 44th Division. On the evening of 13 August, Montgomery rang Harding, asking that this be sent to the combat zone forthwith. Harding went to see Auchinleck, who weakly suggested that he consult Alexander. 'If that's what Monty wants, let him have it,' was Alexander's immediate response.

Despite this reaction, it should not be supposed that Alexander granted Montgomery's every desire automatically without any consideration. Montgomery also claimed 50th Division – which in practice had been reduced by previous maulings to a strength of only one brigade – as his army reserve, but his wish to have the newly arrived 51st Highland Division sent forward as well was refused by Alexander, who believed it was not yet fit for action. The Army Commander was not pleased by this decision but undoubtedly it was the correct one at this time.

Alexander did, however, always grant his subordinate's dearest wish: that of being allowed to fight his own battles without interference. Auchinleck, as de Guingand points out, had had 'a lot to say regarding the major decisions within Eighth Army', and his attempts to direct the fast-moving desert war from a distance had greatly added to that Army's difficulties, as had his tendency to pay protracted visits to Army Headquarters. Fortunately for everyone, Alexander's attitude was entirely different.

On his arrival in the Middle East, Alexander had quickly and clearly appreciated that if Eighth Army was to be reorganized and its confidence restored in the short time available before Rommel attacked, those tasks would have to be left to the dynamic and forceful Montgomery, while he personally ensured – as we have seen that he did – that his Army Commander received every possible moral and material support. The speed and thoroughness with which the desired results were achieved, confirmed Alexander in his opinion, recorded in the Official History,[7] that Montgomery was 'better qualified' to lead Eighth Army 'than any other British Officer of his acquaintance'.

Since he held his belief, Alexander felt strongly that Eighth Army's leader must be allowed to direct his battles free of any interference or distraction. He therefore made sure that Montgomery was shielded from political pressure, which he took on his own shoulders, and, with extraordinary modesty and self-control, he himself made virtually no attempt to influence his subordinate when the fighting recommenced.

This forbearance was the more remarkable in view of the importance of the forthcoming encounters. First came the Battle of Alam Halfa, when Eighth Army and its supporting Desert Air Force, with relatively few casualties, stalled Rommel's final attempt to reach the Suez Canal. Then after immensely complex preparations, including an elaborate deception plan, Eighth Army, though this time at a heavy cost, inflicted a massive defeat on the Axis forces at the Battle of El Alamein. There seems no need, however, to go into all the details of these actions here, for not only have they been recorded in many excellent accounts, but, as Alexander later generously insisted: 'Alam Halfa and Alamein . . . were Montgomery's battles.'

Indeed, prior to Alam Halfa, Alexander's lack of involvement appears to have been taken too far. Judging from his Official Despatch, he had had no knowledge of the basic changes in tactics that had taken place in Eighth Army since he had become C-in-C, Middle East. He appears to have believed that Montgomery was merely following the intentions of General Auchinleck when he had determined on a static defence, designed 'to hold as strongly as possible the area between the sea and Ruweisat Ridge and to threaten from the flank any enemy advance south of the ridge from a strongly prepared position on the Alam el Halfa Ridge'.

In reality, these were entirely new tactics which had been introduced by Montgomery and bore no relation to the intentions of his predecessors. Auchinleck's own Despatch confirms that the whole 'essence of the defensive plan' was 'fluidity and mobility'; Dorman-Smith's Appreciation declares that the battle should be fought out between El Alamein and El Hammam, which lies some 40 miles to the east; and, as already noted, the Operation Orders had specifically directed that Eighth Army should leave the area between the sea and Ruweisat Ridge to retire to the rear strongholds. One of these was Alam Halfa Ridge, but no special importance is attached to it in the Operation Orders; it is not as much as mentioned in Dorman-Smith's Appreciation, and far from being 'strongly prepared', it was held by a weak Indian Infantry brigade, it had hardly any fixed defences, and the Bare Ridge and Point 102 which lay between it and the front line were not defended at all. This was not surprising because there had not been sufficient troops available to guard them until Alexander, at Montgomery's request, had rectified the situation by sending forward 44th Division.

Certainly Alexander's lack of knowledge can easily be excused by the numerous other responsibilities requiring his attention in the brief time before the battle commenced – if indeed any excuse be needed. Nonetheless, it is possible to detect a certain relief in his subsequent reference to 'the confidence I felt in General Montgomery who had handled his first battle in the desert with great ability', and in Rupert Clarke's reflection that at Alam Halfa, Montgomery 'gave the performance of his life'.

By contrast, Alexander took a very great interest in the plans for and the preliminaries to the Battle of El Alamein. He had never liked the luxurious atmosphere of Cairo, and had set up a mobile tactical headquarters outside the city for himself, consisting of a few trusted officers and a small staff. Known as 'the Commander-in-Chief's Camp', this was to be found at first in the shadow of the Pyramids, but it was soon moved forward to just behind the front line. Here, Alexander was able to keep in close touch with his Army Commander, follow all developments, and be on hand to provide assistance, encouragement or inspiration as needed. It was a practice that he would continue – he would find it very valuable during his commands in Vichy French North Africa and throughout the savage campaigns in Italy, but at no time in the future can he have studied the situation with quite so much concern as in the period before and during the conflict at El Alamein.

Alexander had every reason to feel troubled, since his responsibilities had now been increased still further. Reinforcements were arriving in the Middle East but the men needed training and the new Sherman tanks were still having their 'teething troubles'. Alexander helped ensure that both were prepared for the immense task that lay ahead: breaking through a formidable defensive position protected by half a million mines and every form of lethal booby trap that human ingenuity could devise. At the same time he had to convince an impatient Churchill that, as he puts it in his Despatch, 'to attack before I was ready would be to risk failure if not to court disaster.' He succeeded by a mixture of courtesy and firmness which perhaps only he could have achieved.

Alexander's anxieties at this time must have been immense – in order to take advantage of a moon approaching full, the battle would have to be postponed until the night of 23 October, and Churchill was quite right to point out that every day that elapsed would see the Axis defences strengthened. Montgomery had warned that the battle would last some twelve days, and Alexander had to consider the effect of this on the safety of Malta. A convoy, albeit at heavy cost, had succeeded in reaching the island in August, but its situation had again become perilous. It was vital that the Martuba airfields be re-captured by mid-November, in order to provide fighter protection for another supply mission.

To add to his worries, Alexander was still involved in the problems of TORCH. This was originally planned for the end of October, but it was felt, with some reason, that the reception of the landing forces would depend very much on whether Eighth Army had previously gained a decisive victory. It was therefore left to Alexander to determine the final date of the assault. He decided on 8 November, for, as he declares in his Despatch, this would allow Eighth Army enough time 'to destroy the greater part of the Axis army facing us', but not enough for the enemy to send substantial reinforcements to North Africa. 'Both these facts,' he rightly concluded, 'would have a strong effect on the French attitude.'

It was these concerns which, on 29 October, led to Alexander's only interference in Eighth Army's conduct of the Battle of El Alamein. By that date, the enemy had checked Eighth Army's initial westward thrust but Montgomery had countered by changing the direction of his attack. 9th Australian Division had pushed northward on the previous night and Montgomery intended that on the night of 30/31 October he would make a major advance from the Australians' newly won positions, north-west along the coast road.

This would be given the code name SUPERCHARGE and would be carried out by 2nd New Zealand Division, to which a succession of British brigades would be transferred in order to sustain the attack's momentum. The armour would be kept back, ready to follow up as soon as the infantry had broken through. Intelligence reports, however, indicated that German troops were massing in the north, and some of Montgomery's staff, headed by de Guingand, were therefore urging that SUPERCHARGE be delivered further south, where it seemed likely to meet mainly Italian resistance.

At this crucial moment, Alexander, McCreery and Casey arrived at Eighth Army's Headquarters, enquiring anxiously about Montgomery's future plans. Alexander agreed with de Guingand that the direction of the attack should be altered, and McCreery offered to discuss the issue with Montgomery. Alexander would later say that he had no doubt 'Monty was suitably grateful to my Chief of Staff', but he was mistaken; de Guingand, knowing that McCreery's interference would only be resented, persuaded him to leave it to Eighth Army's own staff officers to renew their previous pressure on their chief.

Alexander had also brought with him a telegram from Churchill, declaring his conviction that TORCH could bring about such momentous consequences as risings in Tunisia or even Vichy France, if only Eighth Army had achieved its victory in good time before the landings took place. It was this, rather than any advice given, which really changed Montgomery's mind. When de Guingand approached him after Alexander's departure, he agreed that while the Australians should maintain pressure to pin down enemy forces in the north, he would execute SUPERCHARGE further south, where, he accepted, he could win his battle more quickly, if, as he thought probable, and as turned out to be the case, less completely.

Bearing in mind the urgent needs, not only of TORCH but of Malta as well, Alexander was quite right to express his concern, while the fact that the revised SUPERCHARGE did break through the Axis defences to win the Battle of El Alamein would seem to be a sufficient justification for the change of tactics. Yet it was not an unqualified blessing. The assault did not fall mainly on the Italian infantry after all, because the bulk of this was further south than Intelligence reports had indicated. In order to ensure quick success, Montgomery used his armour, and its effectiveness as a pursuit force was considerably reduced by the heavy losses inflicted on it by the enemy's anti-tank guns. It may even be that victory was not in fact expedited, since the need to recast plans resulted in the operation being postponed until the early hours of 2 November.

Most of all, the change in the location of SUPERCHARGE would contribute to the escape of the enemy's mobile formations. When Eighth Army broke through well away from the coast, many of its units, including its armoured divisions' supply echelons, were still making their way through minefields, and once these were passed, they still had to cross open desert on a very dark night – a dreadfully difficult task for tired troops. Rommel, by contrast, had the priceless benefit of being able to retire down the coast road, which naturally made for easier movement. Had the breakthrough occurred along this road, as Montgomery originally wished, he would have turned the enemy's seaward flank and these advantages and disadvantages would have been reversed.

In fairness though, the main reason why Eighth Army was robbed of total success was some singularly misleading Intelligence, received, strangely enough, from 'Ultra'. Two signals from Rommel were intercepted on 2 November and revealed to Eighth Army on the 3rd.[8] In the first of these, Rommel declared that his men were exhausted, his non-motorized units would probably 'fall into the hands of the enemy' – as would shortly prove the case – and even his motorized forces were threatened, because 'the shortage of fuel will not allow of a withdrawal to any great distance.' The second signal added that he proposed to retire fighting 'step by step'.

Consequently, when, on 4 November, a further 'Ultra' report stated that Rommel intended 'to gain some time' at a position known as El Daba, this seemed entirely in accordance with, in fact confirmation of, the previous interceptions. Montgomery therefore directed all his armour against El Daba, and by the time he learned that the 'Ultra' information was simply incorrect and his tanks had been launched at the wrong target, the remaining Axis mobile units had slipped out of his reach.

Perhaps it mattered little. El Alamein was still a victory for all to see. The Vichy French were sufficiently impressed to ensure the success of TORCH, if not the dramatic predictions of Churchill. The Martuba airfields were captured in time to provide fighter cover for a convoy which finally raised the siege of Malta. The Axis army was so mauled and its leader's resolve so shaken that it would offer little real opposition for another four months. After his dire experiences at Dunkirk and in Burma, after his agonizing responsibilities since coming to Cairo, it is easy to imagine Alexander's feeling of delight and relief as, on 6 November 1942, he signalled to Churchill:

> Ring out the bells! Prisoners estimated now 20,000, tanks 350, guns 400, mechanised transport several thousand. Our advanced mobile forces are south of Mersa Matruh. Eighth Army is advancing!

Notes:
1. The full diary entry can be found in *From Churchill's Secret Circle to the BBC: The Biography of Lieutenant General Sir Ian Jacob* by General Sir Charles Richardson. (Jacob would later become the BBC's Director-General.)
2. *The Mediterranean and Middle East*, vol. III (September 1941 to September 1942), *British Fortunes Reach their Lowest Ebb* by Major General I.S.O. Playfair with Captain F.C. Flynn RN, Brigadier C.J.C. Molony and Group Captain T.P. Gleave.
3. The Appreciation appears as an Appendix to John Connell's *Auchinleck*. The War Diaries can be found in the Public Records Office, Kew. Operation Orders 144, issued by XIII Corps on 29 July, and 71 by XXX Corps on 10 August, are particularly revealing.
4. Dorman-Smith's subsequent career would confirm the most extreme criticisms made against him. On returning to Britain, he reverted to his substantive rank of colonel and remained inactive until March 1944, when he was given command of a brigade in the Anzio bridgehead. It proved a mistake, all three of his battalion commanders protesting about the quality of his leadership. After an enquiry had upheld their views, he retired to Eire, changed his name to Dorman-O'Gowan, and found new employment, giving advice on future objectives to, and conducting tactical studies for, the Irish Republican Army.
5. Jacob's reaction should be noted, as it confirms that his devastating summary of the malaise affecting Eighth Army was in no way influenced by any personal bias against Auchinleck.

6. See in particular Operation Orders 145 (14 August), 146 (17 August) and 147 (27 August) for XIII Corps, and 72 (16 August) for XXX Corps.

7. Volume IV, *The Destruction of the Axis Forces in Africa* by Major General I.S.O. Playfair and Brigadier C.J.C. Molony, with Captain F.C. Flynn and Group Captain T.P. Gleave.

8. All 'Ultra' signals are related in *British Intelligence in the Second World War: Its Influence on Strategy and Operations*, vol. II, by Professor F.H. Hinsley and others. There was an inevitable delay before the interceptions reached the combat zone. They had to be deciphered and translated; errors or gaps resulting from poor reception had to be corrected; the message had to be re-encoded – and only then could it be sent on to the appropriate British Intelligence officer in the field.

Chapter 4

The Army Group Commander: North Africa

In London the news of El Alamein drew tears of joy from Churchill. In Berlin it caused alarm and anxiety, and with good reason, for it triggered a whole series of events which proved disastrous for the Axis cause.

On 8 November, Operation TORCH was executed. Three landings were made under the overall command of Dwight Eisenhower, then a Lieutenant General. In the Mediterranean, II US Corps went ashore at Oran; a mixed British and American formation at Algiers. It was feared that Hitler might cut off these forces by persuading Spanish troops to seize Gibraltar or at least render its harbour and airfield unusable by artillery fire, so the Americans also landed at Casablanca on the Atlantic coast of French Morocco, from which they could provide an alternative line of communications if needed.

The Allies were right to take all possible precautions, though that particular one turned out to be unnecessary. Complete surprise was achieved, as the German High Command, ignoring the advice of Kesselring and the Italians, was convinced that the target of the great fleets of troop transports heading for the Mediterranean from the United States and the United Kingdom was Tripoli, or perhaps Sicily or Sardinia. In Algeria the Vichy French provided less resistance than had been feared; indeed at Algiers itself, the invaders were actively aided by pro-Allied officers. Even so, all the main landings suffered delay and confusion; an attempted parachute landing on the airfields of Oran failed completely; and direct assaults on the harbours of Oran and Algiers resulted only in the death or capture of every man who got ashore. Resistance at Algiers had ceased by 1900, but at Oran and Casablanca fighting was still taking place on 10

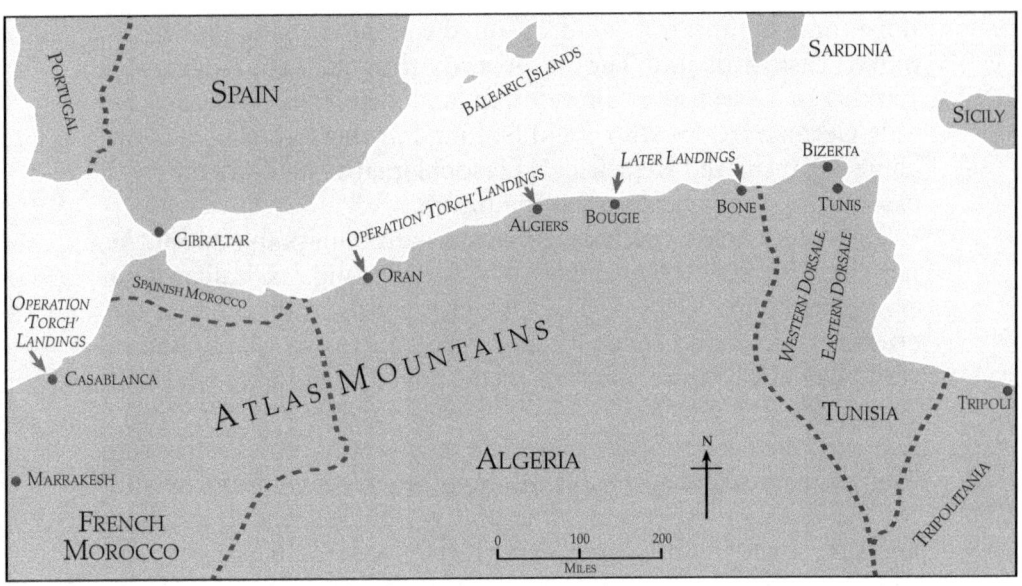

Map 4: French North Africa

November, and would end mainly as a result of events elsewhere.

Happily, Alexander's judgement that TORCH should await an Eighth Army victory at El Alamein now proved decisive, ending any chance of Spanish intervention, as Hitler was sensible enough to realize. It also had a crucial influence on Admiral Darlan, heir apparent to the aged Marshal Pétain as Vichy's Head of State, who happened to be in Algiers, visiting a son dangerously ill with polio. Since his aversion to the British was notorious and his first response to TORCH was to arrest the US Consul-General in Algiers, Mr Robert Murphy, he was clearly no supporter of the Allied cause. On the other hand, he was a realist and he recognized that the tide of war had turned, at least in North Africa. He therefore issued a ceasefire order to all French troops at 1120 on 10 November.[1]

Thereafter, reinforcements quickly arrived to form the British First Army, commanded by Lieutenant General Sir Kenneth Anderson. Aided by further seaborne landings at Bougie and

Bone, and by an airborne drop on the Bone airfield, Anderson moved eastwards into Tunisia. Already though, on 9 November, Junkers Ju 52 transport aircraft had landed at Tunis, carrying the only German troops who could be found at short notice – a parachute regiment and Kesselring's personal guard – and their arrival cast an ominous shadow over the future.

The Axis leaders had indeed reacted with remarkable speed. At midnight on 10/11 November, ten German and six Italian divisions burst into Vichy France, which they overran with savage efficiency. Axis soldiers continued to be sent to Tunisia, by sea as well as by air, because although the Malta striking forces were still decimating convoys to Tripoli, they were unable at first to interfere with this new shorter route. The men sent to both France and Tunisia, however, had previously been intended as reinforcement for the Russian front, and some 400 warplanes, not to mention aerial transport units, were transferred out of Russia to the Mediterranean area. These actions greatly assisted the Russian counter-offensive at Stalingrad, and subsequently considerably increased the difficulties of supplying the German forces which had been trapped there.

Since the German intervention in Tunisia thus led directly to a catastrophe in Russia, and would ultimately result in one in North Africa as well, it might seem to have been misguided, to say the least. Yet Hitler really had little choice but to take the risk. If the Allies could conquer Tunisia speedily, they could attack Tripoli from the rear, thereby dooming Rommel's command. Then, with North Africa secured, they could invade Italy, which the Führer, in an odd echo of Churchill's reference to a 'soft underbelly', called 'the groin of Fortress Europe'. He was rightly concerned that this would knock his increasingly reluctant ally out of the war.

Hitler's strategic beliefs were shared by Alexander and Montgomery. Their relationship at this period was particularly happy, and Nigel Nicolson relates that 'Montgomery would constantly write to Alexander private letters in manuscript about the facts of his situation, his hopes and worries.' In return, he received 'replies, full of encouragement, giving him the wider news, sometimes offering counsel and always help'.

On 18 November, Montgomery wrote to Alexander, declaring bluntly: 'It is most important that the Chiefs of Staff should be left

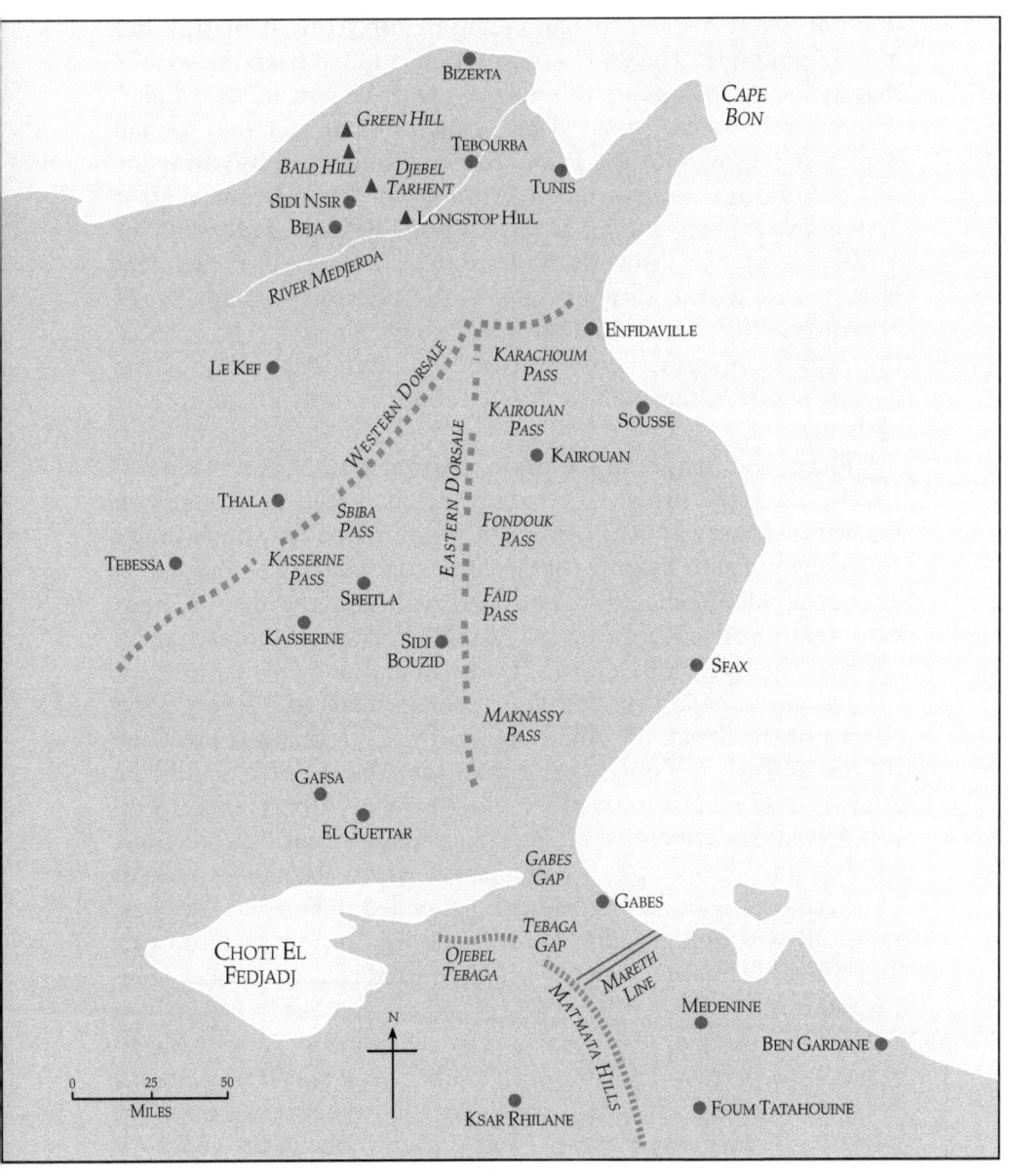

Map 5: Tunisia

in no doubt as to the problem facing Eighth Army in an advance into Tripolitania. The real way to take Tripoli is from the west' – that is by the troops of Eisenhower and Anderson. Alexander, who entirely agreed, assured his Army Commander that he had 'sent a strong wire to the Prime Minister and the CIGS stressing our difficulties', had pressed Eisenhower 'to operate against Tripoli by sea, land and air at earliest possible', and had 'asked for a forecast of Eisenhower's target dates'. It seemed in fact that victory was within Eisenhower's and Anderson's grasp. By 27 November, their forces had advanced to within about 30 miles of the port of Bizerta, while further inland in the valley of the Medjerda River, they had captured Tebourba, only 20 miles short of Tunis.

Unhappily, Anderson's main formation, Major General Everlegh's 78th (British) Division, had dispersed its strength in much the same way as Eighth Army's divisions had done under Auchinleck. Its 36 Brigade on the coast road and its 11 Brigade at Tebourba were some 20 miles apart, with between them a separate armoured column called 'Blade Force', commanded by Colonel Richard Hull, a future field marshal and CIGS.

Given firm leadership therefore, the Germans had a very good chance of thwarting the Allies and on the 27th this was provided by the arrival in Tunis of the man who henceforth would be Alexander's chief opponent. Field Marshal Albert Kesselring, like Alexander, concealed under a cheerful good nature a steadfast resolve, and in his case, a ruthlessness which Alexander lacked. Furthermore, again like Alexander, he tended to be at his very best when all was going badly. He forbade any further withdrawals and his soldiers and airmen quickly ensured that his wishes were carried out.

By 30 November, 36 Brigade, heavily bombed and unable to penetrate a narrow defile between Djebel Azag and Djebel Adjred – Green and Bald Hills as the British called them – had given up all hope of further progress. Next day, the newly arrived 10th Panzer Division heavily defeated Blade Force, then turned on 11 Brigade. 10th Panzer included the first five examples of the new Mark VI 'Tiger' tank, which was armed with the lethal 88mm gun and, despite weighing 56 tons and carrying up to 102mm of armour plate, could still move across country at a speed at least equal to that of almost every other gun-armed tank in North Africa. On 3 December, 11 Brigade was thrown out of Tebourba with the loss of more than a thousand prisoners and much equipment. Fighting continued throughout December around the sinister, double-crested Djebel el Almara – Longstop Hill – but it was finally secured on the 25th by the Germans, by whom it was known in future as Christmas Hill.

Meanwhile, on 7 December, the winter rains had arrived, turning northern Tunisia into a mass of glutinous mud, and forcing the Allies to turn their attention further south. The French by now were wholly committed to the Allied cause, and their XIX Corps, crossing an outlying range of hills known as the Western Dorsale, moved up to the Eastern Dorsale which formed the western boundary of Tunisia's central plain. Here they secured three of the five passes through the hills: Karachoum, Kairouan and Fondouk. On their right flank, II US Corps took the Faid Pass, leaving only the Maknassy Pass, held by the Italians, in Axis hands. Eisenhower now proposed to push forward with a mainly American force to the coast near Sfax, thus severing communications between Tunisia and Tripolitania, but fears that his inexperienced troops would be cut off and destroyed led to the scheme being postponed.

This decision would soon be justified. Kesselring's ground forces had now been formed into the Fifth Panzer Army, and he ordered his tactical commander, General Jurgen von Arnim, a harsh, grim man who had formerly led a corps in Russia, to regain the lost passes. During the latter part of January 1943, von Arnim, aided by strong Luftwaffe detachments, did just that, inflicting over 4,500 casualties.

Luckily, while other Allied advances were breaking down, Eighth Army continued to make relentless progress from Alamein. By 23 November 1942, it had reached El Agheila on the eastern borders of Tripolitania. This, incidentally, was the longest, most rapid retreat in German military history and it is astonishing therefore that most British accounts have only praise for the enemy, but little more than sneers for Eighth Army's achievements.

Thus we are told that the advance was 'a dull and measured affair', 'not one of those mad, headlong, exciting chases'.

Remembering previous madly exciting times when British armour had rushed headlong into the muzzles of anti-tank guns, this would seem to have been advantageous rather than otherwise. We are told that Eighth Army resembled a 'pachyderm' – by which presumably is meant an elephant.[2] Yet Kesselring in his *Memoirs* is full of generous admiration for the way the British were able to supply their troops, as well as some 11,500 RAF and AA personnel who advanced with, almost as part of, Eighth Army; while the German historian Paul Carrell in *The Foxes of the Desert: The Story of the Afrika Korps*, repeatedly describes how the Axis soldiers were forced into premature retirements with 'no time to reorganise or dig in for a defence', how 'Montgomery was pressing on with unusual speed', and how 'the boldness of the British pursuit was conspicuous'.

Perhaps the best answer to the critics, though, is to compare Eighth Army's advance in November 1942 with an earlier one during December 1941 to January 1942, following the relief of Tobruk. No adverse comments are ever made about this – though perhaps they should be, since Auchinleck had unaccountably entrusted the pursuit to XIII Corps rather than to XXX Corps which at that time had been especially trained and equipped for such mobile operations – but in any case Eighth Army then took thirty days to cover some 470 miles by the coast road from Tobruk to El Agheila. In November 1942, an Eighth Army commanded by Montgomery, under the overall control of Alexander as C-in-C, Middle East, advanced some 840 miles by the coast road from El Alamein to El Agheila in just nineteen days.

There was another way in which the two pursuits were very different: the later one did not end at El Agheila. There was possibly a longer pause for reorganization here than was really necessary, because 'Ultra' intercepts had revealed that Rommel had been expressly ordered to hold the El Agheila defences, but not that he had no intention of doing so. Nonetheless, by 16 December those defences were in Eighth Army's hands. By 29 December the Axis forces were back in a new position at Buerat. The men of Eighth Army assaulted this on 15 January 1943; captured it by the 16th; took the formidable Homs-Tarhuna escarpment 'on the run'; and entered Tripoli at 0530 on the 23rd. Even then, some advanced formations were given little time to enjoy their triumph, and had crossed the border into Tunisia by 4 February.

Appropriately enough on that same day, Churchill and Brooke took the salute at a Victory Parade in Tripoli. Alexander stood by Churchill's side, but despite his pride in the men under his command, the main purpose of his visit to Tripoli was to discuss with Montgomery the part Eighth Army should play in the liberation of Tunisia. This was now of increased importance to Alexander, since his responsibilities had been still further increased at the Casablanca Conference in January.

At Casablanca, Churchill, Roosevelt, the British and American Chiefs of Staff, and other high-ranking officials had determined the future aims of the Western Allies. Alexander played only a small part in the decisions reached, but he made a great impression on the Americans, particularly the President. 'The easy smiling grace of Alexander,' according to Churchill, 'won all hearts. His unspoken confidence was contagious.'

Alexander had already gained Eisenhower's friendship at their previous meeting in London and, brief though this was, he had also succeeded in impressing the quiet American with a conviction that he could trust Alexander's advice and judgement implicitly. Consequently, he was very willing to listen when Alexander, quietly but firmly, supported Brooke's arguments against the plan to strike eastward to Sfax. Churchill, who had not favoured it either, was much relieved, reporting to the War Cabinet that: 'It was fortunate indeed that we all met here and that I brought General Alexander to the scene.'

Eisenhower was also delighted when the British Chiefs of Staff proposed that Alexander should be appointed his Deputy, with operational control over all Allied forces in Tunisia, including Eighth Army when it crossed the frontier. Delighted, but also slightly embarrassed, for he would not be promoted to a full 'four star' general until 11 February, and he was very conscious of the extent of Alexander's military experience. So much was this the case that he assured Roosevelt and his Chief of Army Staff, General George Marshall, that he would be happy to serve under Alexander if this was considered desirable. As usual though, politics intervened. It was necessary to appease the Americans, who were not greatly in favour of operations in the Mediterranean; and the French would never have recognized a British officer as the Supreme Commander in any circumstances.

It was of course highly unusual for an officer of Alexander's standing to be asked to abandon his prestigious position as a Theatre Commander in order to serve under a general who was junior to him and totally inexperienced. Yet both Churchill and Brooke were certain that he was the only man who had that mixture of patience and firmness which would be needed to resolve the highly dangerous situation in North Africa. They also knew that he would accept his orders with equanimity – as, needless to say, he did without a murmur. He stepped down from the height of C-in-C, Middle East in favour of General Sir Henry Maitland Wilson, previously head of the Persia-Iraq Command. Instead he became 'Deputy Commander-in-Chief of the Allied Forces in French North Africa' and 'Commander of the Group of Armies operating in Tunisia' – it was designated the Eighteenth but in point of time it was the first ever Allied Army Group.

Alexander's mission was stated as being 'the early destruction of all Axis forces in Tunisia', which was to be followed by the invasion of Sicily. The occupation of that island would open the Mediterranean to Allied shipping and at last end the necessity for convoys to pass all the way round the Cape of Good Hope. It might also deal the final blow to a tottering Italy. In addition, Allied pressure on Italy should reduce Axis pressure on Russia. This would become the more urgent in late February, when, recovering with remarkable resilience from the disaster at Stalingrad, the Germans embarked on a new offensive which would culminate, on 15 March, in their recapture of Kharkov.

So fine a strategist as Alexander was well aware of the importance of Sicily, but any future commitments were quickly cast into the background by more immediate concerns. Alexander's appointment had been scheduled to begin on 20 February. A few days previously, however, he went to Algiers, accompanied by McCreery, who would remain his Chief of Staff, and a team of officers for Eighteenth Army Group. After consultations with Eisenhower, he moved on to Anderson's First Army Headquarters, following which he toured the front line to assess the situation. He quickly realized, perhaps with more resignation than surprise, that he had once again to rectify a highly unpromising situation.

Despite the arrival on the scene of Eighth Army, Kesselring had remained confident. Eighth Army's supply difficulties had not ceased with the capture of Tripoli, for the Germans had blocked the harbour and demolished the port facilities so thoroughly that the first supply ship only arrived on 2 February and large quantities of stores only on the 14th. The Axis commander thus had good reason to suppose that on his southern front 'a lull would continue at least for several weeks'.

Kesselring's determination to resist had never wavered, but now Rommel, who had shown little resolve recently, recovered his old aggressive spirit. Encouraged by his junction with his comrades in Tunisia, and the prospect of engaging inexperienced troops instead of his usual veteran opponents, Rommel proposed to strike at II US Corps which, from its forward position at Gafsa, west of Maknassy, threatened the rear of his right flank.

For this move, Rommel wished to use not only his own armoured divisions, 15th Panzer and the Italian Centauro, but also his former 21st Panzer, recently transferred to von Arnim, and von Arnim's original 10th Panzer Division. Von Arnim, on the other hand, wished to use 10th and 21st Panzer to strike westward from the Faid Pass towards the American positions at Sidi Bou Zid. Kesselring, who, like Alexander, would become used to balancing the requirements of demanding subordinates, decided that von Arnim's attack should go in first, but thereafter he should hand over 21st Panzer at least to assist Rommel's advance.

On 14 February, Fifth Panzer Army, under the command of von Arnim's Chief of Staff, Lieutenant General Heinz Ziegler, well supported by Kesselring's dive-bombers, struck at Sidi Bou Zid. Intercepted signals had indicated that the attack would come through Fondouk, and although more orthodox Intelligence contradicted this, 'Ultra' was considered sacrosanct in some quarters, then and later. As a result, not only were the Americans taken completely by surprise, but reinforcements were held back in the belief that Ziegler's assault was only a diversion. In three days the Germans destroyed two tank, two artillery, and two infantry battalions from II US Corps. Ziegler then advanced north-westward to Sbeitla, which he captured in the late afternoon of 17 February; while Rommel moved up on his left flank to Gafsa, which the Americans had abandoned on the 15th, together with vast stores of petrol and ammunition.

This was the scene which greeted Alexander on his tour of the front line – horribly familiar after his experiences at Dunkirk and in Burma. As he reported bluntly to Brooke: 'The general situation is far from satisfactory. British, American and French units are all mixed up on the front especially in the south. Formations have been split up. There is no policy and no plan of campaign. The air is much the same. This is the result of no firm direction or centralised control from above.'

So concerned was Alexander that he took command prematurely on 18 February, two days earlier than had been intended. This, of course, was what Montgomery had done on his arrival in the Middle East, but whereas Montgomery's action has been violently condemned, no one has ever blamed Alexander for following his example. This might appear rather unfair to the Eighth Army Commander, but perhaps it should really be seen as a reflection of Alexander's noble character. Montgomery, often offensive, invariably tactless, made enemies even of some who most admired his abilities; Alexander made friends even of some who most strongly disagreed with him.[3]

At least, though, fate had given Montgomery just enough time to alter the absurd plans of Auchinleck and his adviser before the Battle of Alam Halfa began. When Alexander took over in Tunisia, he had no chance to do anything other than urge the troops he visited to hold firm and try to hearten them by his own calm assurance, before further blows fell upon them.

Rommel, his spirits dramatically raised by recent events, now proposed to thrust north-westward through the Western Dorsale with all the Axis armour, his objective being the main American base at Tebessa with its huge supply dumps. Kesselring agreed but the Commando Supremo in Rome ordered Rommel to strike northwards instead towards Le Kef, thus cutting in behind the Allied front line.

Von Arnim had protested strongly against having to hand over his tanks. He reluctantly released 21st Panzer but, despite express orders from Kesselring, he retained half of 10th Panzer, including its supporting Tiger Tank unit, and dispatched the other half only after a considerable delay. Nonetheless, on 19 February, Rommel directed 21st Panzer on Le Kef through the Sbiba Pass, and sent 15th Panzer and Centauro towards the Kasserine Pass, from which they could advance on both Le Kef and Tebessa.

It was at this point that Alexander took the first of two steps which would have a vital effect on the battle. He had anticipated the probability of an enemy advance on Le Kef and ordered Anderson 'to concentrate his armour for the defence of Thala' which lies to the north of the Kasserine Pass. Reinforcements, British and American, infantry and artillery, were rushed to both Thala and Sbiba, and at the latter the defenders put up such a sturdy resistance that Rommel abandoned hope of any further advance. American forces also held out at Kasserine, and it was not until units from 10th Panzer had joined Rommel that he finally broke through at 1630 on 20 February.

By that time, US troops had blocked the secondary road to Tebessa and Brigadier Charles Dunphie's 26th (British) Armoured Brigade had taken up station south of Thala. The Brigade's motor battalion, Lieutenant Colonel Gore's 10th Rifle Brigade, together with a squadron of tanks and some anti-tank guns, moved forward and covered the retirement of the Kasserine defenders by a stubborn delaying action.

On the 21st, 26th Armoured Brigade slowly retired to Thala, but, as darkness fell, a surprise raid was made on a newly arrived British infantry force by German tanks, led by a captured British Valentine, which tricked the defenders into believing that this was a straggling Allied column. The attackers were eventually forced to withdraw but they took with them 700 prisoners, which brought the number captured in the offensive as a whole to about 4,000.

Yet in the midst of his successes, Rommel kept glancing anxiously over his shoulder. On 16 February, Eighth Army's advanced units had captured Ben Gardane, an Axis stronghold on the Tunisian coast. Next day, Medenine was taken, as were its four landing grounds. On the 18th, Foum Tatahouine fell. These conquests, Rommel noted uneasily, were achieved 'rather earlier than we had bargained for' – another interesting comment on Eighth Army's allegedly ponderous progress.

Eighth Army now began to build up its supply bases in the area in preparation for an assault in mid-March on the solid French-built defences of the Mareth Line, intended ironically to protect

Tunisia from the Italians who were now among the troops holding it. Then late on 21 February, Alexander took his second vital step. He sent a signal to Montgomery, asking that Eighth Army put increased pressure on the enemy immediately, so as to help prevent further problems at Kasserine.

Montgomery received this appeal early next day. According to General Richardson, now Eighth Army's Director of Operations, he promptly declared: 'Alex is in trouble; we must do everything we can to help him.' Eighth Army's forward units were ordered up to the Mareth Line at once, and the Kittyhawk fighter-bombers of the Desert Air Force stepped up their attacks. 'It was Monty at his most generous,' Richardson concludes.

It was certainly a generous gesture. Montgomery sent a cheerful signal to Alexander that they might be able to get Rommel 'running about' between them 'like a wet hen', but he was well aware that his action was liable to bring the enemy down on his advanced troops at a time when half his army was still back in Cyrenaica and even his nearest reserve division was 200 miles away at Tripoli. Tanks and anti-tank guns were hastily rushed forward and the danger had passed by 4 March, but Montgomery would admit to de Guingand afterwards that he 'had sweated a bit at times'. The whole incident not only makes nonsense of suggestions that the Eighth Army Commander was unwilling to take the slightest risk; it again demonstrates the mutual trust and cooperation – the teamwork, it might be called – between 'Alex' and 'Monty'.

Alexander replied to the 'wet hen' signal by saying he was 'greatly relieved' – as well he might be. When Rommel met Kesselring late on the 22nd, his superior was 'particularly struck by his ill-concealed impatience to get back as quickly and with as much unimpaired strength as possible to the southern defence line'. That same evening, Rommel reported to Hitler that he was abandoning further attacks in the Western Dorsale. His signal was intercepted by 'Ultra' and revealed that Rommel's major motive was 'the situation at Mareth' which 'made it necessary to collect my mobile forces for a swift blow against Eighth Army before it had completed its preparation.'[4]

While Rommel fell back from the Western Dorsale, harried by strikes from Hurricane fighter-bombers, von Arnim, encouraged by the arrival of reinforcements, embarked on a full-scale offensive against First Army on 26 February. He achieved a fair amount of success, especially in the coastal area, taking 2,500 prisoners in all at a cost of about 1,000 casualties. His main thrust, however, was made by seventy-seven tanks, fourteen of them Tigers, plus supporting infantry, towards the vital road centre at Beja. This overran an isolated battalion of 128th (British) Brigade – the 5th Hampshires – and a battery of field artillery at Sidi Nsir, but was trapped next day by the remainder of 128 Brigade in a narrow marshy valley that the British called 'Hunt's Gap'. Here, for three days, von Arnim's tanks were subjected to a continuous bombardment from field and anti-tank guns, and from the Hurricane fighter-bombers of 225 and 241 Squadrons. All except six were put out of action, though admittedly only twenty-two of them were total losses.

By 2 March, von Arnim's offensive had clearly failed, though fighting continued in the north for the rest of the month. Rommel, who had wished to use the Tigers against Eighth Army, was openly contemptuous and instructed von Arnim to 'put a stop to the fruitless affair'. He was in a position to give such orders because Kesselring had promoted him to head Army Group Afrika which had been set up to control the activities of both Fifth Panzer Army and Rommel's own original command, now known as First Italian Army. This he handed over to General Giovanni Messe, who had led an Italian corps on the Russian front with sufficient ability to have been awarded a Knight's Cross by Hitler; his first task was to carry out Rommel's long-desired assault on Eighth Army at Medenine.

At 0900 on 6 March, First Italian Army attacked with 10th, 15th and 21st Panzer, two German and two Italian infantry divisions, and as much artillery as could be brought to bear. But Montgomery had prepared what was called at the time 'a masterpiece in the art of laying out a defensive position under desert conditions'. Rommel did no appreciable damage, gained not a yard of ground, destroyed not a single British tank and lost fifty-two of his own, mainly to Eighth Army's anti-tank guns. Three days later he left Africa for ever, a sick, disillusioned man.

At last the initiative had passed to Alexander, who had already made preparations to take advantage of this. His first task had been to correct existing defects. On 20 February, he had laid down the changes that he required: there was to be no more talk of withdrawal; the troops of the different Allied nations were to be allotted separate sectors; divisions were not to be broken up into brigade groups but must fight as divisions; a general reserve was to be created; new formations would receive intensive training from experienced British officers, and brought into battle gradually, being restricted to limited operations until they had found their feet.

It can, of course, be argued that these requirements were very basic. So they were, but then they were designed to correct basic errors. It will be noted that many of the faults were the same as those which Alexander had previously found in Eighth Army, and perhaps it was the feeling that he had seen this scenario before that made his judgements unusually pointed. He was particularly hard on the Americans who, he reported to Brooke, 'simply do not know their job as soldiers and this is the case from the highest to the lowest'.

The assumption of control over them by a British general, heading an Army Group, the personnel of which were almost entirely British, and holding such a critical opinion of them, could hardly have failed to arouse some resentment among the Americans. It was, however, kept remarkably low by a number of factors. One was the fine attitude of Eisenhower, who welcomed Alexander's ideas, not only approving unpopular suggestions such as the transfer of officers from Eighth Army to help in training, but urging their adoption as soon as possible. Another was the equally commendable willingness to learn on the part of most Americans, who had been profoundly shocked by recent events. A third was that Alexander somehow managed to combine patience with firmness in such a way that the Americans' main reaction was a sense of relief at the arrival of such a knowledgeable leader.

A particularly difficult task faced Alexander at the outset. Major General Lloyd Fredendall, commander of II US Corps, appeared to him to have been 'utterly shaken' by the Axis assault, and to lack any ideas of how to improve the calibre of his troops. Had it not been for the political implications, Alexander would have replaced him forthwith; as it was, he hesitated to interfere in what might be considered a purely American affair. Happily, several senior US officers, who also lacked confidence in Fredendall, made their feelings clear to Eisenhower. When asked for his own opinion by the Supreme Commander, Alexander tactfully replied, 'I'm sure you must have better men than that.' On 6 March, Major General George Patton, who had previously commanded the landings at Casablanca, took over II US Corps.

Once again Alexander had acquired a subordinate who was colourful, capable and awkward. Like Stilwell before him, Patton had little love for 'those mealy-mouthed Limeys', but Alexander managed to win him over, though, as it transpired, only for the time being. Alexander did not lack firmness, telling Patton openly that the American troops were 'mentally and physically soft, and very green', urging him to form a training school with mainly British instructors, and even selecting a British officer, Brigadier Dunphie, the defender of Thala, to act as Patton's adviser. At the same time, although Patton's performance at Casablanca had hardly been remarkable, Alexander flattered him by assuring him that he would make the best possible Corps Commander. Patton, who needed little convincing, was delighted. He raised no arguments to any of Alexander's suggestions, accepted Dunphie, who later became a firm friend, and went so far as to declare that he liked Alexander very much.

Alexander had to exercise further diplomatic skills in dealing with the French. His policy of separating French units from American or British ones and grouping them together helped build up good relations with General Alphonse Juin, head of the French XIX Corps, as did some typically gracious personal gestures such as always wearing a XIX Corps emblem which Juin had presented to him. With regard to the French politicians and civil authorities, he treated them all with respect and impartiality; having some of the burden taken off his shoulders by the appointment of Mr Harold Macmillan as Minister Resident at Allied Force Headquarters in Algiers. This future Prime Minister, being a former officer of the Grenadier Guards, found it easy to work with Alexander whose 'modest, calm, confident' manner impressed him greatly. Their friendship would endure and, according to Rupert Clarke, they 'made a splendid team and each owed much to the other'.

Relations between Alexander and Anderson were less harmonious. Alexander was so critical of the First Army Commander, believing him incapable of firm, clear leadership, that he enquired whether Lieutenant General Oliver Leese, Eighth Army's most capable Corps Commander, could be spared to take over First Army. When he discovered that this would not be possible, Alexander added to his responsibilities by establishing a tight control over First Army's tactical operations. This was not perhaps a desirable state of affairs but at least the fighting in northern Tunisia was largely static and Alexander did move his own tactical HQ forward to Le Kef where he would be closer to the front line. Anderson would remain as head of the First Army during the remainder of the Tunisian campaign, but though he would later hold other important posts, he would not receive a command in the field again.

All these factors had to be considered by Alexander when exercising his most important duty: determining the strategy for final victory in Tunisia. He planned three distinct moves. First, Eighth Army would advance along the coast to link up with the rest of his command. Next the Tunisian plain was to be overrun, following which few further reinforcements, by sea or air, would be able to reach the remaining Axis forces in the north. Lastly, after these had been weakened by naval blockade and pounded from the newly captured airfields, they would be destroyed by a final assault from all directions.

On the face of it, the first move appeared by far the most difficult, for nature and man had combined to place impressive obstacles in Eighth Army's path. The chief natural defence of the Tunisian plain was a vast trackless salt marsh known as the Chott el Fedjadj, which blocked any attempt at an outflanking manoeuvre as effectively as had the Qattara Depression at El Alamein. A long tongue of marsh came to within 15 miles of the sea just north of the little town of Gabes, creating a 'bottleneck' called the 'Gabes Gap'. A series of high ridges ran across this from west to east and the intervals between them had been mined and provided with wide anti-tank ditches. The coastal area was protected by a watercourse called the Wadi Akarit, which had been deepened, widened and mined, and had been filled with water from recent rains.

South and south-west of the salt lake, an almost equally impass-able sea of sand known as the Grand Erg prevented all movement, while to the south-east the Djebel Tebaga and the Matmata Hills ran parallel to the coast, ensuring that Eighth Army had a further narrow passage, some 22 miles wide, to negotiate. This was guarded by the Mareth Line, a maze of mutually supporting artillery posts, backed by fortresses as much as 1,200 yards long by 400 yards deep and capable of holding a full battalion. These were protected by 100,000 anti-tank and 70,000 anti-personnel mines, and by watercourses of which the chief was the Wadi Zigzaou, 20 feet deep, varying from 60 to 200 feet in width, mined, full of water, and with its sides artificially steepened.

It was possible for troops to be moved west of the Matmata Hills through a 'gap' bearing the name of its discoverer, Lieutenant Nicholas Wilder of the Long Range Desert Group, but doing so would by no means solve Eighth Army's problems. A force passing through Wilder's Gap and then turning northward, would have to travel some 150 miles through extremely difficult waterless country, and when it reached the northern end of the hills, its way would be blocked by marshes and it would have to turn back eastward towards the coast, south of the Djebel Tebaga. This would take it through the narrowest 'bottleneck' of them all, the Tebaga Gap, just 4 miles wide, protected by strongpoints, minefields and an anti-tank ditch.

Considering the difficulties it faced, it might seem that Eighth Army had been given too hard a task and Alexander should have assisted it by mounting a simultaneous advance by II US Corps, which could come in behind Messe's First Italian Army north of the Gabes Gap, blocking its escape route. In a conference with Eisenhower on 7 March, Alexander did indeed consider this possi-bility, but rejected it, restricting the American role to that of making limited attacks to draw off enemy reserves. For this he has been criticized by his biographer among others, but there were two very good reasons for his decision.

In the first place, Alexander was desperately anxious to ensure that the Americans did not suffer any further disasters which might wreck their slowly growing confidence. Patton had done much to restore discipline in II US Corps, though his martinet methods, such as requiring the wearing of full uniform, including steel helmets, at all times, were far removed from Alexander's gentler approach. But neither Patton nor anyone else could make II US Corps an effective fighting force until it had gained experience in battle. Nicolson tells us that Alexander called Patton 'a dashing steed', but in reality he called him 'a dashing steed that always wanted watching', and he was determined to prevent Patton from asking too much of his men or endangering them by pushing too far forward. Patton would increasingly resent the restriction imposed on him but Major General Omar Bradley, whom Eisenhower had appointed as Patton's Deputy, considered it only sensible 'that we learn to walk before we run'.

The second reason for Alexander's attitude was that both he and Montgomery believed that Eighth Army would find its task far easier in practice than it appeared on paper. 'Ultra' intercepts had indicated that the Italians were losing heart and that Rommel and von Arnim, who had succeeded him as head of Army Group Afrika, favoured a withdrawal from Mareth to the Gabes Gap, or even as far as Enfidaville at the northern edge of the Tunisian plain. There thus seemed reason to hope that a resolute assault near the coast might 'bounce' the defenders out of the Mareth Line; that forces held back to exploit the breakthrough might then storm the Gabes Gap before the enemy could organize resistance; and finally that Sfax, Sousse and perhaps even Tunis might be taken in one continuous series of encounters. It was just a pity that 'Ultra' had not revealed that Hitler, Kesselring and Messe had no intention whatever of abandoning Mareth without a struggle.

Accordingly, Alexander not only set limited objectives for the Americans' first operation, but further irritated Patton by insisting that staff officers from Eighteenth Army Group should supervise his plans. Happily, Alexander's desire that American confidence be restored by a small success was fulfilled. While Major General Ward's 1st US Armoured Division guarded against enemy interference from the north, Major General Allen's 1st US Infantry Division captured Gafsa on 17 March. Allen then advanced to El Guettar but here he found his path blocked by the Italian Centauro Armoured Division, so he halted in accordance with his orders not to engage in a major action.

Encouraged by the capture of Gafsa, Alexander ordered a further limited American advance. Ward moved up to the

Maknassy Pass on the 21st, but he then paused, and when he tried to push through the pass next day he was checked by German mobile troops. American accounts blame Ward's halt on Alexander, who had insisted that all attacks must be properly coordinated and supported, but since Ward's men had been exhausted and heavy rain had bogged down his tanks, it would seem that he would have had to reorganize before pressing on, whatever orders he had received, and that Alexander has therefore again been judged unfairly.

Meanwhile, on 10 March, an Eighth Army unit had also fought a limited action, but one which was to have massive consequences. This was 'Force L', the initial standing for General Philippe Leclerc, who, on 1 February, had joined Eighth Army at Tripoli with over 3,200 French and colonial troops, volunteers all, after a march of a thousand miles over the desert from Chad in French Equatorial Africa. When Alexander had called for increased pressure by Eighth Army to help ease the situation at Kasserine, 'Force L' had moved up the west side of the Matmata Hills to the craggy massif of Ksar Rhilane, about a third of the way from Wilder's Gap towards the Djebel Tebaga. Here on 10 March, it clashed with a strong German reconnaissance force which included tanks.

Fortunately for the Free Frenchmen, although they were too far away for direct assistance from the rest of Eighth Army, they were aided by Eighth Army's partner, the Desert Air Force. Raids by the Kittyhawk fighter-bombers of 250 and 260 Squadrons, and particularly by the Hurricane IIDs of No. 6 Squadron, which were armed with two 40mm anti-tank cannons, drove the enemy away with ruinous losses. Messages of congratulation poured in for the successful pilots, but it is unlikely that they had any idea of how important the precedent was which they had just set.

At 2230 on 20 March, an artillery barrage opened the Battle of the Mareth Line. Eighth Army's attack was made by Leese's XXX Corps, while Major General Bernard Freyberg's 2nd New Zealand Division, heavily reinforced and officially raised to the status of the 'New Zealand Corps', headed for Ksar Rhilane and thence on towards the Tebaga Gap in the hope of distracting attention from the coastal sector. Two infantry divisions and the tanks of X Corps under Lieutenant General Brian Horrocks were held back in order to exploit success once Leese had captured the Axis defences.

Unhappily, there proved little success to exploit. Leese's infantry broke into the defences but their supporting tanks found it difficult to get over the flooded Wadi Zigzaou. Attempts to bring up the armour were made at the expense of the anti-tank guns needed to hold off the inevitable Axis counter-attack, and as a crowning misfortune, bad weather on 22 March grounded the Desert Air Force's light bombers which had been ready to engage the enemy armour. Early on the 23rd, Montgomery accepted that the coastal thrust had failed and that night the surviving attackers fell back over the Wadi Zigzaou.

Montgomery in his turn now asked if Alexander could help him. It was clear that the enemy intended to stand and fight, and Montgomery, on both 21 and 22 March, suggested that Patton should advance to the north of the Gabes Gap, not only to help ease the pressure on Eighth Army, but because this might sever the line of retreat for Messe's men, in which case, 'none, repeat none, of the enemy army facing us could get out of the net'. Alexander was equally aware of the possibilities, but at 2200 on the 22nd, he replied firmly: 'The role you suggest for II US Corps is too ambitious at the moment.' However, he did instruct Patton to deliver a strong armoured thrust further north at the Maknassy Pass.

Alexander's reasons for not favouring a move directly on Gabes were twofold. He believed that II US Corps was 'not sufficiently trained' and that the forces involved might well be engaged from the rear by 10th Panzer Division which von Arnim had held back in reserve. This anxiety soon proved justified, for in the early hours of 23 March, 10th Panzer did strike at Allen at El Guettar. The Germans captured several American positions, inflicting numerous casualties, but then their tanks ran into a minefield, and while so trapped, came under heavy fire; thirty-eight of them were knocked out and the remainder fell back. The attack was resumed in the afternoon but was again repulsed.

American morale naturally soared and Alexander, also greatly encouraged, began to think that an advance on Gabes by II US Corps might well succeed after all. Meanwhile 1st US Armoured Division was carrying out its planned attacks on the Maknassy Pass, the final one on 25 March being led personally by Ward, who was wounded in the face for his trouble. All of them failed, however, and on the 25th, Alexander visited Patton to direct that the American armour should be transferred to El Guettar. He also added 9th US Infantry Division from his reserve to the strength of II US Corps, which he ordered to deliver a full-scale assault towards Gabes. This began on the night of 28/29 March, but though Patton had 88,000 men opposing some 1,000 Germans and 7,000 Italians, backed by the forty tanks of 10th Panzer and the obsolete Italian armour with Centauro, it was also a failure and was called off as darkness fell on the 29th. At least Alexander could find some consolation in reflecting that the Axis forces resisting the Americans had been prevented from adding to the numbers facing Eighth Army.

By then, in any event, the Battle of the Mareth Line was over and won. Montgomery – who we are told repeatedly was a cautious, unimaginative general – had reacted with superb flexibility to the defeat of his coastal thrust, by switching his main weight to his subsidiary outflanking movement, in what would become known throughout Eighth Army as the 'Left Hook'. Horrocks, the Headquarters staff of X Corps and 1st Armoured Division were all sent to join Freyberg's New Zealanders. Tremendous efforts by the drivers of the tank transporters, many of whom had manned long-distance lorries in peacetime, got the armour to the mouth of the Tebaga Gap just in time for an attack in the afternoon of 26 March.

Nothing could provide Freyberg with the additional artillery which he rightly thought necessary, but a solution was provided by the example of Ksar Rhilane. In the past, the Desert Air Force had acted mainly against enemy positions, transport and lines of communication. Now its present commander, Harry Broadhurst, youngest Air-Vice Marshal in the Royal Air Force, despite warnings from his superiors that heavy losses would ruin his career, gallantly agreed that his men could participate directly in the Army assault on Tebaga, at a very low level, where the cannons of their fighters would be most effective. Alexander also played his part by providing Spitfires from northern Tunisia to keep the Axis warplanes at bay and cover the Desert Air Force's low-flying 'blitz'.

For three days, starting on 23 March, Broadhurst's pilots attacked enemy tanks and transport in the Tebaga area. On the

26th, they were ready for Eighth Army's assault and their own greatest effort. In all Broadhurst could provide two squadrons each of Boston, Baltimore and Mitchell light bombers, five squadrons of Spitfires, sixteen of fighter-bomber Kittyhawks or Warhawks, one of Hurricane fighter-bombers and the Hurricane 'tank-busters' of No. 6. In just over two hours these flew 412 sorties, and despite earlier fears, only one Baltimore and thirteen single-engined aircraft were lost, six of the pilots returning safely to their units. Under cover of this barrage, the Eighth Army broke through the Tebaga 'bottleneck', and by the following night First Italian Army was hastily abandoning the Mareth Line to seek shelter in the defences of the Gabes Gap.

Sadly, the failure of the original coastal assault had prevented any chance of these being taken 'on the run' as Montgomery had hoped. On 30 March, II US Corps again attempted to advance from El Guettar to strike Messe from behind. It did compel 21st Panzer to join the defending forces but fierce resistance and the repeated air attacks ordered by Kesselring thwarted every attack on this day and the following one. Feeling that this confirmed his original belief that a major offensive by II US Corps was 'too ambitious' a project, Alexander ordered it to revert to limited diversionary operations. Patton was furious. He dismissed the luckless Ward and exchanged vicious signals with Air Marshal Coningham, head of the North-West African Tactical Air Force, over the lack of protection provided against the Luftwaffe. Their mutual recriminations could only be silenced by the exercise of all Eisenhower's and Alexander's tact and charm.

It was therefore left to Eighth Army to make another assault on an enemy line. This began on the night of 5/6 April, and the following night Messe ordered a general withdrawal, leaving 7,000 prisoners, mainly Italians, behind him. The garrisons in the southern part of the Eastern Dorsale fell back with him and on 7 April, Eighth Army at last made contact with II US Corps.

Alexander still had hopes of cutting off Messe's retreat. He had placed 34th US Infantry Division under Patton's command with instructions to clear the Fondouk Pass, through which he intended to send his army reserve, Lieutenant General Crocker's IX (British) Corps. Once again he would be disappointed. The Americans proved unable to capture the Pass, and after repeated failures, Alexander, on 8 April, ordered 6th (British) Armoured Division to do so regardless of casualties. It did indeed have heavy tank losses and although it broke through to join Eighth Army at Kairouan, south-west of Sousse, it was too late to trap First Italian Army.

Happily, by this time, Eighth Army's advance was handicapped mainly by the almost embarrassing number of prisoners it was taking – they were coming in at the rate of 1,000 every day. Sfax fell on 10 April, Sousse on the 12th, and by the evening of the 13th, Eighth Army had covered 150 miles since taking the Gabes Gap, and had completed its conquest of the central Tunisian plain.

It was not the final act of the campaign but it was the decisive one. The loss of the central Tunisian landing grounds meant that the Axis warplanes had to be grouped together on a limited number of airfields, where Allied raids soon reduced them to impotence. The loss of Sfax and Sousse restricted their convoys to a narrow funnel leading to Tunis and Bizerta, which quickly engaged the attention of submarines from Malta and bombers from North Africa. The Italian merchant marine had delivered 90,000 tons of food, fuel, tanks and guns to Tunisia without loss in November 1942; in April 1943, only 27,000 tons of supplies and 2,500 troops reached their destination, and over half the vessels making the attempt were sunk. In the first few days of May, some three-quarters of the cargoes sent went to the bottom and only 2,000 tons passed safely over what had become known as the 'death route'.

Axis efforts to deliver supplies by air suffered similar losses to the Desert Air Force's Kittyhawks and Warhawks. On 18 April, four American units shot down twenty-four Junkers Ju 52 transports, besides causing thirty-five more to crash-land on the coast, where five of them were finished off by a night-fighter Hurricane squadron. Next day, two South African Kittyhawk squadrons destroyed eight Italian transport aircraft and badly damaged four more. Finally, on the 22nd, the Kittyhawks of Nos 2 and 5 Squadrons South African Air Force sighted some twenty huge, six-engined Messerschmitt Me 323s, each carrying ten tons of petrol; they sent sixteen of them blazing into the sea and for all practical purposes ended attempts to supply Tunisia from the air. Cut off from any chance of rescue, desperately short of fuel, ammunition and even food, the position of the Axis armies was hopeless. Even the unquenchable Kesselring accepted that their 'whole resistance would break down within a few days'.

Alexander was equally aware that, as he declared in an Order of the Day of 21 April, the Allies had got their enemies 'just where we want them – with their backs to the wall'. However, he also warned that 'this final battle will be fierce, bitter and long', so was naturally concerned to find the best way of ending it as quickly and cheaply as possible. On 10 April, Montgomery had urged that either First or Eighth Army should deliver the 'final assaults on the enemy's last positions', while the other should 'sit tight and merely exert pressure', but 'on no account must we split our effort and launch two or more thrusts none of which can be sustained.' He was probably not pleased when Alexander replied next day that First Army would make the 'main effort in the next phase' and he was to send his 1st Armoured Division to assist it. Yet Alexander was undoubtedly correct. First Army had an easier line of attack through country more suited to the employment of armour, and this was proved when diversionary attacks which Alexander did order Eighth Army to make, petered out by 29 April.

Alexander was perhaps secretly relieved that Patton had given up command of II US Corps in order to concentrate on plans for the landings in Sicily, but Bradley, who had succeeded him, now added to his superior's problems. He had, in fairness, valid grounds for complaint, for though Eighteenth Army Group's planners intended XIX French Corps to exert pressure in the south between First and Eighth Armies, they had found no place for II US Corps. Bradley protested to Eisenhower, who in turn, made it clear to Alexander that, for political reasons, it was essential that American soldiers take part in the culmination of the campaign. Alexander, quickly appreciating the necessity, directed II US Corps to capture Bizerta. Bradley therefore skilfully transferred his men to the northern flank of First Army, where Alexander visited him, discussed his mission in considerable detail, and, according to Macmillan, quietly suggested alterations to some of his proposed tactics.

First Army's offensive began on 22 April, and had ended by the 28th. Limited progress was made and heavy casualties suffered, but 78th (British) Division, aided by the tanks of the North Irish Horse, finally captured Longstop Hill on the 27th. On its northern flank, 34th US Division, again with the help of tanks, captured Hill 609, the Djebel Tahent, after an epic struggle. Its loss, combined with pressure from 9th US Division, forced von Arnim to withdraw from Green and Bald Hills as well. These encounters left the Germans with only some sixty tanks, which were so short of fuel and ammunition that some would later have to be destroyed by their own crews. Alexander's operations have been criticized – they were rudely compared to a 'partridge drive' by Montgomery – but they had prepared the way for the final triumph.

Confident that one more assault would suffice, Alexander, on 30 April, visited Montgomery, intending to arrange a further transfer of Eighth Army personnel to the north. Yet Air-Vice Marshal Broadhurst, who was present at their conference, confirms that the order was never given. The trust and teamwork between 'Alex' and 'Monty' was still complete and the Eighth Army Commander offered the reinforcements before they could be requested. 7th Armoured Division, 4th Indian Division and 201st Guards Brigade set out before dark that same day, and covered the 300-mile journey in only two days.

Broadhurst also reveals that Montgomery suggested to Alexander that he should concentrate on a single major attack: 'You'll be through in 48 hours,' he promised. To his great credit, Alexander, far from resenting such gratuitous advice, accepted it without even consulting Eisenhower first. He ordered subsidiary advances by Bradley in the north and the French XIX Corps, with 1st Armoured Division on its left flank, in the south, but the Eighth Army units were added to the British 6th Armoured and 4th Infantry Divisions in IX Corps to strike the principal blow in the Medjerda Valley. Since Crocker had been injured during a weapons demonstration, Horrocks was also transferred from Eighth Army to lead the assault.

At 0300 on 6 May, a tremendous artillery bombardment, followed by heavy air raids, fell on the enemy defences in the Medjerda area. Under cover of these, 4th Indian Division had broken through by 0730 at the cost of only about 100 casualties, and although 4th (British) Division found progress more difficult,

7th Armoured was thrusting out beyond the ground gained by the infantry by 1000, and 6th Armoured had followed suit by noon. Their subsequent advance was less rapid than Alexander had hoped, but at approximately 1515 the first British armoured cars entered Tunis, and Bizerta fell to Bradley at almost the same moment.

Alexander made haste to complete his victory. 7th Armoured swung north from Tunis, trapping Fifth Panzer Army between itself and the Americans. By midday on 9 May, the Germans in the north were out of ammunition and had no option but to surrender. South of Tunis, 6th Armoured cut across the base of the Cape Bon Peninsula, thus preventing an enemy retirement there – though shortage of fuel would probably have prevented this in any case. On 12 May, von Arnim surrendered to Lieutenant Colonel Glennie, CO of 1st Battalion, Royal Sussex Regiment, and at midday on the 13th, Messe, who had just been made a field marshal – a promotion well earned by his earlier stubborn resistance, if scarcely appropriate in its timing – ordered First Italian Army to give up the fight. The number of men in prisoner-of-war camps was later stated at over 238,000, but no doubt this included many who had been taken earlier. General Fraser in *And We Shall Shock Them: The British Army in the Second World War*, estimates that in these final surrenders, 'over 100,000 German soldiers passed into Allied captivity – a greater number than taken at Stalingrad a few months before – and nearly 90,000 Italians.'

Messe, meanwhile, had personally hurried south to capitulate to the renowned Eighth Army rather than to the forces closing in from the rear. Eighth Army had certainly performed magnificently throughout the Tunisian campaign, but the ultimate credit for the success of that campaign must be given to Alexander. He had directed its strategy throughout; he had changed doubt into confidence; he had held together his very different subordinates; and he had reconciled the needs of his very different national formations. No one has ever attempted to deny him this credit, and for once an unkind fate failed to find a distraction elsewhere which might overshadow his achievements.

Alexander would later be created a viscount and later still, appropriately perhaps, for services in a purely political role, he would be advanced in the peerage. He took his title from his most commendable success, and he will always be remembered, deservedly, as the Earl Alexander of Tunis.

Notes:
1. Darlan would not gain any personal benefit from his action. On Christmas Eve, he was shot dead by a youthful anti-Vichy fanatic named Bonnier de la Chapelle, who in turn was hastily court-martialled and shot two days later.
2. In fact, a 'pachyderm' is defined as a member of any species of 'hoofed quadrupeds that do not chew cud'. An elephant is certainly a pachyderm. So is a racehorse.
3. Montgomery would be the first to confirm this, acknowledging with astonishing honesty that he did not possess the 'fine qualities' of Alexander 'whom we all love'. 'I ruffled people's feelings,' he admitted. 'Alex smoothed them down.'
4. Rommel's signal is quoted in Professor Hinsley's *British Intelligence in the Second World War*.

Part 2

The Liberator of Italy

Chapter 5

Success in Sicily

Ahead lay 'Fortress Europe'. Its nearest bastion was Sicily, which, it will be recalled, the Allies had already determined to assault as soon as the North African campaign was concluded. Alexander had once again been given heavy responsibilities. Eisenhower would remain Supreme Commander, but it was to Alexander that the planning and subsequent conduct of Operation HUSKEY, as the liberation of the island was code-named, had been entrusted, and while the strategic and political effects of success could well be immense, a failure of this first invasion of the Axis heartlands would be likely to have equally devastating consequences.

There were many who considered that failure was not at all unlikely, including, discouragingly enough, Mountbatten's Combined Operations Staff. Alexander was instructed to capture an island of 10,000 square miles, with a population of four million. He would be opposed initially by the Sixth Italian Army, containing four field divisions and six static coast defence divisions, backed by the Hermann Göring Panzer Division and 15th Panzer Grenadier Division, which between them had 160 tanks and 32,000 men. These forces, led officially by the 66-year-old General Alfredo Guzzoni, but in practice by Kesselring, were supported by Luftflotte 2, now under Field Marshal Wolfram Freiherr von Richthofen, a cousin of the famous First World War flying 'ace'. Moreover, the Straits of Messina between Sicily and the Italian mainland are only 2 miles wide at one point and 5 miles wide on average, so the Axis powers, having supplied Tunisia over much greater distances, should have little difficulty in providing the defenders with any reinforcements they might need.

In addition, Sicily was ideal defensive country. Away from the few main roads, advances normally had to be made on a 'one-tank'

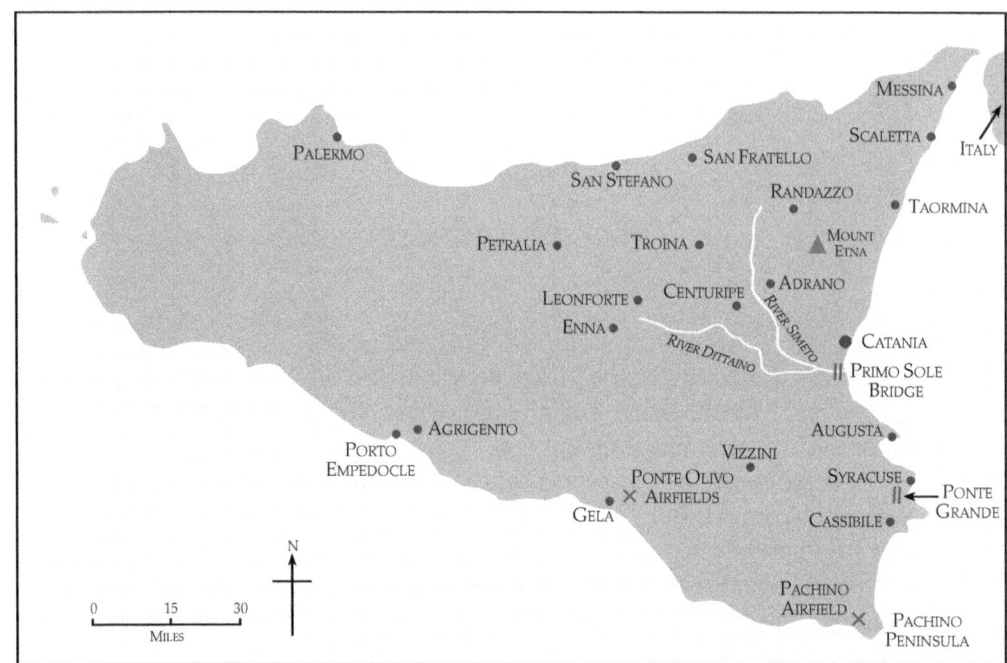

Map 6: Sicily

front, over narrow, winding lanes with high stone walls on either side. In between, the island, apart from its small coastal plain, was rugged and mountainous, and in the north-east, guarding the vital port of Messina, it became a maze of cliffs, ridges and gorges, dominated by the massive volcano, Mount Etna, surrounded by its great fields of lava which could cut like a razor, and injuries from which had a nasty habit of turning septic. No wonder then, that thoughts of Gallipoli in an earlier conflict, and of Dieppe in the present one, lurked in the back of all minds.

Alexander's greatest problems, however, were those of time and space. His command for HUSKEY was designated Fifteenth Army Group, a figure obtained by adding together the numbers of the two armies which it controlled. One was Montgomery's Eighth Army, which contained Leese's XXX Corps and Lieutenant General Miles Dempsey's XIII Corps; the other was a new American Seventh Army under Patton, which then consisted of Bradley's II US Corps and a separate American division, the 3rd, under Patton's direct control. To get these forces ashore would require the largest invasion fleet so far launched, together with strong air support. Close liaison between Alexander and the Air and Naval Commanders, Air Chief Marshal Tedder and Admiral of the Fleet Sir Andrew Cunningham, was vital, but, since their headquarters were widely scattered and until mid-May they were all concentrating on the final defeat of the Axis armies in Tunisia, this was far from easy to achieve.

Attempting to plan the Sicilian campaign was particularly difficult for Alexander in view of his myriad responsibilities as the ground force commander in Tunisia, and it is not surprising that he delegated the task to a special unit under Major General Charles Gairdner, known as 'Force 141'.[1] This produced a plan whereby the British would make three widely dispersed landings on both sides of the Pachino Peninsula in the south-east of the island and on its south coast, to be followed by another, three days later, on the east coast; meanwhile the Americans would make further separate assaults on western Sicily, mainly in the vicinity of Palermo. The plan did not appeal to Alexander, who suggested that the task forces should be concentrated and directed against the south-east of Sicily, but Gairdner assured him that the ports in that area would not be able to handle the volume of shipping needed.

The plan was then passed on to Montgomery, to whom it appealed even less. Both he and Admiral Sir Bertram Ramsay, once the organizer of the Dunkirk evacuation, but now the naval officer responsible for supporting Eighth Army, believed that the multiple landings would only succeed if Axis resistance was weak; if not then they could be overwhelmed one after the other. Montgomery acted promptly and though his arrogant and tactless attitude may well be deplored, it is difficult not to admire his forthright refusal to pay 'lip service' to a scheme which he believed would prove disastrous. On 24 April, he signalled to Alexander that they 'must plan for fierce resistance, by the Germans at any rate', and, in view of the way they were fighting in Tunisia, probably by the Italians as well. He therefore insisted that Eighth Army must land on one single front in the south-east of Sicily stretching from the Pachino Peninsula to just south of Syracuse.

Alexander, having already favoured concentrating all his forces in the south-east, and also believing, wrongly as it transpired, that the Italians would indeed fight well in defence of their homeland, was naturally sympathetic, but Tedder and Cunningham objected strongly. This was mainly because Eighth Army would not now be landing in the Gulf of Gela in the south of Sicily and so would leave the Ponte Olivo airfields free to make damaging attacks on the assault shipping. Such was their hostility that when Leese attended a conference at Algiers on 29 April to put forward Montgomery's views, no one was there to meet him at the aerodrome and he had to get a lift to the city in a lorry. At the meeting, the assembled senior officers 'listened politely' to him but would not discuss the matter further unless Montgomery was present in person. Only Alexander, says Leese, 'was splendid and stood up for me from the start'.

Montgomery then declared that the 'answer to the problem' was to cancel the proposed American landing in western Sicily and 'use it in the Gulf of Gela'. This would enable the Ponte Olivo airfields to be captured quickly, protect Eighth Army's left flank and simplify the provision of fighter cover for the landings. It seems that Alexander was informed of this suggestion when he visited Montgomery on 30 April. It is quite certain that on 2 May, Montgomery flew to Algiers, where he 'sold' his ideas to Eisenhower's Chief of Staff, Major General Walter Beddell Smith. He in turn convinced Eisenhower, and that evening Montgomery signalled to Alexander, who had been prevented from attending the conference by bad weather: 'Eisenhower will accept this plan if you agree and recommend it.' Next day, despite continuing objections from Tedder and Cunningham, Alexander did agree – Nigel Nicolson says 'resignedly' but it is hard to see why, for the plan exactly reflected the wishes which he had expressed when he had heard Force 141's original proposals.

The final plan did not solve all difficulties. The American landing would have to be supported over open beaches, but this problem was greatly eased by American production skills. Large numbers of the 1,500-ton Landing Ship Tanks (LSTs) and the smaller Landing Craft Tanks (LCTs), both of which could ground on a beach and then lower ramps for the use of guns, armour and lorries, were arriving in the battle area. So were Landing Craft Infantry (LCIs) which could similarly set men ashore. So were

DUKWs (inevitably called 'Ducks'), six-wheeled amphibious trucks which could carry men and equipment direct from ships to inland bases without the need to unload on the beach. And Montgomery was only too pleased to confirm that American supplies could be unloaded through the ports on Sicily's east coast, once these had been captured by Eighth Army.

The proposed American landing at Palermo had of course been sacrificed. Captain Liddell Hart regrets its loss, claiming that, had it proceeded, Patton 'would have been well on the way to the Straits of Messina, the enemy's line of reinforcement or retreat – whereby all the enemy forces in Sicily could have been trapped.' It is permissible, however, to doubt this statement. Apart from the dispersal of ground and air strength involved, the bulk of 15th Panzer Grenadier Division and two mobile Italian divisions had been stationed in the west of Sicily in such a position that they could have attacked a force advancing from Palermo to Messina from flank and rear. It is worth pointing out that no American authority would ever question the wisdom of concentrating both Allied armies in the south-east. Beddell Smith considered that Palermo had no strategic value except as a port for the receipt of supplies. So did Bradley (and, incidentally, Kesselring); while Eisenhower, some years after the war, would state that he still believed the decision to land the Americans on the south coast was absolutely correct.

Perhaps, though, the best confirmation that Alexander and Montgomery had been right is shown by the fact that once the senior Naval and Air Force officers had got over their resentment at the dictatorial attitude of the Eighth Army Commander, they took the same view as Eisenhower. The Navy agreed that the plan adopted 'undoubtedly reduced the risks of failure'. Tedder went so far as to claim that he personally 'had always favoured it'.

In view of the difficulties in getting an agreed plan for the landings, it was perhaps reasonable that Eisenhower and his Service chiefs should have preferred to await their success before deciding how best to exploit it. When they all met with Churchill, Brooke and Marshall at Algiers in late May, however, Alexander showed that he for one had already considered the matter. Churchill confirms that Alexander twice stated that the south-eastern ports and airfields were crucial, but 'once we had a firm grip on these we could ignore the remainder of the island for the time being'. He also suggested that 'as a part of the plan', and clearly before the whole island was subdued, a landing should be carried out on the mainland side of the Straits of Messina, thus severing 'the very windpipe of Sicily'.

Once again, Alexander had proved a fine strategist. Had such a landing taken place, it could have prevented any reinforcement or evacuation of the Axis forces in Sicily. This was Kesselring's greatest fear, as he later admitted. It was an idea to which Alexander reverted in mid-July during the course of the Sicilian campaign, but, sadly, he received no backing from his Supreme Commander or his fellow service chiefs. Cunningham expressed his support at Algiers but thereafter seems to have lost interest; no joint consultations were ever held to examine the subject. Eisenhower was unenthusiastic from the start – reluctant to entangle Allied troops in Italy until Sicily had been secured. By the time he changed his mind on 14 August, it was too late: the enemy evacuation of Sicily was already underway.

At least Alexander could assure Churchill at the Algiers conference that the preliminaries for the invasion of Sicily were proceeding satisfactorily. The most important were raids on airfields in Italy, Sicily and Sardinia which had secured Allied command of the skies by the time Operation HUSKEY began. Alexander also had an indirect part in a brilliant, if macabre deception ruse which was put into effect on 30 April, when the body of 'Major William Martin of the Royal Marines' was washed ashore on the Spanish coast. Among this fictitious personage's false papers was a letter to Alexander from the Vice Chief of the Imperial General Staff, Lieutenant General Sir Archibald Nye, indicating that the Allied objectives were Greece and Sardinia. The German High Command, provided with copies by agents in Spain, obligingly sent reinforcements to those areas, but, sadly, Kesselring was not deceived. A fine airman, he was certain the Allies would invade only where they could be protected by friendly fighters – which must mean Sicily.

Despite this disappointment, tactical surprise was achieved. As the task forces headed for Sicily on 9 July, a strong wind increased to gale force, whipping up fierce plunging seas. Yet Eisenhower, Alexander and Cunningham, all temporarily based at Malta, were as one in their belief that the operation should continue. Their moral courage was rewarded. That night, the storm subsided and in the early hours of 10 July, the superbly organized British and American naval forces set the soldiers ashore at almost the scheduled times on the right beaches – where they found that the bad weather had lulled their enemies into relaxing vigilance at just the moment when they needed to be most alert.

Only in the air did the plans go badly wrong. The storm which had so paradoxically assisted the seaborne assaults, gravely hampered the airborne landings which had been arranged to precede them. The pilots of the American Dakotas which were detailed to drop parachutists in the area of the Gulf of Gela had had very little time for training, and that only in daylight. Hampered by strong winds, uncertain moonlight and their own inexperience, they scattered their precious passengers over some 50 square miles, and although this may have helped to confuse the defenders, it is difficult to see the operation as anything other than a waste of highly capable and specially chosen fighting men.

On the Eighth Army front, 134 gliders took off from North Africa with the objective of seizing the Ponte Grande, a key bridge giving access to Syracuse from the south, while Wellington bombers raided targets in the area and night-fighter Hurricanes attacked any searchlights they might find. The route of the gliders and their towing aircraft passed over the south-east of Malta, where Alexander watched them flying low overhead 'with the roar of their engines partly carried away by the gale and their veiled navigation lights showing fitfully in the half light of the moon'.

Unhappily, the formation which had seemed so assured to Alexander, broke up as it approached its target. Some thirty of the gliders were towed by RAF Albemarles or Halifaxes, but the majority by Dakotas, the pilots of which were as inexperienced as their colleagues who carried the US parachutists. Sixty-nine gliders were released too soon, falling into the sea where most of the troops were drowned. Almost all the rest landed far from their target and only twelve, all towed by RAF crews, came down near the bridge. Eight officers and sixty-five men seized it and held off repeated enemy attacks until 1530 on 10 July, when the nineteen survivors were relieved by the vanguard of the advancing Eighth Army.

By the end of the day, Syracuse had been captured with its port facilities intact. The whole of the Pachino Peninsula was also in British hands, and the Italian coastal divisions, made up of Sicilian troops who had little love for Mussolini, were surrendering in embarrassing numbers. By the 11th, the Pachino airfield, which had been ploughed up, was being restored by the sappers, and early that morning, Flying Officer Keith of 72 Squadron safely landed his Spitfire there to refuel and rearm after combat, though the aircraft had to be dragged to the nearest road before he could take off again. The morning also saw the arrival of Montgomery in a DUKW, urging that the aerodrome be made ready as soon as possible. Two days later, it was operational and the first Spitfires were arriving to provide fighter support for the ground troops. Meanwhile Eighth Army had captured the port of Augusta on the 12th and the Italian Napoli Division had all but disintegrated.

The Italian forces facing Patton were much more resolute. A small group of light tanks made a gallant counter-attack on the town of Gela on the morning of the 10th, but was driven off. Next day, the Livorno Division, the Hermann Göring Division and a formation of Tigers made a series of converging thrusts which overran the American outposts. Determined resistance, backed by a devastating barrage from the supporting warships, shattered all the attacks but Patton prudently arranged for the bulk of the 82nd US Airborne Division to be flown in from North Africa as reinforcements. The transports arrived at about 2245 on the heels of a heavy air raid. The warships and AA gunners on shore had been warned of their coming, but after the first wave had been dropped safely, a single gun opened fire. Thereupon every weapon on ship or land joined in. Some aircraft turned back for North Africa but twenty-three were shot down, thirty-seven more were badly damaged and almost one hundred officers and men were killed.

Fortunately, the danger had already passed. Next day, 12 July, the Hermann Göring Division moved eastward to assist in stemming the more menacing British advance. Part of 15th Panzer Grenadier Division was already fighting Eighth Army north of Augusta. The remainder now hurried from western Sicily to the area of Gela, but before it could oppose the Americans, they had recovered their balance with remarkable speed and were pushing northward. By the end of the day their beachhead was secure and the invasion phase of HUSKEY had been successfully concluded.

Reluctantly, the Axis commanders accepted the situation. On 13 July, Guzzoni gave orders that the main part of Sicily should be abandoned and the defenders should withdraw slowly to a line running from just south of the town of Catania on the east coast, westward along the Simeto and Dittaino Rivers to Leonforte, then swinging northwards to San Stefano on the northern coast, from which the position took its name. His decision was confirmed by Kesselring, who had just flown to Sicily to visit the front line.

Kesselring also appreciated that Sicily would eventually have to be evacuated and so informed Mussolini. The German High Command reached the same conclusion, as did Hitler. All, however, agreed that the San Stefano Line should be held as long as possible and, with this in mind, reinforcements should be sent to the island. On his visit to Sicily, Kesselring had watched a regiment of 1st Parachute Division being dropped, most efficiently, south of Catania. The rest of the division was now ordered to Sicily. On 15 July, 29th Panzer Grenadier Division also started to arrive, as did XIV Panzer Corps Headquarters under the one-armed General Hans Hube whose task was to take over tactical command of all German and, unofficially, all Italian forces. To ensure a safe line of supply and potential retreat, the Germans arranged a ferry service across the Straits of Messina, which Colonel Ernst Baade – appointed Commander, Messina Straits by Kesselring on 14 July – set about making secure by the provision of over 500 anti-aircraft and coastal guns.

The Axis leaders had, quite unintentionally, dispatched their reinforcements at just the right moment. Judging from the notes he had made prior to the landings,[2] Montgomery's original intention had been to push up the east coast, taking Syracuse, Augusta, Catania and finally Messina, while the Americans protected him against attacks from any enemy forces in western Sicily. Considering its shortage of transport – priority in the assault ships had been given to tanks, guns and ammunition – and considering the unsuitability of Sicily for mobile warfare in any case, Eighth Army had so far performed with high credit. It had also made nonsense of the description of its leader as slow-moving and methodical, so often repeated in American accounts. Ironically, it might have been better for everyone if that portrait had been accurate.

For, though he had already taken Syracuse and Augusta, Montgomery now changed the direction of his main advance. Seeing an opportunity to cut off the forces facing Patton, he signalled to Alexander on 12 July: 'Intend now to operate on two axes.' He would send XXX Corps inland towards Leonforte and the neighbouring town of Enna, and felt sure that once it had reached them, 'the enemy opposing the Americans will never get away.' Only XIII Corps would be left to try to break through to Catania.

In order to compensate for the diversion of XXX Corps, Montgomery attempted to speed up the XIII Corps advance by means of an airborne assault on the Primo Sole bridge which carried the main road to Catania over the Simeto River. The 1st Parachute Brigade of 1st (British) Airborne Division left North Africa in 107 Dakotas on the night of 13/14 July, accompanied by anti-tank and sapper units carried in gliders towed by Halifaxes or Albemarles. Though the Royal Navy had been advised of their approach, this again unluckily coincided with a raid by the Luftwaffe, and a number of aircraft were shot down or forced to turn back. Most of the parachutists were dropped far from the target and only 200 men and a few anti-tank guns reached the bridge in the early hours of 14 July. Here they were savagely attacked by the German parachutists stationed in the neighbourhood of Catania, but they held on all day and even when driven off the bridge that evening, they prevented the enemy from destroying it. Next day, the advance guard of XIII Corps arrived, and the bridge was finally secured on the 16th. By that time though, the road to Catania was firmly blocked and no further progress could be made.

Nor did XXX Corps attain its objective, partly, by an unkind trick of fate, because the Americans had recovered so well that they had pushed the defenders out of the trap before it could close. Having once been committed, however, the Corps could not be switched back to the Catania area quickly enough over the inadequate road system. Montgomery therefore persisted with his northward wheel to Leonforte, from which he intended to swing XXX Corps eastward to Adrano, and thence north of Mount Etna, to cut off the enemy facing XIII Corps at Catania. Meanwhile he wanted Bradley's II US Corps to thrust forward on his left flank so as to protect Eighth Army's rear.

Though Seventh Army was capable of far more than a mere supporting role, this move had much to recommend it in principle. Unfortunately, Montgomery soured it from the start. The easiest way northward was over Route 124, which was the only good road to Enna and Leonforte. As this had been allotted to the Americans by Alexander, Bradley had naturally planned to use it for his own line of advance. Bearing in mind that American transport vehicles were better than those of the British, there seems little doubt that he could have done so most effectively. Unhappily, he was not given the opportunity: Montgomery, on his own initiative, directed XXX Corps onto the road instead. Alexander was not consulted, but being presented with a 'fait accompli', he felt that he would only increase the confusion by restoring Route 124 to its rightful users. Reluctantly therefore, he approved Montgomery's action.

Bradley, thus forced to mount his own offensive further to the west, was rightly displeased, and matters were made no better by the inability of XXX Corps, in the face of heavy German opposition, to take the important road junction of Vizzini before the late afternoon of 14 July. It then moved on to Leonforte but did not reach it until the 19th, or capture it until the night of the 21st. In the process, it passed to the east of Enna, an Eighth Army responsibility after the change of the inter-army boundary, thereby exposing the flank of II US Corps, which was forced to clear the town itself. Only the fact that Bradley and Leese were personally on excellent terms prevented a major breakdown in relationships between the Allies.

In the circumstances, it was greatly to the credit of the Americans, and a final proof that they had become experienced, battle-hardened professionals, that not only did they capture Agrigento and Porto Empedolce to the west of their original bridgehead on 16 July, but Bradley was able to keep pace with Leese in the advance northward despite fierce resistance by 15th Panzer Grenadier Division. On 23 July, Bradley reached Petralia on the inland east-west Route 120 and he cut the coast road, Route 113, on the same day.

By that time though, much of the benefits of this move had been lost. Bradley had always believed that, having reached the coast, he should turn eastward towards Messina. Montgomery, whose advance on Adrano was meeting increasing resistance – so much so that he felt compelled to summon 78th (British) Division from North Africa to provide him with fresh troops – had by now come to the same conclusion. On 19 July, he signalled to Alexander, asking that an American division thrust along the coast towards Messina, though, with unusual tact, he declined Alexander's offer to put this under his own command. Two days later, he was urging that the Americans as a whole should execute this movement while Leese renewed his pressure in the direction of Adrano. Unfortunately, it was soon apparent that the Americans would not be able to advance towards Messina for some little time to come, as a result of a decision made by Alexander. Montgomery did not take this kindly and the incident marks the moment when he would join the ranks of Alexander's critics.

It has often been said that Montgomery could make Alexander do whatever he wanted and it appears that privately he may have held the same opinion. What has not been understood is that Alexander usually accepted Montgomery's view simply because he usually believed that view to be correct. If he did not, as for instance when he considered First Army should make the final assault on Tunis, not Eighth Army as Montgomery desired, he did not hesitate to overrule his subordinate.

Nonetheless, Montgomery had become accustomed to getting his own way and was increasingly high-handed as a result. Yet it was just at this time that he found that Alexander was able to oblige him less and less often; even if Alexander entirely supported his Eighth Army Commander on strictly tactical grounds, he might still have to act otherwise in order to comply with political directives or the wishes of Britain's allies – as now happened in Sicily. Montgomery, whose sole concern tended to be for the men under his command, and who was certainly never a politician – both good reasons why his troops trusted him – could not or would not appreciate Alexander's wider responsibilities and wider vision. He became more and more intransigent and would go so far as to advise Patton that if he got an order from Army Group which he did not like, he should 'just ignore it'.

Not that the Seventh Army Commander needed much encouragement to oppose Alexander's wishes. Patton's distaste for Montgomery is well known but he regarded him as 'a far better leader than Alexander', whom he claimed 'cut a sorry figure at all times'. In North Africa Patton had deeply resented Alexander's criticism of American deficiencies and had interpreted the restraints imposed on II US Corps as an attempt by Alexander to keep all the glory for himself. Now, in Sicily, Patton accused Alexander, somewhat inconsistently, of lack of leadership and 'sitting on the fence'. It seemed that whatever poor Alexander did or did not do, it found little favour with Patton – but then Patton's own behaviour in Sicily scarcely suggests that he was capable of balanced judgements at this time.

Indeed, the most charitable explanation of Patton's conduct is that the pressure of circumstances had strained his always volatile temperament to breaking point. Towards the end of the campaign, his self-control snapped completely. On two different occasions, on 3 and 9 August, he violently assaulted shell-shocked men in hospital whom he thought were malingering and who, it is worth remembering, could not retaliate without suffering severe punishment. When Eisenhower learned what had happened, he was furious and ordered Patton to apologize, but when he asked Alexander if he wanted Patton replaced, Alexander replied that Patton was too good a commander to be removed in the middle of a campaign.

Alexander's wisdom and generosity were typical of the man, but it is permissible to wonder what his reaction would have been had he known of earlier horrible incidents that had resulted from Patton's lack of judgement. Desperate to instil a fighting spirit into his Seventh Army, he had, before the landings in Sicily, delivered a ferocious 'blood and thunder' speech which included such expressions as 'When we meet the enemy we will kill him. We will show him no mercy.' On 14 July, in two quite separate incidents, a sergeant and an officer of 45th US Infantry Division showed no mercy to over seventy Italian prisoners who were shot in cold blood. At their courts-martial, both pleaded that they believed they were only obeying Patton's orders. Sergeant West was sentenced to life imprisonment but released in just over a year. Captain Compton was acquitted and was later killed in action. There can be no doubt that Patton had never intended such tragic consequences, but he showed little regret for them, merely telling a horrified Bradley that nothing could be done about it and he should 'certify that the dead men were snipers or had attempted to escape or something'.[3]

In between the shootings and the assaults came Patton's 'obsession' with Palermo, as American historians have described it. On 17 July, he flew to Alexander's Headquarters in Tunis to insist that he be allowed a more important role in the campaign. His demand was understandable, but for some extraordinary reason he was adamant that his main effort should be directed not against Messina, as Bradley and, belatedly, Montgomery wanted, but towards the port in western Sicily where it had once been intended that he should land. Alexander agreed and, as already mentioned, Montgomery was most displeased.

'The over-running of the west,' declares Nicolson in *Alex*, 'was a necessary part of the campaign, to provide Patton with a port instead of the open beaches to which Montgomery's plan had restricted him.' Yet even ignoring the fact that Patton was being supplied through Syracuse and Augusta, to say nothing of the recent American capture of Porto Empedolce, Palermo was useless as a port since the enemy had most effectively blocked its harbour by sinking some forty ships in it. Neither Bradley nor Major General Lucien Truscott whose 3rd US Infantry Division was detailed to take Palermo, believed that its occupation had the slightest value. Which is not to say that Alexander's decision was incorrect. He had to soothe Patton's feelings for the sake of inter-Allied relations which he rightly regarded as of immense importance. As in Burma, political needs had to take precedence over purely military requirements.

Certainly the American conquest of western Sicily was dramatic and dashing – as it could hardly fail to be. The Italian field divisions had been ordered to retire behind the San Stefano Line on 16 July and the Americans were unable to prevent their doing so. That left only the men of the ineffective and demoralized coastal divisions whose main aim was to surrender as quickly as possible. The casualty list sums up the situation: American losses, killed and wounded – 272; Italian losses, killed and wounded – 3,000; Italian prisoners – 52,000. When Palermo fell on 22 July, its conquerors were welcomed by jubilant crowds shouting: 'Long Live America! Down with Mussolini!'

Alexander's immediate reward was to find that the man whose

wish he had granted was taking part in discussions over future strategy without bothering to consult him. On 25 July, Patton was invited to Syracuse by Montgomery, and there they agreed that Seventh Army should employ its full strength against Messina, for which it would be given the use of both the coastal Route 113 and the inland east-west Route 120 leading to Messina by way of Troina and Randazzo. Meanwhile XXX Corps, headed by the fresh 78th Division, would renew its advance on Adrano and then move north over difficult roads which skirted Mount Etna, to join the Americans at Randazzo. Though this plan clearly envisaged that Seventh Army should take Messina – Montgomery suggested that it should then push southwards to engage the enemy defending the Catanian plain from the rear – Patton's lack of balance again became evident. Not realizing perhaps that Montgomery could be extremely flexible, he felt that this change of attitude must be some trick and indulged in a new obsession: he must at all costs reach Messina before the British.

There followed a rather sad little incident. Alexander arrived in Syracuse. He was justifiably annoyed that he had not been advised of the proposed plan and was not mollified by being told rudely by Montgomery that everything had already been arranged by Patton and himself. He angrily demanded the details. Having been given them, however, he quietly approved them. He has, of course, been accused of a weak lack of grip and a failure to direct a campaign for which he was ultimately responsible. It would seem, however, that he should rather be praised for his moral strength. He could have demonstrated his own importance by demanding changes, but to do so would have been foreign to his nature and it would have served no useful purpose. Alexander approved the new plan for one reason only – he believed it was a good one – though it was somewhat optimistic of him to tell Brooke that the converging advance on Randazzo might split the enemy strength in two and enable each half to be rolled up separately as had happened in Tunisia.

Since Patton needed some time to reorganize his forces before bringing them back from western Sicily, Alexander set 1 August as the date for the new offensive and, on 28 July, moved his Headquarters to Cassibile, south of Syracuse, in order to supervise it. But in the meantime the dramatic news of the fall of Mussolini had altered the whole aspect of the Sicilian campaign. It convinced Hitler and Kesselring that the island could not be held much longer, and Kesselring therefore ordered his tactical commander, Hube, to make preparations for a planned withdrawal to the Italian mainland.

The details of the withdrawal were dictated, but also assisted, by the geography of north-eastern Sicily. The island gradually tapers to a point in the vicinity of the intended embarkation area around Messina, which meant that the farther Hube retired, the less width of front his soldiers would have to defend. He intended to make a sequence of retreats, holding first one, then a second reserve line behind the San Stefano one. Then he would occupy three evacuation lines, and as he fell back to each of these in turn, he would send a proportion of his men, both Germans and Italians, to the ferries waiting to carry them to the mainland. The remainder of the campaign would thus take on a pattern of periods of savage resistance, followed by rapid retirements to rear defences.

It was to comply with such a planned retreat that the stubborn defenders of Catania at last abandoned the town, which was captured on 5 August. On the northern coast road, Patton's men had pushed on to San Fratello by 3 August, but could make no further progress until the early hours of the 8th, when the enemy fell back to prepared positions in the rear. On the inland route to Randazzo, the Americans advanced on the little town of Troina on 1 August, but the Germans only abandoned it on the 6th, and then voluntarily. The finest achievement was that of 78th (British) Division, which had begun its own operations on the night of 29/30 July, prior to the main offensive. Its objective was Centuripe, the key to Adrano, which could only be approached by a single steep, winding mountain road, with deep ravines on either side. Nonetheless, after tremendous and brilliant endeavours, the Division stormed Centuripe on 3 August, and moved on to Adrano which it entered after dark on the 6th.

These events convinced Kesselring that any further delay would be dangerous and he ordered Hube to begin the evacuation as soon as possible, not even waiting to obtain Hitler's consent – though in fact the Führer accepted the situation without protest – and the first troops started to cross to the mainland on the night

The Commander-in-Chief, Middle East, August 1942.

2. Above and right: Pioneers of the *SS-Totenkopf Division* crossing a canal during the German invasion of the Low Countries. They are ferrying across a 3.7 cm PAK 35/36 anti-tank gun under cover of a smoke screen.

3. A British 25-pounder gun crew in action against the invaders.

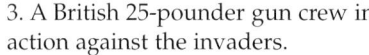

4. Above: Dunkirk beach with British troops awaiting transport.

5. Left: Abandoned British transport.

6. Below: German victors gather at a former British beach HQ. The Union Jack still flies in pathetic defiance.

7. Left: Alexander, Wavell and Slim

8. Above: The Governor of Burma, Sir Reginald Dorman-Smith, and Alexander.

9. Bottom left: Alexander and General Bruce Scott.

10. Right: General Thomas Hutton.

11. Bottom right: General 'Vinegar Joe' Stilwell.

The Defenders of Burma

12. Japanese troops during their advance on Rangoon.

13. Japanese troops in action among the oil derricks at Yenangyaung.

14. The Middle East, August 1942: Alexander, Churchill, Montgomery, Brooke.

15. Alexander hammers in the final spike to complete the rail link through Syria to Turkey.

16. Allied forces land in French North Africa.

17. Alexander with the Minister Resident at Allied Force Headquarters, Algiers, Harold Macmillan.

18. Eighth Army completes the 'left hook' which outflanked the Mareth Line.

19. Armoured cars of the 11th Hussars enter Tunis.

20. Field Marshal Albert Kesselring, Alexander's most formidable opponent.

21. A conference between Montgomery, Alexander and Patton in Sicily.

22. Alexander at the wheel of his jeep in Sicily, accompanied by his aide, Rupert Clarke.

23. British troops come ashore in Sicily.

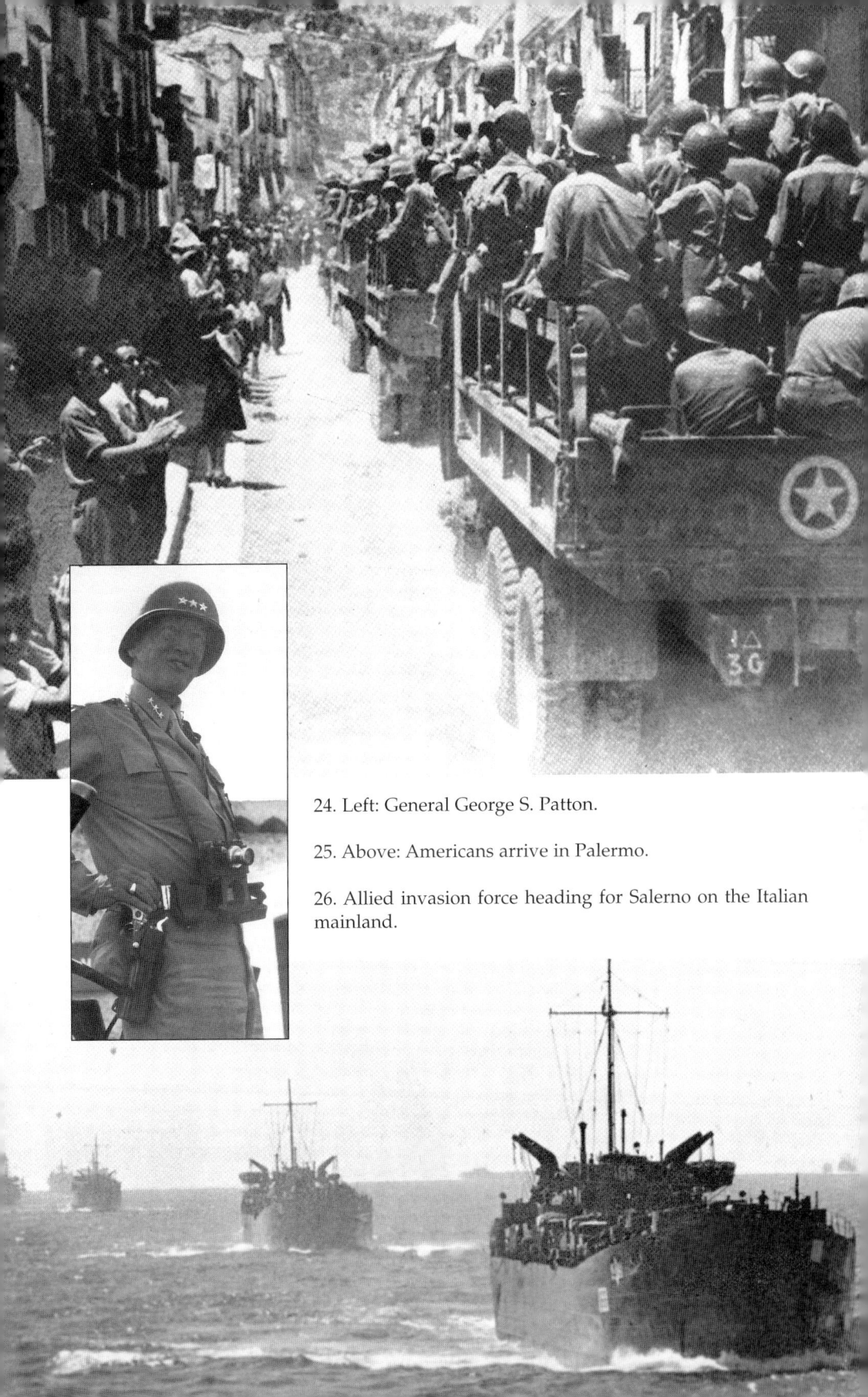

24. Left: General George S. Patton.

25. Above: Americans arrive in Palermo.

26. Allied invasion force heading for Salerno on the Italian mainland.

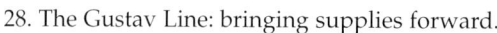

27. Tanks of the British 7th Armoured Division in action near Mount Vesuvius.

28. The Gustav Line: bringing supplies forward.

29. General Truscott and Alexander.

30. Montgomery and Eisenhower.

The Liberators of Italy

31. General Mark Clark.

32. General Leese.

33. Anzio: Allied landing craft approaching the beaches.

34. Cassino: the wrecked monastery after the bombing.

35. German soldiers defending the ruins of the monastery at Monte Cassino.

36. The Polish flag is hoisted on the final capture of the monastery.

37. American troops move up to the Gothic Line.

38. Right: Alexander and General McCreery just before the last Allied offensive in Italy.

39. Above: Victory celebrations.

of 11/12 August. Thereafter the end came quickly. Randazzo was captured on the 13th, Taormina on the east coast on the 15th, and, on the evening of the 16th, the Americans entered Messina – the liberation of Sicily was complete.

It might have been thought that Alexander, the land forces commander, would have received due praise for this achievement. Instead he has been subjected to blame, not only from Montgomery and Patton but from one of his fellow commanders as well. Nicolson says that Alexander 'had a particularly sympathetic relationship' with Admiral Cunningham. If so, the sympathy was entirely one-sided, for Cunningham would later contemptuously dismiss Alexander as 'a mountebank' who was 'not fit to be a supreme commander' and 'had no opinions of his own that he was not prepared to change'.

It is perhaps understandable that Cunningham, always very much the man in charge for all to see, should have had little in common with a commander who publicly stated that the task of his Headquarters was to serve the armies which made up his Army Group. It is also easy to appreciate how Alexander's modesty, and his generosity in giving credit for his own achievements to his subordinates, might suggest weakness or lack of control to those who did not know him well. Yet Cunningham's contentions did not stop there. He also disapproved of Alexander's strategy. In particular, he felt that once Eighth Army had been blocked at Catania, Alexander should not have permitted the wheel inland, but should instead have made use of the Allies' 'priceless asset of sea power and flexibility of manoeuvre' by carrying out amphibious landings on Sicily's eastern coast.

As a mere soldier, Alexander might have found it difficult to answer the claim of an admiral of the fleet that he 'had no knowledge of the sea and little of the air'. Happily, the Navy's own Official Historian, Captain Stephen Roskill, has done so for him. A major new amphibious operation, Roskill declares with masterly understatement, 'would certainly have been no simple matter.' It would have taken much time and trouble for the necessary troops to break off combat and re-embark for another landing; the enemy's coastal defences would have rendered the mission 'very hazardous'; and, most significantly, 'to the north of Catania the coast becomes so precipitous, and the few beaches have such poor exists, that it was scarcely possible to land or deploy a substantial assault force.'

Though Roskill does suggest that small amphibious raids could have been arranged north of Catania to harass and disorganize the enemy, similar minor assaults elsewhere indicate that these would have been unlikely to achieve satisfactory results. In northern Sicily, where both the coast and the beach exits were far more suitable, Patton had tried to speed up his advance by three such missions in the early hours of 8, 12 and 16 August respectively. The first landed in the wrong place and failed to cut off the enemy units, which were already retiring voluntarily at the time the attack took place. The second was fiercely engaged, lost all its tanks and artillery and had to be rescued by major American forces moving down the coast road. It did help to persuade the Germans to fall back twenty-four hours earlier than planned, but they promptly rectified the situation by holding their next defensive position for twenty-four hours longer than originally intended. The third only came ashore after the main American advance had already passed the landing beaches.

Had British troops been set ashore north of Catania prior to the Germans' withdrawal on 5 August, there would have been no question of Eighth Army breaking through to their aid and they must have suffered very heavily. Had they been set ashore after that date, they could at best have accelerated the withdrawal. In fact, the British did make a landing on the night of 15/16 August at Scaletta, 8 miles south of Messina – only to find that the German rearguard had previously abandoned the area. The commandos were hampered by demolitions and by damage caused by the Allies' own naval gunfire, but they followed up the retreating enemy to become the first British unit to reach Messina. This they did early on the 17th, just before Patton personally made a dramatic entrance.

Indeed, at the risk of being ungracious, it might be suggested that it would have been better if Cunningham had concentrated his attention on matters under his own control. He had, for instance, been warned repeatedly of the dangers to airborne operations from 'friendly' naval gunfire and the need for more restraint and better aircraft recognition, but he had constantly declined to as much as discuss the problem.

Nor was this the only lack of foresight that Cunningham had displayed. By 3 August, Intelligence reports had convinced Alexander that an enemy withdrawal to the mainland was under consideration. He passed on his information to Cunningham and Tedder, adding that they had 'no doubt coordinated plans to meet this contingency'. He was being optimistic. No plans had been made, no conferences held and, as Cunningham would honestly admit later, the Navy had given very little thought to the matter. Since, when Alexander's reminder was received, Eisenhower was in Algiers, Tedder in Tunis and Cunningham himself in Malta, it proved too late then for any 'plans to meet this contingency' to be prepared. Though, of course, if Alexander's suggestion of a landing on the Italian side of the Straits of Messina had not been ignored, then the contingency might never have arisen in the first place.

The task of hindering Hube's escape was therefore left to the Allied airmen, who had plenty of other duties to perform. RAF Wellingtons did do considerable damage in bombing raids at night – so much so that from 14 August, the enemy ferried troops out only in daylight. During the day, however, Baade's massive array of AA guns ensured that the air attacks inflicted only very light losses, and a delighted Kesselring could inform his relieved Führer that some 39,500 Germans and 62,000 Italians had been rescued; the Italians had lost almost all their vehicles but the Germans had retained 47 tanks, 94 guns, some 9,600 lorries and 17,000 tons of equipment and ammunition.

It was a disappointing end to the campaign, but it detracts little from that campaign's achievements. The Allies had had odds of four to three in their favour and had been backed by a dominant air force; on the other hand, they had been fighting in difficult country which greatly favoured the defenders. They had suffered approximately 22,800 casualties, of whom 8,400 were killed or missing. The figures for German casualties vary widely but it seems they were much the same as those of the Allies, and although they had previously evacuated their wounded, they had left 5,500 men behind as prisoners of war. The Italian Sixth Army had suffered losses of at least 130,000, most of whom had surrendered. The first bastion of 'Fortress Europe' had fallen, with all that this meant to the morale of both sides, in just thirty-eight days.[4]

Moreover all the strategic objectives of HUSKEY, as laid down at the Casablanca Conference, had been achieved. The passage of Allied shipping through the Mediterranean was now secure. The pressure on Russia had been relieved: on 13 July, the news from Sicily had caused Hitler to cancel the offensive he had launched against Kursk eight days earlier – it was never to be renewed – and the departure of Luftwaffe units to the Mediterranean area had further weakened the enemy on the Eastern Front. But the most spectacular result of HUSKEY was the effect it had had on Italy.

On 24 July, Mussolini had called a meeting of the Fascist Grand Council for the first time since the war had begun, and this supposedly docile body had passed a motion calling for a drastic reduction of his powers. Next evening, Mussolini was received by King Victor Emmanuel III, who told him that he was the most hated man in Italy, demanded his resignation, and ordered him taken into custody, officially for his own protection. The King then summoned Marshal Pietro Badoglio, a long-time critic of Mussolini's regime, and instructed him to form a new government. Badoglio assured Hitler, Kesselring and anyone else who would listen to him that Italy would preserve the Axis Pact, but, in reality, his only aim was to end the war which was ruining his country, while at the same time preventing it from being taken over by the partner he was preparing to desert.

The period from early August to early September therefore saw a bewildering series of negotiations between the new Italian Government and the Western Allies, which must at all cost be kept secret from Hitler. It quickly became clear that what was being proposed was not only a peace treaty but a treaty of alliance, under which Italy would join her erstwhile enemies as a co-belligerent; this, as everyone agreed, being the only way – if indeed there was any way – in which the Germans could be driven out of the country. It was thus very important for Badoglio to know the terms Italy would be granted if he took such a drastic step.

Unfortunately, at the Casablanca Conference, Churchill and Roosevelt had declared that Germany, Italy and Japan would be offered no terms of any sort; nothing less than 'unconditional surrender' would be accepted. Apart from making nonsense of the

Western Allies' propaganda that they were opposed not to the peoples of the Axis powers but to the leaders who had misled them, this idiotic slogan theoretically made any negotiations impossible. A month therefore passed in hypocritical manoeuvres, designed to reassure Badoglio that if he surrendered 'unconditionally', he would, in fact, receive favourable conditions. By 2 September, it had become urgent that this farce should be terminated without delay.

At this point, Alexander made his only real contribution towards resolving the issue, but, as it turned out, an important one. Negotiations had been transferred to his Headquarters at Cassibile. It was suggested by Macmillan and Eisenhower's British Head of Intelligence, Brigadier Kenneth Strong, that Alexander, whose name was already legendary among the Italians, should put pressure on Badoglio's representative, General Guiseppe Castellano, who was maintaining that, while the Italian Government had accepted the Allied terms in principle, he was not authorized to sign anything.

Alexander, much amused by his role, visited the Italian delegation in a resplendent uniform, his tunic covered with medal ribbons, and with gold spurs on his boots, ostensibly to express his satisfaction over the imminent completion of the surrender formalities. On being told that nothing was yet settled, he pretended to fly into a rage, warned them of the dire consequences of further procrastination, and insisted that they convey his demands to Rome. His imposing appearance – and his personality – proved decisive. Next day, Badoglio bowed to the seemingly inevitable and gave his authority. Castellano signed the instrument of surrender in the presence of Eisenhower, Alexander, Cunningham and Tedder, while Beddell Smith signed on behalf of the Western Allies.

The great news was at first kept secret, so that the Germans would only learn about it on the eve of the major Allied invasion of southern Italy. When it was announced late on 8 September, the Italian fleet sailed for Malta, being attacked next day by the Luftwaffe which sank the flagship, the battleship *Roma*. Some 300 Italian warplanes flew to Allied aerodromes to surrender. Even before the announcement, the loss of Sicily had convinced the Germans that they should abandon Sardinia and Corsica. The evacuations were authorized on 8 and 12 September respectively and were carried out with typical efficiency.

It was not until 13 October that Italy officially declared war on Germany and few of her soldiers or airmen showed much desire to see action against their former comrades in arms. Nonetheless the Germans were faced with the enormous task of disarming, and in most cases taking prisoner huge numbers of obviously unreliable Italian troops, stationed not only in their homeland but in Russia, southern France, Yugoslavia, Albania and Greece – and then assuming their responsibilities. In most cases these aims were achieved without much trouble, but the Italians fought stubbornly and successfully in the mountainous area of Greece and on some of the Greek islands. In Yugoslavia, many of the Italians voluntarily surrendered their weapons to the local guerrillas, who took advantage of the confusion to occupy most of the Adriatic coast and islands, requiring a major German counter-offensive to regain them. In both Yugoslavia and Albania, several thousand Italians took to the hills to become guerrillas themselves – as they would later do in northern Italy.

Yet if the Italians did comparatively little fighting against the Germans, at least only a few die-hard Fascist units would still be fighting against the Allies. After his disasters in Russia and North Africa, Hitler had finally come to realize that he was incurring far too many casualties, and for the evacuation of Sicily he had expressly decreed that men must have priority over equipment. The Italians may not have been of the same high standard as the Germans, but the loss of well over a million and a half soldiers must have come as a colossal blow to him. The campaign in Sicily may have had its tactical setbacks and disappointments for the Allies, but strategically it was an overwhelming and far-reaching success.

Notes:
1. So called from the number of the room in the Hotel St George, Algiers, in which its first meetings were held.
2. Quoted in *Monty: Master of the Battlefield 1942–1944* by Nigel Hamilton.
3. Full details of this episode can be found in *Hitler's Last General: The Case Against Wilhelm Mohnke* by Ian Sayer and Douglas Botting. Mohnke was a SS officer whose troops were twice involved in the murder of Allied prisoners. The Sicily shootings are described in

the course of an examination of the responsibility of senior commanders for the acts of their subordinates.

4.   To put matters into perspective, it might be mentioned that in July
     and early August 1943, another amphibious campaign was being
     waged in the Pacific, where the Americans had invaded New
     Georgia Island – or specifically its north-western extremity, which
     contained the vital Munda airfield. This was held by just 8,000
     Japanese who were outnumbered by well over four to one. Even
     excluding preliminary operations, it took thirty-five days to secure
     Munda, whereupon the surviving defenders escaped by sea.

Chapter 6

Success in the South

Alexander and the men under his command had liberated Italy from her own domestic tyrant. They now faced the much more difficult task of liberating her from an efficient and ruthless German army of occupation. As he embarked on it, Alexander might have been tempted to murmur his private code word 'Bargo', for he was again confronted with an intensely confused situation – only this time, one caused, not by enemy action, but by the differing ideas and wishes of the leaders of the Western Allies.

The main problem was that the British and Americans held conflicting views on the importance of activities in the Mediterranean. Both agreed that the knockout blow against Germany must be struck elsewhere. The troops needed to deliver it must be assembled in Britain, from which they would invade occupied France; they would then advance as quickly as possible to their enemy's economic heart, the Ruhr, the capture of which would make the end of the war only a matter of time. At the 'Trident' Conference, held in Washington in May 1943, the date for the cross-channel operation, code-named OVERLORD, was provisionally scheduled for 1 May 1944. It was the action to be taken before that date that caused heated discussion.

To Churchill and Brooke, it seemed both sensible and essential to use the large forces already in the Mediterranean to apply such pressure there that the Germans would be compelled to send troops from North-West Europe and, incidentally, from Russia, to the threatened area. The Americans were all in favour of weakening resistance to OVERLORD and did not object to Mediterranean campaigns in principle, but General Marshall in particular was greatly concerned that, if these were not strictly controlled, they would weaken, not the Germans but the Allies, by diverting too many men, vehicles, ships and aircraft away from the vital main theatre. The Americans had already agreed to the assault on Sicily, but the directive sent to Eisenhower at the end of the 'Trident' Conference merely stated vaguely that thereafter he should 'plan such operations in exploitation of HUSKEY as are best calculated to eliminate Italy from the war and to contain the maximum number of German forces'.

Whatever operations Eisenhower decided upon, they would have to take place within a strictly limited timescale, for the Americans insisted not only that no further reinforcements should be sent to the Mediterranean, but that many of the units there should return to Britain in good time to take part in OVERLORD. This transfer was to be effected by 1 November 1943 at the very latest, after which Eisenhower and his subordinates would be deprived of the services of three British and four American divisions, all of them experienced, plus three groups of medium bombers and the bulk of their troop-carrying aircraft, landing ships, landing craft and DUKWs. When it is remembered that the HUSKEY operation itself would not commence for another six weeks, it is not surprising that Eisenhower's planners envisaged only the possible occupation of Sardinia and Corsica; any suggestions for attacks on the Italian mainland were made hesitantly and without much conviction.

Once HUSKEY was underway though, attitudes quickly changed. First, it became clear that the Italians were not fighting in Sicily with anything like the determination they had shown in North Africa and the occupation of the island was likely to be achieved in a comparatively short time. Then came the momentous news of the fall of Mussolini and the opening of negotiations by the Badoglio government with a view to Italy joining the Allies. The advantages that could be gained by an invasion of the mainland suddenly seemed much more readily attainable.

Nearest to hand were the strategic prizes. The port of Naples would provide the Allies with a base which would effectively secure their supply lines, but more important was the group of aerodromes at Foggia, near Italy's Adriatic coast. With these in their hands, the Allied Air Forces could complete their aerial blockade of the enemy, by attacking targets previously out of range of their heavy bombers, not only in southern Germany but in Eastern Europe and the Balkans – in particular perhaps, the Rumanian oil fields. Beyond

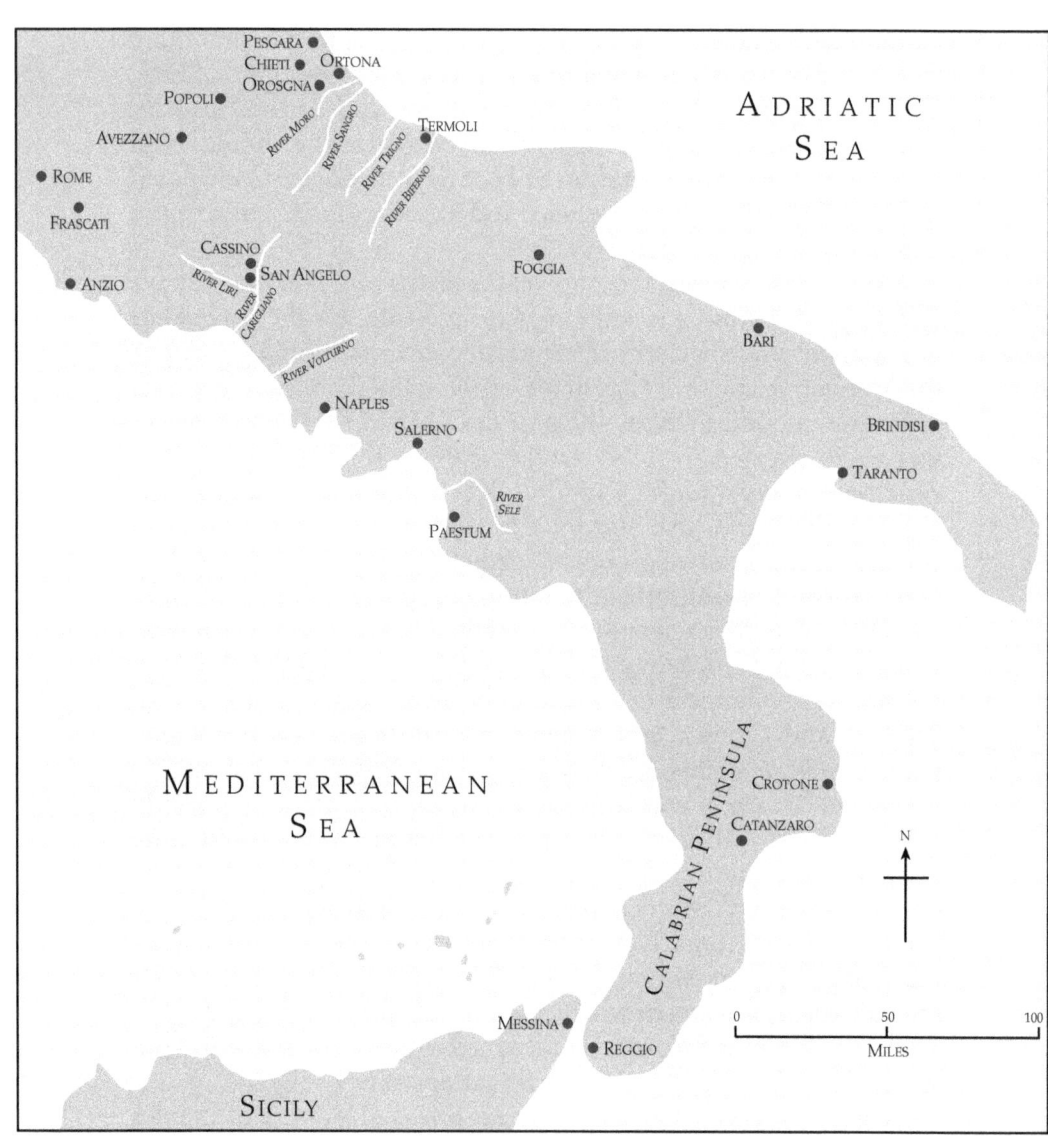

Map 7: Southern Italy

the immediate objectives lay Rome. Although its airfields were also of considerable strategic value, the main benefits accruing from the capture of the Italian capital would be political. 'He who holds Rome, holds the title deeds of Italy,' pronounced Churchill, and its loss would be a tremendous blow to the morale of the Axis powers, especially to that of Hitler's other European satellites.

General Marshall, the most resolute opponent of increased Allied commitments in the Mediterranean, now found himself on the horns of a dilemma. He was much too good a strategist not to desire these potential benefits, but at the same time he did not wish to achieve them at the cost of delaying the build-up for OVER-LORD. He therefore desired to gain the prizes as quickly as possible and began urging Eisenhower to show greater daring. His demands, combined with the growing evidence that Italy was on the point of collapse, resulted in the production of a whole series of hastily prepared and often mutually contradictory plans, which became steadily more unrealistic.

Since many of these plans never came to fruition, the first one that need be mentioned is Operation BAYTOWN. This was originally formulated on 17 July and envisaged the main body of Montgomery's Eighth Army crossing the Straits of Messina. Two separate smaller landings elsewhere in the 'toe' of Italy by the British V and X Corps were also discussed. Taranto on Italy's 'heel' was suggested as the target for the American Fifth Army of General Mark Wayne Clark, an officer who had handled a number of difficult staff appointments with conspicuous success, possessed a strong personality and was shortly to prove his considerable personal courage, but had had no experience of commanding even a division in action. Both Clark and Montgomery would come under Alexander, to whose Fifteenth Army Group responsibility for land operations was again entrusted.

On 27 July, encouraged by the fall of Mussolini, Eisenhower put forward other options, which were finally confirmed on 16 August. Clark would land not at Taranto but, as Marshall had suggested, in the Gulf of Salerno, south of Naples. Operation AVELANCHE, as this mission was called, would be carried out by both a US and a British Corps. It would be supported by a parachute drop by the American 82nd Airborne Division north of Naples, which would seize the bridges over the Volturno River, so as to prevent the arrival of German reinforcements. Both subsidiary landings on the 'toe' would be cancelled, V Corps being kept in reserve, while X Corps provided the British contingent for Fifth Army. BAYTOWN would still proceed but in strictly limited strength, and a shortage of assault shipping would mean that it would have to take place about a week before AVALANCHE, which in turn was planned for 9 September.

By the time the Italians had signed the formal instrument of surrender on 3 September, still further operations were in the course of preparation. The Italians had promised to secure Naples and also ports on the 'heel'. Intelligence indications that there were only weak German forces in that area led to the proposal that the men of the 1st (British) Airborne Division, for whom no troop-carrying aircraft were available, should be landed by sea at Taranto. This was Operation SLAPSTICK which would take place on the same day as the Salerno landings. The Italians also gave assurances that they would drive the Germans out of Rome. They asked for Allied help in the form of a seaborne landing at the mouth of the Tiber and an airborne drop on the airfields near the city. In view of the Allies' other commitments, there was no time to arrange the former in any event, but, to the dismay of Mark Clark, Eisenhower deprived him of the services of 82nd US Airborne Division, so that this could assist his new allies to hold their own capital. This was Operation GIANT II,[1] which was due to take place in the late evening of 8 September.

It is clear that Alexander did not agree with many of the assumptions on which the various plans had been based. He privately warned trusted members of his staff that he could see no likelihood of the Italians opposing the Germans effectively. He publicly expressed concern that the Germans were building up their military strength in Italy – as was known from 'Ultra' interceptions, to which Alexander always paid personal attention – and that this was likely to imperil the Salerno operation in particular. It is difficult to feel that he was other than anxious about the directions he was receiving from Eisenhower.

It might therefore be argued with some justice that Alexander should have taken a stronger line, making it very clear that he considered many of the orders which were being issued to be impracticable. There were perhaps two main reasons why he did not. He firmly believed that once decisions had been finalized, it was a soldier's duty to carry them out to the best of his ability; and he was determined to preserve Allied solidarity, so the last thing he wanted was to quarrel with an American Supreme Commander. Had the forceful McCreery still been Alexander's Chief of Staff, he might have taken open issue with Eisenhower, but after the fall of Tunis, McCreery had been promoted to lieutenant general and left to take up an active command, ultimately of X Corps. His successor was Major General Alexander Richardson, a capable staff officer but lacking operational experience and, like his chief, far too nice a gentleman to wish to embarrass the Supreme Commander in this way.

Alexander was less tolerant of Cunningham, complaining to Eisenhower that his naval colleague so dominated his staff that they would do nothing without consulting him, thereby causing frequent delays. What especially irked Alexander was the delay in providing sufficient landing craft and naval assistance for BAYTOWN. Already it had been decided that there were insufficient facilities to allow XXX Corps to take part in the invasion, which meant that it had to be carried out solely by XIII Corps. At the time it took place, the Italians had as yet not even signed the surrender agreement and Lieutenant General Miles Dempsey, the XIII Corps Commander, had flatly refused to proceed before his requirements were met. Montgomery supported Dempsey and Alexander backed both of them. It is typical of Alexander that, while he always valued inter-service cooperation, he was not prepared to place this above the needs of the soldiers for whom he was responsible.

Cunningham was greatly angered by this affair. Presumably it helped to bring about his later hostile assessment of Alexander, but for the moment, it had the desired result. Cunningham, to his credit, flew to Sicily to sort out the problems, and a delighted Dempsey would shortly confirm that he had offered 'to do anything that the Army wanted'. In the early hours of 3 September, XIII Corps crossed the Straits of Messina. Intelligence reports had suggested that opposition would be weak, but small units, landed secretly on the mainland to confirm this, had failed to do so, and the Eighth Army staff, remembering the false information that had been circulated in the past, were not willing to 'chance it'. The landing took place under cover of a massive artillery bombardment which, as it transpired, was quite unnecessary because the enemy had prudently retired from the area. Critics have heaped much ridicule on this episode, but it should be noted that Alexander was never among their number. He firmly believed that war was inherently wasteful but it was better to waste any amount of metal than risk that much more precious commodity – men's lives.

Tactically, the operation went well. The port of Reggio was taken almost undamaged, 3,000 Italians were captured, and Eighth Army began to move northwards. In practice, two of Eighth Army's divisions began to move northwards, 5th (British) along the western coast road and 1st Canadian on the eastern one. These, the only possible lines of advance, twisted and turned over innumerable hairpin bends, hemmed in by steep cliffs and crossing immense ravines, through which rivers raced to the sea. 'Never,' declares de Guingand feelingly, 'was a country more suited to delaying action.' The Germans took full advantage of this, wrecking the roads, bringing down the overhanging cliffs, blowing up the bridges and ambushing the sappers as they sought to repair them. Small amphibious landings behind the enemy lines on 3/4 and 7/8 September did little to speed the advance. Nonetheless by the 10th, after a journey of 100 miles as the crow flew and as much as 250 miles by road, Eighth Army had reached its immediate objective, Catanzaro, where gulfs cutting into the Calabrian Peninsula reduced it to a width of some 30 miles – a feature known, with scant regard for anatomical accuracy, as the 'neck' of the 'toe'.

Despite this achievement which, in view of the difficulties faced, was not inconsiderable, Montgomery was thoroughly discontented. He was frankly disgusted by the hasty, ill-considered ideas that had been poured out by his superiors, and deplored the nebulous thinking which had resulted in his having been given no indication of what BAYTOWN was intended to achieve. And he agreed with his staff that BAYTOWN was a pointless exercise in any event – it would not divert enemy forces from the Salerno landings because the Germans would certainly retain their main strength in the area of Naples, relying on rearguards and the dreadful terrain to impose delay on Eighth Army.

As before the invasion of Sicily, Montgomery wished the Allied effort to be concentrated. Far from being opposed to the Salerno landings, as some have stated, he had expressed his approval to Brooke as early as 27 July, though he would have preferred it if the assault could have been delivered further to the north. What he most desired, though, was that AVALANCHE should be carried out by both Fifth and Eighth Armies, and that Italy's 'toe' should be ignored, leaving any troops there to 'wither on the vine'.

Alexander was not indifferent to such arguments but, recalling the resentment caused by Montgomery's dogmatic demands before HUSKEY, he was not prepared to support them for a second time, thereby risking a further disruption of Allied unity. His opinion was strengthened by the fact that the perennial shortage of landing craft would in any case have made it impossible for Fifth and Eighth Armies to land at Salerno together; they would have had to go ashore separately, with an interval of time between them. BAYTOWN therefore went ahead and Montgomery, who tended to look at all problems from a purely military point of view, most unfairly regarded Alexander's wider concerns as evidence of a lack of decision.

Montgomery's exasperation with his superior was apparently completed by a conversation held at Reggio airfield, to which Alexander had flown, on 5 September. At this, Montgomery learned, for the first time, of the signing of the Italian surrender document and the arrangements that had been made to take advantage of it. As Montgomery relates in his *Memoirs*: 'Alexander was most optimistic and was clearly prepared to base his plans on the Italians doing all they said . . . I told him my opinion was that when the Germans found out what was going on, they would stamp on the Italians.'

Since, as we have seen, Alexander also feared that the Italians would never fight the Germans effectively, he cannot have been nearly as optimistic as Montgomery supposed. It would appear that the Eighth Army Commander, like Brooke before him, did not realize that it was Alexander's deliberate policy to inspire everyone around him by radiating a confidence which he might not necessarily feel. Possibly Alexander would have been better advised to have had a quiet, private talk with his subordinate on the lines that he also doubted the wisdom of many of Eisenhower's ideas, but that they must just get on with the job and do their best to ensure that it was carried through successfully. Montgomery would surely have responded. It may be that Alexander feared that Montgomery would not be sufficiently discreet to keep such comments to himself. More probably, he simply felt that, even when given in confidence, they would show disloyalty to his friend, the Supreme Commander.

The sad result of Alexander's forbearance was that Montgomery did not show the same loyalty to his own friend, the Army Group Commander. He concluded, impulsively, that Alexander did 'not understand the conduct of war'. Quite inexcusably, his frustration would take the form of telling Clark, when they met at Salerno, that if Alexander gave him any instructions with which he did not agree, then he 'should not hesitate to protest'. Montgomery had said much the same to Patton in Sicily, but this time his words would bear bitter fruit.

Allied hopes that the Italians would stand up to the Germans had vanished long before that happened. When Mussolini fell, Badoglio and the Chief of Staff of Italy's Commando Supremo, General Vittorio Ambrosio, loudly proclaimed that their country would remain faithful to her alliance with Germany. Kesselring, who had always cooperated with the Italians, took them at their word, but Hitler did not believe them for a single moment. In a cold, unforgiving rage, he began preparing the necessary steps for a German military occupation of Italy when Badoglio's expected 'treason' occurred. With a rather ghastly irony, his plans were given the code name ACHSE, the German for AXIS.

On 1 August, a German infantry division appeared at the Brenner Pass, between Italy and Austria, purportedly to assist the Italians in the event of an Allied invasion. Ambrosio, who had previously agreed in principle to its entry, decided that it would be dangerous to refuse permission now. The new arrivals promptly secured the pass, through which other German formations began to pour. If Ambrosio was going to prevent them from taking control of northern Italy, he would have to act at once, but he did not dare to do so until the Italians had completed their negotiations with the Western Allies.

As a result, by the time that Eighth Army crossed the Straits of Messina, there were eight German divisions in the north of Italy. Together they formed Army Group 'B' under the control of Rommel, hastily recalled from commanding the Axis forces in the

Balkans – though the Germans tried hard to conceal his presence from the Italians, all of whom, of whatever political persuasion, regarded Rommel with loathing and distrust. The return of the German units from Sicily meant that they had eight divisions in southern Italy as well – increased to nine when the one in Sardinia was withdrawn. These, on 17 August, became the German Tenth Army, led by General Heinrich-Gottfried von Vietinghoff, who in turn was responsible to Kesselring. Also under Kesselring came General Kurt Student, whose 2nd Parachute Division flew in to the Rome airfields and who, in addition, took responsibility for 3rd Panzer Grenadier Division and a tank battalion from 26th Panzer Division which were already in the Rome area.

The Allies' long-term aim of weakening German forces in more vital areas was thus being achieved, for all the German reinforcements had either been intended for, or had been transferred from North-West Europe or the Russian Front. Unhappily, the immediate result of the German build-up was to paralyse the Italian authorities. Their inactivity was made all the greater by Eisenhower's natural reluctance to inform them of the date of the major landings before the surrender had been announced officially, and their consequent ignorance that this was planned for the early hours of 9 September. In an attempt to gain more time for countermeasures, Badoglio, on the morning of the 8th, signalled to Eisenhower that it was 'no longer possible to accept an armistice'.

To the Allied Supreme Commander, this seemed like blatant treachery and he warned Badoglio that he was going to announce Italy's capitulation in any case. This he did at 1830. Since Badoglio was well aware that Hitler would disbelieve any Italian denials, he broadcast a similar announcement at 1945. Alexander would later report that Badoglio spoke 'in a depressed and subdued voice'. Well he might!

The Italians' state of unpreparedness had already become obvious to Major General Maxwell Taylor, then the Artillery Commander of the 82nd US Airborne Division and later to lead the equally famous 101st US Airborne Division, who had gone secretly to Rome to check on the feasibility of the GIANT II parachute landings. General Giacomo Carboni, controlling the five Italian divisions entrusted with the defence of Rome, made it quite clear that he did not believe that the operation would succeed, that it was impossible to neutralize the German anti-aircraft batteries as had been suggested, and that the only result would be a battle which would bring about the destruction of the capital – an outcome which he was not prepared to contemplate. Taylor accordingly signalled the agreed code word 'Innocuous', cancelling 82nd Airborne's mission.

Senior Allied officers – but not Alexander – would later be very critical of Taylor's decision, their disfavour increasing in direct proportion to their distance from the scene of action. Captain Liddell Hart makes much play with Kesselring's assertion after the war that: 'An air landing on Rome and a sea landing nearby . . . would have automatically caused us to evacuate all the southern half of Italy.' Yet, even ignoring the fact that Kesselring personally felt that the sea landing was impracticable in view of the lack of fighter cover, his comment was clearly based on the assumption that the Italian Army would have joined in the fight against him; as his Chief of Staff, Lieutenant General Siegfried Westphal declared: 'The two divisions we had near Rome were far from sufficient for the double job of eliminating the strong Italian forces and repelling the Allied landing.' For that matter, they should have been insufficient to counter Carboni's troops alone, had these shown a will to resist. Few did, and it seems unlikely that the airborne landing would have given them the necessary 'stimulus', as some have argued, considering that the Italians themselves had already doubted its chances of success.

After making his capitulation announcement, Badoglio, together with his king and most of his high-ranking army officers, fled to Pescara on the Adriatic coast, whence they sailed in an Italian warship to seek safety with the Allies. Their subordinates – deserted by their leaders, left without any proper instructions, shocked and humiliated by the surrender of which they had been given hardly any warning, enjoying for the most part reasonably good relations with their German counterparts – can surely not be blamed too harshly for their lack of resolution.

By contrast, the Germans, as might have been expected, showed ample resolution. At about noon on 8 September, Allied bombers had attacked Kesselring's Headquarters at Frascati, near Rome, for a whole hour. The Germans suffered about a hundred casualties, and much damage and loss was inflicted on the town, but the field marshal and his chief staff officers were unhurt, and as soon as they learned of Badoglio's broadcast, put Operation ACHSE into effect with admirable efficiency. Student's two divisions closed in on Rome, while Kesselring, through the medium of Westphal, opened negotiations with the Italian authorities. Taking advantage of the Italians' concern for their lovely capital, he employed a skilful mixture of promises that if the Italians handed over their weapons and defensive positions, Rome would be declared an open city, and threats that if this was not done promptly, Rome would be bombed without mercy. Also, in defiance of the instructions he had received from OKW, he agreed that once the Italians had been disarmed, they could return to their homes. By 1630 on 10 September, all Italian resistance in central Italy – it was somewhat spasmodic at best – had ended.

The Germans proved equally capable of 'stamping on the Italians' elsewhere. In the south, von Vietinghoff followed Kesselring's policy of disarming the Italian troops, then letting them go home. The only opposition came from the Italian Divisional Commander in the Salerno area, who paid for it with his life. In the north, Rommel was also successful in the short term, but, with unnecessary brutality, he did obey OKW's orders, wasting time and manpower in transferring any Italians he could capture to Germany. Those who escaped hid their weapons or retired with them to the hills, to form the nucleus of what would later become a savage resistance movement.

Whatever his outward show of confidence, it seems clear that Alexander did not really anticipate that the Italians would do much in the way of confronting their former partners on the battlefield, but he did believe, as he advised Brooke, that they might provide assistance in the form of strikes, sabotage and the seizure of ports and key points. Nothing of the kind was done and on 12 September the Germans completed their take-over of Italy when SS Captain Otto Skorzeny, sent out specially by Hitler, dramatically rescued Mussolini from his place of detention, a hotel high in the Apennine Mountains. He was flown to Germany and set up as head of a new puppet government, notionally controlling what was known as the North Italian Republic, which consisted of that part of his country still under German occupation.

This would steadily diminish in size. On 9 September, the 1st

(British) Airborne Division captured the port of Taranto virtually intact, though early next morning the fast minelayer *Abdiel* drifted over a magnetic mine while at anchor in the harbour. The explosion broke her in two and she sank in a few minutes, with heavy casualties among the 400 parachutists still on board. The landing force then advanced to capture Brindisi on the 11th and Bari on the 14th. The Germans had accepted the loss of the Italian 'heel', so no difficulty was experienced holding these ports until late September, when two divisions arrived as reinforcements and the area was taken over by Lieutenant General Charles Allfrey's V Corps, which in turn formed part of Eighth Army. It was not, however, possible for the parachutists to move far beyond the ports because the hurried preparations for their mission had left them short of supplies and without vehicles apart from a few jeeps. Even when this situation was rectified, there remained a desperate shortage of petrol, and since 1st Airborne lacked tanks and supporting artillery, it could not push too far northward without risking serious consequences should the enemy concentrate against it in strength.

Just how serious those consequences might be was demonstrated by the AVALANCHE landings, which also began early on 9 September. Clark's Fifth Army contained both the British X Corps under McCreery and the US VI Corps of Major General Ernest Dawley. The two divisions of X Corps, flanked on their left by British Commando and American Ranger units, landed in the northern part of the Gulf of Salerno, their immediate objectives being Salerno harbour and the airfield at Monte Corvino. The Americans came ashore on their right, south of the little Sele River, at first with only one division, though a second disembarked next day. Fifth Army's ultimate objective was Naples, which, it was confidently forecast, would be secured within three days.

The Salerno beaches were ideal for landing craft, but the area had two potent disadvantages: it was surrounded by an arc of hills, from which the Germans could observe and their artillery could shell every Allied movement; and the enemy had anticipated that the Allies would land there. Coastal batteries opened fire on the assault craft before they could touch down. The escorting British warships retaliated but the American warships only followed their example after the troops were ashore, since Clark had decided against a preliminary bombardment in the hope of gaining surprise. Moreover the sector was defended by 16th Panzer Division, which controlled four infantry battalions as well as some eighty Mark IV Specials and forty self-propelled guns.

The reason behind the German anticipation was the same one that had decided the Allies to go to Salerno in the first place – it was just within the range of the British Spitfire and American Mustang fighters. Had the Allies landed further north, they could have been guarded only by the twin-engined American Lockheed Lightnings but, even if assisted by the carrier-based fighters, there were not enough of these to provide adequate cover, and Tedder's requests that more be forthcoming from bases in Britain had been refused. Kesselring and Westphal would both state later that their prediction that the Allies would only land where they could be given fighter protection, had greatly simplified their problems, and Captain Liddell Hart is very scornful of Eisenhower's and Alexander's 'consistency in observing such conventional limitations'.

Since both Clark and Montgomery had advocated a landing in the Gulf of Gaeta, north of Naples, where there was an easier line of advance from the beaches but where full air protection could not be provided, and since Alexander was willing to risk a landing at Taranto which was also outside the range of the single-engined fighters, there might seem some justification for this complaint. It should be remembered, however, that AVALANCHE had been planned at a time when it was not known that the Italians would surrender, whereas the Taranto operation had been hastily improvised to take advantage of their having done so. Admiral Cunningham had favoured the Taranto mission, but previously both he and Tedder had refused to contemplate a landing north of Salerno. Alexander, always eager to preserve good relations with the other services, and with bitter memories of the sufferings his men had endured at Dunkirk and in Burma when enemy air forces had dominated, can scarcely be blamed for not attempting to over-rule them.

Indeed, the troops at Salerno were soon to be more than grateful for whatever aerial support they could get. It was not until the morning of 10 September that X Corps captured Monte Cornvino airfield, and German artillery fire ensured it would remain unusable. Salerno fell that night, but no further progress could be made as 16th Panzer concentrated the bulk of its strength against the British who represented the greater threat to the German hold on Naples. This enabled the Americans to expand their bridgehead and begin to close the gap between the two Allied corps by occupying the area around the mouth of the Sele River; but the morning of 11 September saw Fifth Army still hemmed into a narrow strip of coast, with enemy reinforcements arriving.

First on the scene was 29th Panzer Grenadier Division, followed closely by the Hermann Göring Division which could add twenty tanks to the defenders' strength, and 26th Panzer Division, though this was now in practice only an infantry unit, having transferred its armour to Student. 3rd and 15th Panzer Grenadier Divisions were also hastening to the battle area, but luckily Kesselring's appeal for the aid of two panzer divisions from Army Group 'B' was turned down by Rommel, whose refusal was subsequently approved by OKW. Despite this, on the evening of the 11th, von Vietinghoff ordered the first German counter-attacks. An American advance towards Ponte Sele, possession of which bridge would have secured the link-up between the two corps, was thrown back in confusion, while on the British front, a forward position was surrounded and 450 prisoners taken.

It is much to his credit that Alexander realized the imminent danger sooner than anyone else; he had, after all, experienced plenty of crises previously in his career. As early as the evening of 10 September, he signalled to Montgomery, asking if he could put pressure on the enemy facing him so as to reduce the build-up of German strength at Salerno. The nature of the country and a shortage of supplies made this a difficult task, but, de Guingand tells us, 'Montgomery responded wholeheartedly and with speed.' Next day, the port of Crotone was captured intact, while the Desert Air Force – which had retained its former title despite its employment in Europe – occupied nearby airfields, from which its Kittyhawk fighter-bombers could join in the attacks on the enemy engaging Mark Clark.

Alexander also urged that the efforts of every available aircraft, strategical as well as tactical, should be directed towards aiding Fifth Army, and that the Navy should send more warships to assist in the bombardment of enemy columns. It was now that his own consideration for inter-Allied and inter-Service relations reaped its reward. No doubt Eisenhower, Tedder and Cunningham would have responded to his requests in any case, but they did so with exemplary promptness. On 12 September, fighters and fighter-bombers were in action over the battlefield from dawn to dusk. On the previous day, Lightning fighters had arrived at a landing strip newly constructed by Allied engineers within the bridgehead at Paestum, where they would shortly be joined by Spitfires and Warhawks. Meanwhile heavy and medium bombers pounded the German lines of communication.

According to Alexander, these 'tremendous air attacks', which increased in fury over the next few days, 'seriously interfered' with enemy movements and 'prevented his concentration of the necessary forces to launch large-scale attacks'. This was just as well for the enemy attacks which were launched proved dangerous enough. On 12 September, 16th Panzer and 29th Panzer Grenadier Divisions thrust forward through the point of junction between the British and the American corps. Next day, they turned on the latter and forced it back almost to its landing beaches. The American field artillery, backed by naval gunfire, checked the advance just in time, and the Allied air raids prevented its renewal.

During this attack, Clark had driven right up to the front line in a jeep to rally a battalion which had started to give way – an action for which he was deservedly awarded a Distinguished Service Cross. For all his individual gallantry, however, Clark was so concerned over his Army's precarious situation that early on the 14th, he ordered emergency plans to be prepared, whereby his Headquarters could be re-embarked and VI US Corps evacuated and transferred to the X Corps bridgehead, or vice versa as necessary. Clark's suggestions were only speculative and were strongly opposed by McCreery, at least one American divisional commander and subsequently by Cunningham, but the fact that they had even been considered caused great concern to Alexander when he heard of them.

Alexander was already on his way to the beachhead in a destroyer, arriving on the morning of the 15th. He was met by Clark's Deputy Chief of Staff (British), Brigadier Charles Richardson, who had formerly been Montgomery's Director of Operations. 'It has often been said,' relates Richardson, 'that his [Alexander's] mere arrival at a crisis was in some mysterious way

worth an extra division, and I certainly felt it on this occasion.'
Richardson's account also shows why Alexander had this effect:
his calm, unruffled composure was wonderfully reassuring. As they
walked up the beach together, Alexander remarked, 'I've had no
lunch yet, so we'll have that now.' They sat down together and 'had
a picnic'. Only when they had started eating did Alexander ask
about the situation. He was probably secretly much relieved to
learn that Richardson believed the crisis had passed.

This was indeed the case. On the night of 13/14 September, a
regiment of 82nd US Airborne Division had been dropped behind
the American lines after all anti-aircraft guns onshore or afloat had
been ordered to remain silent; unlike the tragic occasions in Sicily,
this order was rigidly obeyed, even though the Luftwaffe chose this
inconvenient moment to deliver a heavy raid on the beachhead.
Next night, another of 82nd Airborne's regiments further reinforced the Americans,[2] while 7th (British) Armoured Division
started to go ashore in the X Corps sector.

By the time Alexander arrived therefore, the most serious danger
facing the Allies was a failure of nerve – which his presence guar-
anteed would not occur. As had happened on his taking over
Eighteenth Army Group in North Africa, however, he had the
depressing duty of assessing a senior American officer as unfit for
his post. He told Clark, who agreed with him, that the VI US Corps
Commander, Major General Dawley, was 'a broken reed'.
Alexander had the power to relieve Dawley but again he preferred
to report his impressions to Eisenhower, leaving him to take action.
Dawley was duly replaced by Major General John Lucas.

In contrast, Alexander strongly praised Clark's calmness and
resolution, but he was most displeased about the withdrawal plans,
even though these were intended for use only in the last resort.
Inevitably, the news had leaked out in an exaggerated form and
appeared to be confirmed by the fact that the unloading of the
supply ships in the American sector had temporarily been stopped
on the 14th, though it had been restarted in the evening.
Remembering how Auchinleck had all but destroyed the morale of
Eighth Army single-handedly by his obsession with withdrawal
plans, Alexander, tactfully but very firmly indeed, ended all suggestions that either of Fifth Army's Corps might be evacuated in any
circumstances whatsoever.

Meanwhile, actions taken by Alexander earlier were combining to complete the success of AVALANCHE. 15 September saw the arrival of the British battleships *Warspite* and *Valiant* which Cunningham had sent in response to Alexander's request. That evening, they opened fire on targets of opportunity with great effect, both materially and morally. On the 16th, the Germans resumed their major attacks but Allied artillery fire, more than substantially backed by the battleships' heavy guns, broke all of them. That afternoon, the Luftwaffe gained some revenge when a raid by Dornier Do 217s carrying radio-controlled glider-bombs, so damaged *Warspite* that she had to be towed back to Malta – but it was too late to affect the issue. On the 16th also, the Eighth Army, in response to an order from Alexander received two days earlier, came up on Clark's right flank. That evening, von Vietinghoff recommended withdrawal from the battle area. Kesselring accepted his advice, and next day, after one last assault to cover their retreat, the Germans fell back.

The Tenth Army's War Diary records sadly that the failure of its attacks and consequent decision to retire had been caused by 'the fire from naval guns and low flying aircraft, as well as the slow but steady approach of the Eighth Army'. As all of these had resulted from actions taken by Alexander, it seems unnecessary to elaborate further on the importance of his contribution towards turning a near disaster into a hard-won victory.

With his soldiers securely based on the Italian mainland, Alexander could direct his attention to future objectives. On 21 September, he indicated that these would be obtained in four stages, though the last of these, the occupation of key positions some 150 miles north of Rome, was obviously one for the fairly distant future. On the other hand, the first, the consolidation of the area from Salerno to Bari, had already been all but achieved in practice. It was completely achieved by the transfer, which now took place, of Eighth Army to the Adriatic coast, with its supply lines running through the ports on the Italian 'heel'.

Had Rommel sent his two panzer divisions to join von Vietinghoff, as requested, they could not have arrived in strength before Clark's reinforcements had reached him and he had joined hands with Eighth Army. It seems unlikely therefore, that they would have altered the result of the Salerno battle, but presumably the fighting there would have lasted longer and probably they would have enabled Kesselring to stand firm north of Salerno, in which case he would have deprived Alexander of his second-stage objectives, defined as 'the port of Naples and the Foggia airfields'. As it was, Eighth Army captured the vital aerodrome complex on 27 September, and on 1 October, Flying Fortresses of the United States Army Air Force left this to strike at the aircraft factories in Wiener Neustadt in Austria, hitherto exempt from such attacks.

On 1 October also, Fifth Army finally entered Naples. It was a shattered, ruined city, the retreating Germans having wrecked the power stations and the sewage and water systems, and a very dangerous one, for booby traps and time-bombs were everywhere. Its splendid port facilities had also been wrecked with savage efficiency, but the indefatigable army engineers set to work immediately, and within a fortnight Fifth Army was being supplied through Naples instead of over the Salerno beaches.

Alexander's third-stage objective was the capture of Rome, but on 4 October Hitler made a decision which frustrated that desire for many weary months, yet at the same time enabled Alexander to achieve his overriding aim of diverting German troops from other fronts. The Führer never liked giving up territory under any circumstances, and was much heartened by the fight his Tenth Army had put up at Salerno, and the casualties Clark's men had already incurred – nearly 7,000 British, some 5,000 American – which would, Hitler hoped, discourage the Allies from further amphibious adventures. He ordered Kesselring to stand firm south of Rome and promised to send him reinforcements.

Kesselring, who had been averse to giving up Rome without a fight in any case, responded energetically. Across the Italian peninsula at its narrowest part, his engineers began the construction of the Gustav Line, running from the mouth of the River Garigliano on the western coast to the mouth of the River Sangro in the east. In front of it, other defensive positions were constructed with a view to preventing the Allies approaching it before bad weather could come to the defenders' aid. Kesselring had another valuable ally in the geography of Italy. From the central range of the Apennines, swift rivers rushed down to the Mediterranean and the Adriatic, providing a series of natural barriers, each of which the Allies would have to overcome in turn.

Geography also dictated the form of the Allied advance, the two Armies proceeding separately on either side of the Apennines. On the Adriatic coast, the first obstacle encountered by Eighth Army was the Biferno River. Montgomery neatly outflanked this by landing a force of commandos at Termoli, just north of its mouth, on the night of 2/3 October, capturing the port intact. One brigade of 78th (British) Division then also landed at Termoli, while another thrust over the river to join the commandos in establishing a bridgehead. Kesselring, in person, ordered that this be eliminated, and on 5 October, a heavy counter-attack by 16th Panzer, well supported by the Luftwaffe, came close to doing so; but it was held, another brigade from 78th Division came in to Termoli during the night, and on the 6th, the Germans fell back to their next line of defence, the River Trigno. Eighth Army broke over this, in the face of fierce resistance, on the night of 2/3 November. On the 4th, the enemy slowly and reluctantly withdrew, and by 19 November, Eighth Army had secured the southern bank of the River Sangro and was confronting the main defences of the Gustav Line.

On the west coast, Fifth Army crossed its first major obstacle, the Volturno River, after dark on 12 October. Again the enemy fought with great determination and it was not until the 16th that a retirement was authorized by Kesselring, and then only because he had previously decided to fall back on this date to the Bernhardt Line, a defensive position somewhat in advance of his main one. Fifth Army attacked its key feature, Monte Comino, on 5 November but was repulsed. Further inland some small gains were made, but by the 15th, Clark had been compelled to call off his offensive altogether.

Alexander had hitherto left it to his Army Commanders to decide their own courses of action. Now, perhaps somewhat belatedly, he took steps to coordinate these. Unhappily, he could not switch forces from one Army to another, thus bringing overwhelming strength to bear at a crucial point, as he had done so decisively in North Africa. The Germans, as they retired, had done everything in their power to wreck all the roads, including those across the Apennines, whereas the ones behind their own lines were largely undamaged. Kesselring would therefore be able to transfer his troops much more rapidly than Alexander could hope to do.

On 8 November, Alexander called a conference at his Headquarters in Bari, at which he set in train movements by both his Armies, either of which might achieve a breakthrough to Rome. The first blow would be struck by Eighth Army on the Adriatic coast. Alexander intended that it should cross the River Sangro to secure the defensive line beyond it on the Li Colli Ridge. It would then cross the River Moro and seize the port of Pescara and the town of Chieti, some 10 miles inland to the south-west. Beyond these, the line of advance would be restricted by spurs of the Apennines running down to the sea, with rivers in between them. These would give the Germans a whole series of perfect defences, so the intention was that Eighth Army would swing westward down Route 5, the main road across the Apennines leading from Pescara, through Chieti, Popoli and Avezzano to Rome. Even if this move was checked, it should draw in German reinforcements and, Alexander hoped, 'loosen up' opposition to Fifth Army.

Eighth Army's assault was originally planned to start on 20 November. Ten days later, when German attention had been directed eastward, Alexander intended that Fifth Army would resume its attempts to break the Bernhardt Line, and having done so, would penetrate the Gustav Line by way of the Liri Valley, south of Cassino, which seemed the weakest part of the defences. To assist in speeding up Fifth Army's advance, an amphibious landing would be made at Anzio, south of Rome, codenamed Operation SHINGLE. Since, despite the claims of Patton and Cunningham, such outflanking moves had proved far from successful in the past, it was agreed that SHINGLE would only take place if and when Fifth Army had come within 30 miles of Anzio.

Alexander's strategy was a sound one but, as can be seen with the benefit of hindsight, probably doomed to failure from its inception. From mid-October, his soldiers had been increasingly handicapped by a foe more relentless than any human one. Fine days were becoming ever more scarce and the rain more heavy, more persistent and colder. Snow and sleet mingled with the downpour and vicious, biting winds swept down from the mountains. During December, five men from 78th (British) Division froze to death and there were 113 cases of exposure.

In these circumstances, the attackers suffered from every possible disadvantage. Their supporting airmen could fly less and less often.

The ground became a sea of thick, clinging mud, preventing any movement other than on the damaged roads, where it was scarcely easier. Rivers became raging torrents, drowning men and sweeping away the temporary bridges erected by the sappers to replace those the Germans had destroyed. A shortage of supplies increased the difficulties, and it must be said that Alexander was badly served by his Administrative staff. When transport vehicles broke down in the dreadful conditions, there were insufficient spare parts available for them, so they had to be sent back to Egypt for repair. Even the capture of the Foggia aerodromes proved a handicap, because petrol, bombs and material for strengthening and extending the runways had to be provided, and the requirements of the airmen competed with those of the soldiers.

Nor did it help Alexander that his potential strength was now considerably reduced. He was able to delay the departure from the Mediterranean of the landing craft needed for SHINGLE, but not that of a large number of his most experienced men. XXX Corps would no longer form part of Eighth Army since its two infantry divisions had been earmarked for OVERLORD. X Corps gave up 7th Armoured Division. 1st (British) Airborne Division, 82nd US Airborne Division, one American armoured and two American infantry divisions also left for North-West Europe. And, to make matters worse, their departure coincided with an increase in the number of enemies that Alexander's remaining troops would have to face.

On 21 November, Hitler rewarded Kesselring's determined resistance by appointing him C-in-C, South-West, in charge of all German forces in Italy. Rommel left the country and his divisions were reorganized into a new Fourteenth Army under General Eberhard von Mackensen, joining with Tenth Army to form Army Group 'C'. Kesselring still needed to keep troops in northern Italy to control this area but for this he could always use units withdrawn for rest and recuperation, replacing them in the front line with fresh divisions from what had now become his reserve.

Ill fortune dogged Alexander's schemes from the start; he even went down with an attack of jaundice. Eighth Army's offensive was hampered by the elements before it ever began. Elaborate deceptions had been devised to convince the defenders that the main assault would be delivered by XIII Corps in the mountains on

Eighth Army's left flank, but these were ineffective because Kesselring was aware that the appalling weather that prevailed in late November meant that major advances could only be made either along the coastal road or on Route 81 which ran parallel to it, some 15 miles inland; he had ordered the defences here to be strengthened accordingly.

Montgomery did indeed plan to use these roads. V Corps, containing 78th (British) and 8th Indian Divisions, would take the coast road to Pescara. The veteran 2nd New Zealand Division, which had done so well in North Africa, had now rejoined Eighth Army; it came under direct Army control and would advance down Route 81 towards Chieti. Both moves gained bridgeheads over the Sangro, V Corps in the early hours of the 20th, the New Zealanders on the night of 22/23 November, but continuously dreadful weather prevented either from being expanded before, on the 23rd, the river rose dramatically, demolishing the temporary bridges by which the attackers had crossed.

Not until the 27th did the rains relent. The Desert Air Force then carried out heavy raids in preparation for major assaults on both routes on the following evening. These were duly delivered under cover of a massive bombardment by artillery and from the air. The tanks of 44th (British) Armoured Brigade climbed onto the Li Colli Ridge on the 29th, followed by the infantry of 78th Division. By nightfall on the 30th, the whole of the Li Colli defensive position was in British hands and the German 65th Infantry Division had been badly mauled, losing over 1,000 men as prisoners.

Already, though, the defenders' advantage of being able to use undamaged roads was beginning to take effect. Kesselring had ordered 26th Panzer Division from the Fifth Army front and 90th Panzer Grenadier Division – a revival of Rommel's famous 90th Light – from northern Italy to reinforce the Sangro front. These now counter-attacked with great determination, preventing any further advance for the time being. There was still no secure supply line over the Sangro but on 6th December, a high-level bridge – called the 'Montgomery Bridge' – was completed by the heroic sappers, and Eighth Army was able to push forward to cross the Moro River two days later.

Montgomery's next objectives were the port of Ortona on the way to Pescara and the town of Orsogna on Route 81.

1st Canadian Division, transferred from XIII to V Corps to replace the exhausted 78th Division, was directed to capture Ortona, with 8th Indian on its left flank. XIII Corps took over the New Zealanders who were sent against Orsogna, with 5th (British) Division on their right. But the weather and the fresh German reinforcements were too much for them. Three full-scale divisional attacks by the New Zealanders failed to capture Orsogna and the attempts were finally abandoned, in pouring rain, on Christmas Day. The Canadians, fiercely opposed by 90th Panzer Grenadier, were unable to reach Ortona until late on 20 December, only to find that units of the 1st Parachute Division had been brought forward to garrison it. The Canadians only secured the town on 28 December after ferocious street-fighting. By then, it was clear that the lateral road to Rome was out of Eighth Army's reach and Alexander accepted Montgomery's advice that the offensive should be discontinued.

At least Eighth Army's operations had caused the Germans to transfer troops from the western coast. Fifth Army had also received reinforcements, though mainly inexperienced ones, from Sicily, enabling Clark to form a new II US Corps under Major General Geoffrey Keyes. All his forces, however, would face the same problems as had Eighth Army: resolute defenders in ideal, prepared positions, and exceptionally bad weather, which, for a start, compelled Clark to postpone his first move until 2 December.

On that date, covered as usual by a powerful artillery barrage and heavy air attacks, X (British) Corps resumed the assault on Monte Comino. It took four days of hard fighting to capture the peak and a further four to clear its far slopes, and it cost X Corps over 1,000 casualties. Meanwhile on 7 December, II and VI US Corps advanced on X Corps' right. The struggle continued into the New Year, with the Germans being gradually pushed back to the Gustav Line, but progress was painfully slow and expensive. By 18 December, it was clear to Clark that he would never reach the Liri Valley in time to assist the proposed SHINGLE landings, which, he therefore warned Alexander, would have to be cancelled.

Alexander's first attempt to capture Rome had failed, but the disappointment this naturally caused must not be allowed to mask the extent of Alexander's overall success. He had established his armies in Italy, his own decisions at Salerno being very largely responsible for this. He had attained the Allies' primary strategic objectives, chiefly Naples and Foggia. He had then continued to advance until he had liberated one-third of the Italian mainland. And he had also achieved his overall requirement of diverting German forces from other vital areas.

There was a price to be paid if this benefit was to continue and Alexander was well aware of it – he had repeatedly warned Churchill and Eisenhower that it would be necessary to 'keep the Germans on their heels', as he put it, until OVERLORD could be launched. This meant that he would have to carry on attacking throughout the coming winter. Or at least whoever commanded the Allied Armies in Italy would have to do so, for on 10 December, Eisenhower was informed that he would be OVERLORD's Supreme Commander, and his selection meant that other changes would also have to be made. In the first place a new Supreme Allied Commander, Mediterranean would have to be chosen. Churchill favoured Alexander but Brooke believed that Alexander's past experiences uniquely fitted him to lead Fifteenth Army Group. He therefore persuaded the Prime Minister to leave Alexander in that role and appoint Wilson as Eisenhower's successor. It is probable that Alexander was not unhappy with the decision, for Rupert Clarke states that everyone who was close to him knew that 'his heart was on the battlefield and with his soldiers'.

Alexander lost the assistance of a number of valued colleagues or subordinates at this time. His Chief of Staff, Major General Alexander Richardson was given command of a division, being replaced by Lieutenant General John Harding, happily recovered from severe wounds received during the fighting for Tripoli. Tedder and Dempsey returned to Britain and, on 30 December, Leese took over Eighth Army from Montgomery, who had been chosen to command OVERLORD's land forces.

It was the end of the partnership between 'Alex' and 'Monty' which had witnessed the turn of the tide for the Western Allies in the Second World War and to which each had made an immense contribution. Of late, as has been seen, their relationship had become less happy, but the strongest disagreements never marred their personal feeling for each other. To Montgomery, the superior whom he honestly, if mistakenly, accused of being hesitant and indecisive, was still 'a very good friend of mine', 'a very dear person'; while, for his part, Alexander retained a fondness for his troublesome and inconsiderate lieutenant, despite his faults: 'I always like him best when I am with him.'

Nor, it is a pleasure to relate, did either forget what he owed to the other during those months in the Desert and Tunisia when they had formed an almost perfect team. 'All I have to do,' declared Alexander, 'is tell Monty what I want and he goes ahead and does it. I never have to worry about him.' 'My great supporter throughout,' declared Montgomery, 'was Alexander. He never bothered me, never fussed me, never suggested what I ought to do, and gave me at once everything I asked for – having listened patiently to my explanation of why I wanted it. But he was too big to require explanations; he gave me his trust.'

Alexander had been an even greater supporter than Montgomery ever realized, for it was he who had recommended his Army Commander to Brooke for that OVERLORD appointment. Montgomery was overjoyed. On his way home, he visited Churchill, who was recovering from pneumonia at Marrakesh in Morocco, and the Prime Minister was 'gratified and also relieved' to find him thrilled and uplifted by the great task ahead of him. Bursting with energy, he insisted on walking up a hill to a famous viewpoint, while the rest of the party made their way by car. 'He leaped about the rocks like an antelope,' relates an amused Churchill, 'and I felt a strong reassurance that all would be well.' Alexander, confronted by the prospect of a series of bitter clashes throughout an Italian winter, might well have envied him.

Notes:
1. Operation GIANT had been the code word given to the Division's original mission to seize the Volturno River bridges.
2. The Division's third regiment was dropped behind the German lines at this time, in an attempt to disrupt their communications, but it was widely scattered and had little, if any, effect.

Chapter 7

Deadlock

Since he had taken over the post of Commander-in-Chief, Middle East in August 1942, the men under Alexander's leadership had steadily occupied more and more enemy or enemy controlled territory: the western part of Egypt, Cyrenaica, Tripolitania, Tunisia, Sicily, southern Italy. Now everything changed. Now gains were limited to a few miles at best, often only a few hundred yards. Across the narrowest part of Italy, from the Adriatic to the Mediterranean, the crooked curve of the Gustav Line barred the Allied advance on Rome.

Construction of this had begun in the autumn of 1943 and from November onwards had been the personal concern of Hitler. Based on natural features such as mountains or rivers, it consisted of a series of dugouts and pillboxes, protected by steel and concrete, linked by trenches and frequently by underground passages. Nor did these form only a single 'line'; instead there were a whole number of such connected positions, one behind the other, the rear ones cleverly sited so as to enable counter-attacks to be made on any advanced posts that had been lost. Existing buildings were strengthened and incorporated into the defences if possible, so that many mountain villages became formidable fortifications in their own right. Equally, any buildings which blocked fields of fire were ruthlessly removed. The approaches to the front line were liberally covered with barbed wire and, as always, a profusion of anti-personnel mines and booby traps could be counted upon to take a hideous toll of any number of attackers.

On the Adriatic coast, the outlying parts of the line had fallen to the Eighth Army's advance over the Sangro and Moro Rivers, but new defences had been established beyond the ground gained, while positions such as Orsogna which Eighth Army had failed to capture, were strengthened still further. Beyond Orsogna, the Gustav Line ran south-westward through the Abruzzi region, past Monte Amaro, at 9,170 feet one of the highest peaks of the Apennines, to Monte Cairo, 5,500 feet, and its outlying spur Monte Cassino, 1,700 feet. Here, where the mountains ended suddenly and dramatically, the Gustav Line had to be sited on low ground, the valley of the Liri River, but on the southern edge of this, a smaller but still difficult range, the Aurunci Mountains, provided natural strength to the last stretch of the defences leading down to the Mediterranean.

It was in this area that the two most likely lines of advance on Rome were to be found, both of them dating from a time when that city was mistress of most of the then known world: Route 7, the famous Via Appia, followed the coast, but it was hemmed in by the Aurunci range; and Route 6, the Via Casilina, seemed a better prospect. This passed through the little town of Cassino, which lies just south-east of the mountain of that name, then crossed the rich agricultural land of the Liri Valley to head north-westward straight to Rome. Unfortunately, the Allies could not use the valley until two very different obstacles had been overcome.

The first of these, blocking the valley's mouth, was a southward-flowing river system that acted as the Gustav Line's outer moat. East of the Monte Cairo-Monte Cassino feature, this was formed by the Rapido River, the valley of which, north of Cassino town, had been flooded when the Germans had blown up a dam, making it impassable for tanks and transport vehicles without the laying of an artificial surface. Just south of Cassino, the Rapido joined the River Gari which officially gave its name to the combined water-course, but the soldiers in practice continued to call it the Rapido, which seemed appropriate as it now moved extremely rapidly through a deep channel which was very difficult to cross. Into it flowed the Liri, after which the troops did accept a further change of name by which the river completed its journey to the sea under the title of the Garigliano.

The other obstacle was still more serious. Monte Cassino, topped by an enormous monastery, originally founded by Saint Benedict in AD 529, jutted out into the Liri Valley, towering almost verti-cally above Route 6 which ran close to its foot, and providing the Germans with a superb observation post over the whole area. The

Allies would never be able to use this road to Rome until they had captured the mountain which controlled and dominated it.

If the Allies had had greatly superior numbers and conditions had been perfect, these defences, manned by a highly trained, resolute and well-led enemy, would have proved difficult enough. As it was, Alexander commanded eighteen divisions, while Kesselring commanded fifteen. Admittedly, these were quite a bit weaker in numbers than their Allied equivalents but there were eight more divisions in northern Italy which could relieve or reinforce them if needed; they had all the advantages of defending fixed positions; and those advantages were increased by the weather. As winter set in, snow, rain and freezing winds produced conditions that verged on the primitive. Sophisticated supporting vehicles were useless in a sea of mud and essential equipment for the soldiers engaged in combat at close quarters could only be brought forward by mules or by the men themselves.

In these circumstances, it was inevitable that gains were made only slowly and at heavy cost. It was inevitable that the infantry suffered horribly, as much from the elements as from the enemy. It was inevitable that some broke under the strain and there was a rising number of deserters, though many of these were in reality 'shell shock' cases who were found wandering about behind the lines in a state of stupor. Many excellent accounts exist of the soldiers' courage and endurance, of their privations and misery. It is only regrettable that these so often try to contrast the former with, and to blame the latter on the alleged incompetence of their senior commanders.

The brutal truth was that Alexander could only have spared his troops their ordeals by following the example of the warriors of classical times and refraining from warfare during the winter. But this was impossible, for Alexander's duty was to keep up pressure in Italy to prevent enemy forces there being used to reinforce other fronts. As it was, during the first five months of 1944, the Germans sent six new divisions to join those already stationed in northern France and the Low Countries. Had they been able to add any of the very capable formations in Italy to this strength, it might have had calamitous results. On the other hand, if Alexander could break through the impressive fortifications guarding the approach to Rome, this would probably force Hitler to send more divisions to Italy and would quite certainly have an immense moral effect on both sides.

Alexander was always ready to adopt measures which would reduce his men's suffering. For instance, it was during the closing weeks of 1943 that an improved system of air support began to be practised. Called 'Rover David' after the Christian name of Wing Commander Haysom, the Head of Operations in the Desert Air Force, this consisted of mobile observation units in close contact with the headquarters of the various forward brigades, controlling a squadron of fighters or fighter-bombers, known as the 'Cab Rank', which could be directed to attack, at very short notice, targets requested by the Army. The main disadvantage of this system was that it required the services of a considerable number of aircraft, but the Allied Air Forces by now enjoyed sufficient resources to make its adaptation well worthwhile.

Alexander was also greatly concerned with improving the supply situation, and urged the Allied airmen to attack marshalling yards, repair depots and rail or road bridges which would help to cripple Kesselring's lines of communication. At the same time, he took steps to rectify his own unsatisfactory system, reluctantly dispensing with certain officers and bringing in others, chiefly Major General Brian Robertson as his Chief Administrative Officer.

The tragedy was that these measures proved of little use for the time being. 'Rover David', 'Cab Rank' and the attacks on Kesselring's supply lines were alike largely nullified by the weather. The improvements made by Robertson and his staff could not alter the fact that in the mountains during winter, a lorry was less valuable than a jeep; a jeep less valuable than a mule. Nonetheless, Alexander's armies would have good reason to be grateful for the changes he had made and the ideas he had adopted when the coming of spring enabled them to become fully effective.

Nor need Alexander have reproached himself on the basic plan he had devised for breaking the Gustav Line. Even Captain Liddell Hart, who continuously, and usually unfairly, carps about the Italian campaign, concedes that this was 'well designed in broad outline'. The main offensive was entrusted to Mark Clark, whose strength Alexander had increased at the expense of Eighth Army. Preliminary moves would be made north of Cassino by Juin's newly arrived French Expeditionary Corps – developed from the XIX French Corps which we met in North Africa – and across the Garigliano by McCreery's X (British) Corps. These, it was hoped, would divert German forces to the flanks before Keyes delivered the main thrust with his II US Corps over the Rapido into the Liri Valley.

This attack was originally planned for the night of 18/19 January. On the 22nd, a revived Operation SHINGLE would be executed by VI US Corps at Anzio. Churchill had persuaded the Americans to allow the necessary assault craft to remain in the Mediterranean for a further length of time and Alexander had increased the strength of the landing force from its original one division to two infantry divisions, two tank battalions and supporting units, which would be followed up by two more divisions, one of them armoured. It was anticipated that by the time the landings took place, the mobile divisions which the Germans kept in reserve would be hurrying southward to aid their comrades in the Gustav Line – only to have to turn back again to meet the new threat at Anzio. It was felt that the resultant confusion and the risk that its line of communications might be cut would so unsettle von Vietinghoff's Tenth Army that Clark would be able to break through the Liri Valley. He would then join forces with the troops at Anzio, after which Rome would be a prize ready for the taking.

It was not to be. There were many reasons for this, but it is suggested that one of the most important was poor Intelligence which would, indeed, bedevil Alexander throughout the next five months and of which we will see plenty of other examples.[1] Alexander was notified that the Germans were exhausted, low in morale and desperately eager to rest and refit. He was given an accurate estimate of the divisions that Kesselring could theoretically send to Anzio and the times of their arrival, but he was also advised that Clark's pressure, combined with the threat that SHINGLE posed to the Germans' supply lines, would be sufficient to ensure that this would not happen in practice.

It was a wildly optimistic assessment. The defenders of the Gustav Line had confidence in their strong positions, were not nearly as tired as had been made out, and would resist with their usual fierce resolution. The character and mood of the enemy High Command had also been badly misread. When VI US Corps landed at Anzio, some of Kesselring's staff did urge him to pull back from his southern front, but he refused to panic and it is not hindsight to suggest that his previous record had given no indication that he was likely to do so.

At first, though, all seemed to be going reasonably well. Juin advanced on the night of 11/12 January, and despite bad weather, his men, who were very experienced in operating over mountainous terrain, drove the Germans back some 10 miles. Lieutenant General Fridolin von Senger und Etterlin, commanding XIV Panzer Corps, which guarded the southern half of the Gustav Line, was forced to commit his reserves in order to stop any further progress.

Next, on the evening of 17 January, X (British) Corps began its attack over the Garigliano. Surprise was achieved and by dawn on the 18th, both McCreery's divisions had secured bridgeheads, which they held against counter-attacks. It was difficult to expand them, however, because German artillery fire prevented the building of a bridge capable of taking tanks until the early hours of the 20th, and even then the approaches to it were shelled so repeatedly that it could only be used after dark. By that time in any event, fresh enemy formations were arriving. Kesselring, assured by his Intelligence staff that an Allied amphibious landing, which he felt certain would take place at some time or other, was unlikely to occur in the near future, had reluctantly sent 29th and 90th Panzer Grenadier Divisions and detachments from the Hermann Göring Division to block X Corps' advance.

For Alexander, news of the German move was most encouraging, suggesting that his intention of stripping the Anzio area of defenders was working. But then the plan started to go wrong. The attacks so far had been only preliminary ones, designed to help prepare the way for the decisive thrust in the Liri Valley of II US Corps. The idea was that 36th US Infantry Division should cross the Rapido and close in from both sides on the village of San Angelo, standing on a small bluff about halfway between Cassino to the north and the junction of the Liri with the Rapido to the south. Once an adequate bridgehead had been established, 1st US Armoured Division would pass through it and advance up the valley.

Unfortunately, the Americans only completed their capture of outlying German positions on the east bank of the Rapido by 15 January, and although the time of the assault was postponed to

2000 on the 20th, this still gave very little opportunity for proper preparations. Intelligence summaries had not advised the Americans of just how formidable were the defences, including extensive minefields, which awaited them on the far bank, and it was not then appreciated how enemy observation posts on Monte Cassino could detect any move that was made in the Liri Valley. The Americans showed little concern, for they believed that the thorough, methodical preparations made by Eighth Army, and indeed X (British) Corps before embarking on river crossings, were examples of over-caution, but McCreery was most unhappy and warned Clark that he would have a disaster.

His prediction quickly came true. Despite the usual bad weather, American aircraft and American artillery delivered powerful preliminary bombardments, but these had little effect on the strongly protected German batteries. A subsidiary attack south of the Liri River by 46th (British) Division from X Corps was unable to effect a crossing and was wisely called off with minimal casualties. 36th US Infantry Division struggled gallantly to establish and maintain bridgeheads over the Rapido throughout 21 and 22 January, but being unsupported by tanks or heavy weapons and under intensive and continuous shellfire, its task was a hopeless one. By the evening of the 22nd, the last Americans were hurled back across the river, having suffered losses assessed by Clark at 143 dead, 663 wounded and 875 missing.

Far from having put pressure on the Germans by breaking through the Gustav Line, the fighting on the Rapido had raised enemy confidence just at the time when it would be tested by the landings at Anzio. A brief period of good weather for once favoured the Allies, surprise was total, and by nightfall on 22 January, VI US Corps had put ashore at least 36,000 men and 3,000 vehicles. Resistance had been negligible, some 200 prisoners had been taken and Allied casualties were only 154, few of them fatal and mostly suffered in minefields.

As we have seen, however, Alexander's original intention had been that SHINGLE should play merely a supporting role to Clark's advance into the Liri Valley, causing confusion and providing an additional threat at the crucial moment. Now the American defeat on the Rapido meant that the troops at Anzio would be operating on their own.

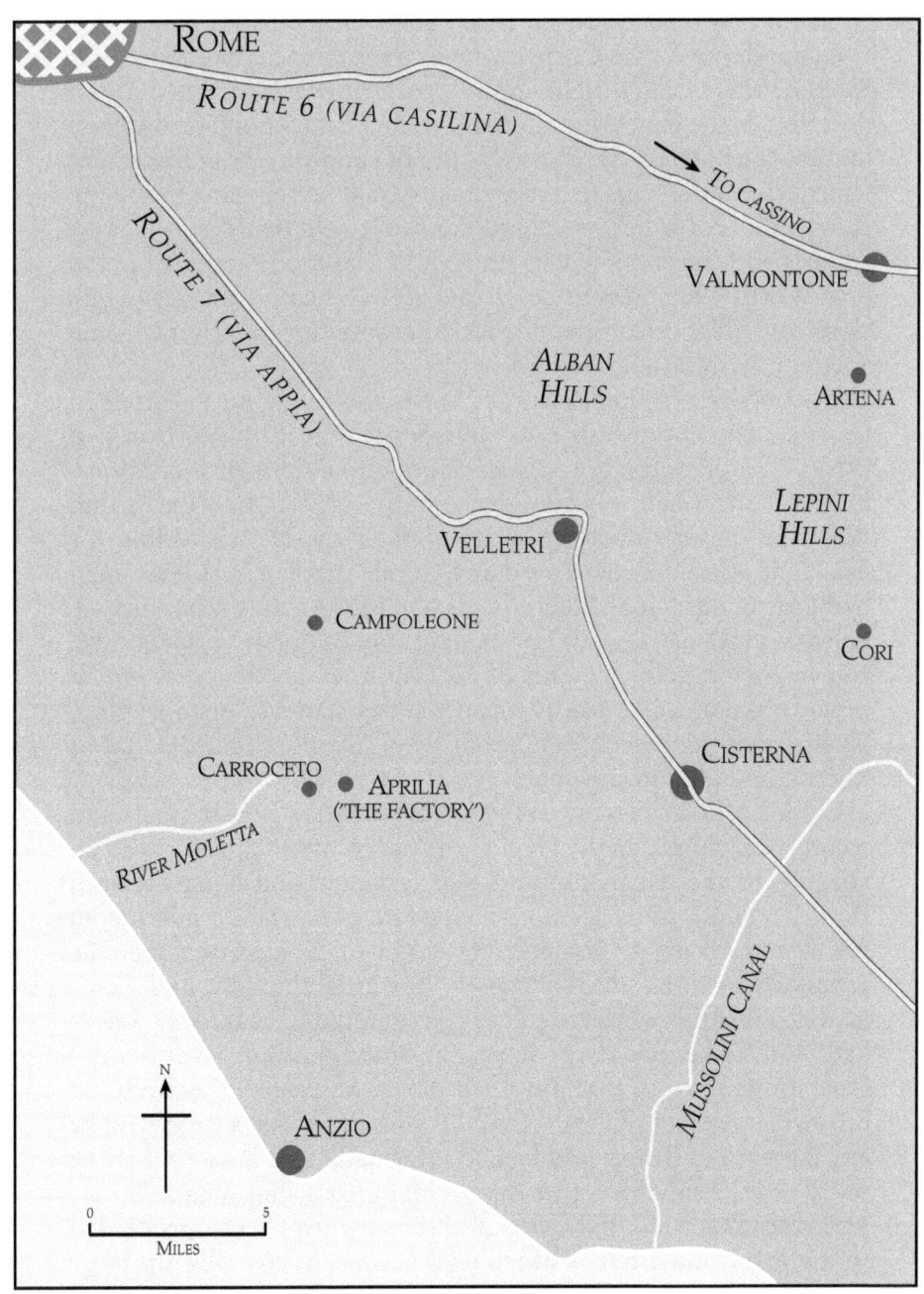

Map 8: The Anzio Beachhead

This fact was painfully clear to Major General John Lucas, the Commander of VI US Corps, who, as a result of his experiences at Salerno, was already highly pessimistic. He was concerned about the effect of the inevitable German counter-attacks and he doubted that the air raids on the enemy's lines of supply and reinforcement which Alexander had tried to arrange would be very effective in the equally inevitable bad weather. Nor did it help that Lucas was no admirer of Churchill; he had studied the Gallipoli campaign in the First World War and considered that SHINGLE bore an alarmingly close resemblance to this, not least because 'apparently the same amateur was on the coach's bench'.

It is only fair to point out that Lucas was by no means alone in his anxieties. Innumerable accounts insist that if only Patton had led VI US Corps, there would have been no doubts or hesitations. In fact, Patton had less confidence in SHINGLE than Lucas did. When he said goodbye to Lucas prior to the latter's sailing for Anzio, he effectively destroyed any morale that Lucas still retained by blurting out, 'John, there is no one in the Army I hate to see killed as much as you, but you can't get out of this alive. Of course, you might be badly wounded. No one ever blames a *wounded* general.' Clark, if more restrained, was scarcely encouraging. 'Don't stick your neck out, Johnny,' he warned Lucas. 'I did at Salerno and got into trouble.'

Clark's official instructions to his subordinate were to 'seize and secure a beachhead in the vicinity of Anzio', after which he was 'to advance to the Alban Hills', 3,000 feet high and lying between Routes 6 and 7 some 15 miles south-east of Rome, 25 miles from Anzio and 60 from Cassino. It was not made clear whether the advance was to be 'into' or merely 'towards' the hills, and Clark made no mention of the need to proceed rapidly. Moreover, Lucas had been told explicitly by Brigadier Brann, head of Fifth Army's Operations section, that any such move must depend entirely on his own assessment of the situation. Nor did Clark's orders make any mention of Rome, and he had informally told Lucas before he sailed that he should 'forget this goddam Rome business'.

As a result, Lucas, in the virtual absence of any enemy, proceeded to dig in on his original beachhead perimeter, to build up large reserve stocks of supplies and ammunition, and to await the arrival of his follow-up divisions, before pressing on. He has been roundly condemned for his attitude and indeed there does seem little doubt in retrospect that if he had sent columns forward, they could have entered Rome, reached the Alban Hills and cut Route 7 certainly, and possibly Route 6 as well.

Yet there also seems little doubt in retrospect that such an action would soon have led to a catastrophe. This could only have been avoided had the Germans panicked and fallen back from the Gustav Line. As already noted, Kesselring resolutely refused to consider this. So did Hitler, who demanded that the Line be held 'at all costs' and there should be 'the most bitter struggle for every yard'. In these circumstances, it would have been impossible for the Allies to establish a firm base at Anzio, while at the same time keeping their long, narrow supply lines to their troops in Rome and the Alban Hills secure in the face of assaults from all sides.

When Kesselring visited the Anzio front late on the 22nd, he initially felt that the Allies had missed 'a uniquely favourable opportunity'. His reaction, though, was inspired by relief; on consideration he would reflect that the landing force had not been strong enough to do more than hold the beachhead. This was certainly an opinion shared by Clark. Most convincing, however, are the views of the two original divisional commanders at Anzio, particularly bearing in mind that neither had much respect for Lucas. Major General Truscott of 3rd US Infantry Division, who had won distinction in Sicily and would later take over VI US Corps himself, states that an advance to the Alban Hills 'without establishing a firm base to protect our beaches would have been sheer madness and would almost certainly have resulted in the eventual destruction of the landing forces'. Major General Penney of 1st (British) Infantry Division believes 'we could have had one night in Rome and eighteen months in PoW camps.'

Alexander's own original objectives for SHINGLE were not concerned with Rome, but were designed to threaten the rear of the German forces in the Gustav Line by severing their lines of communication. To this end, he did envisage an advance to occupy the Alban Hills but only on the assumption that this would assist Fifth Army to 'break through' the enemy's 'main defences' on the Line and link up with VI US Corps 'at the earliest possible moment'. The repulse of II US Corps had completely altered the situation and Alexander accepted that Lucas could not possibly seize the Alban

Hills until he had consolidated his bridgehead and reinforcements, particularly of armour, could reach him.

Nonetheless, Alexander, as he states in his Official Despatch, did consider that 'Lucas could have been more adventurous.' He was very anxious that VI US Corps should be seen to be taking some positive action and should give as convincing an impression of strength as it could. By doing so, he hoped that it would continue to keep the defenders of the Gustav Line 'looking over their shoulders' and that units would be sent back from the southern defences to help contain the Anzio bridgehead, thereby increasing the chances of renewed offensives by II US Corps proving successful.

Alexander twice visited Anzio soon after the initial landings – specifically on 22 and 25 January. He quickly became concerned about the negative atmosphere that he found there. Lucas had previously expressed reservations to his Army Group Commander, but Alexander had mistaken pessimism for modesty, and felt he had done enough by assuring Lucas that: 'We have every confidence in you. That is why you were picked.' His trips to Anzio quickly revealed his error, so he attempted to hearten Lucas by displaying a confidence which he may not have felt and by bestowing praise which he may deliberately have exaggerated; on his first visit, he congratulated Lucas on having carried out the landings, which, he said, 'have certainly given the folk at home something to talk about'; on his second, he described the establishment of the beachhead as 'a splendid piece of work'.

At the same time, Alexander, as he reported to Churchill, stressed to Lucas and to Clark, who was also present on both the 22nd and the 25th, 'the importance of strong-hitting mobile patrols being boldly pushed out to gain contact with the enemy'. In particular he suggested limited advances down the two main roads leading inland from Anzio, northward to capture the town of Campoleone and north-eastward to capture Cisterna. This would give the Allies more room to manoeuvre, and better communications since these places controlled vital road junctions. Cisterna, indeed, was situated on Route 7 and its loss would thus cut a main supply line to the German Tenth Army, thereby achieving one of the aims of the Anzio operation.

Churchill would later strongly rebuke Alexander for having merely urged these courses of action instead of expressly ordering them, as he would have been entitled to do. Once again though, this was a matter of politics. When dealing with the Americans, Alexander preferred to suggest, rather than command, and the same considerations prevented him from taking a firmer line with Lucas. Nonetheless, his signal to Churchill indicated that he believed that Clark and Lucas did intend to carry out his suggestions.

As indeed they did, but not immediately. In the beachhead area, the left flank was protected by the Moletta River and the right flank by the Mussolini Canal. Whereas if VI US Corps moved forward, it would reach ground on both flanks which, Intelligence reports advised, would provide easy approaches for German armour. In fact, this was simply not the case. On the west, the terrain contained a mass of scrub-filled gullies, up to 50 feet deep, impassable to tanks; on the east, it became waterlogged after rain, and was crossed by 20-foot irrigation ditches. Since Lucas did not know this, however, it is understandable that he was reluctant to risk counter-attacks by hostile armour before the arrival of his own 1st US Armoured Division on 27 January.[2] Patrols were sent out to probe towards Campoleone and Cisterna on the 25th, but they were checked well short of their objectives. The build-up of German forces in the Anzio area was already underway.

Kesselring was eager to engage VI US Corps as quickly and with as much strength as he could manage. The Luftwaffe was first on the scene. Air raids began on the 23rd and, despite worsening weather, increased the following day, a particularly savage attack being made on three clearly marked and illuminated hospital ships, of which one was sunk and another damaged. Kesselring also sent Luftwaffe AA units to Anzio but these were not intended to operate against Allied aircraft but to use their dual-purpose weapons to establish an anti-tank screen around the beachhead.

Behind this screen, Kesselring rushed troops from the Gustav Line and central and northern Italy to contain the Anzio perimeter. He was urged on by Hitler, who, remembering how close the Germans had come to success at Salerno, was eager to deal what he called the 'abscess' at Anzio a devastating blow that might scare the Allies out of making any further landings either in Italy or, more importantly, in North-West Europe. By 23 January, the first units of 3rd Panzer Grenadier and the Hermann Göring Divisions were already taking up positions around Anzio. By the end of the month, elements of eight divisions were surrounding the bridgehead, command of them being entrusted to von Mackensen's Fourteenth Army. Von Vietinghoff's Tenth Army was reduced to ten divisions, which were ordered to stand on the defensive, and six remained in northern Italy. In addition, Hitler dispatched to Italy one division from Yugoslavia, three independent regiments from Germany, and another division and two heavy tank battalions from France.

Alexander was thus continuing to fulfil his ultimate strategic aim of attracting German forces from more vital areas and his immediate strategic aim of weakening the enemy in the Gustav Line. These successes, though, were achieved at the expense of Alexander's tactical objectives of Campoleone and Cisterna. He continued to believe that they could still be attained, since his Intelligence had assured him that only light enemy units were holding these areas, covering major positions being prepared further back. Unhappily, and it is tempting to add, needless to say, this report was incorrect.

Clark, who returned to the bridgehead on 28 January, agreed with Alexander, and even Lucas felt that his own strength was now sufficient for such a double advance. The initial units of 1st US Armoured and 45th US Infantry Divisions had now come ashore and by the end of the month Lucas controlled 70,000 men, 27,000 tons of stores, 508 guns, 356 tanks and 18,000 other vehicles.[3] Yet both his attacks failed. A British assault on Campoleone, supported by the tanks of 1st US Armoured, was checked just short of the town and resulted only in the creation of a long, narrow and obviously vulnerable salient. An American attack on Cisterna was thrown back with heavy losses and during a preliminary raid by US Rangers – the equivalent of the British Commandos – two battalions ran into an ambush; of their 767 men, 761 were killed or taken prisoner. The initiative had passed to the enemy. 'I had hoped that we would be hurling a wildcat ashore,' laments Churchill, 'but all we had got was a stranded whale.'

Of course, had the diversion of troops to Anzio weakened the Gustav Line sufficiently to allow the Allies to break through it – as von Vietinghoff feared might be the case – these setbacks would have been unimportant. On the evening of 24 January, 34th US Infantry Division, with the French Expeditionary Corps on its right

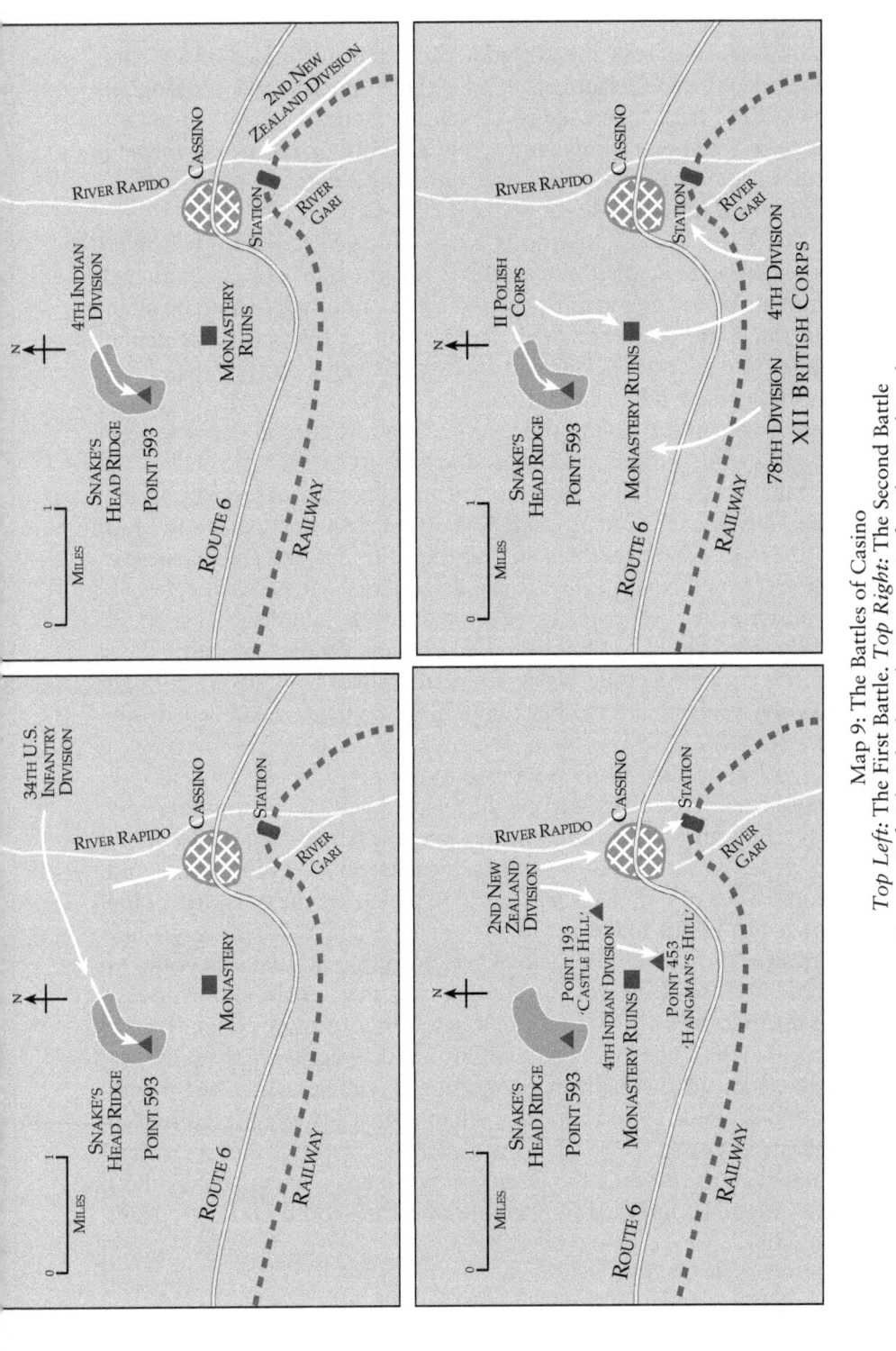

Map 9: The Battles of Casino
Top Left: The First Battle. *Top Right:* The Second Battle
Bottom Left: The Third Battle. *Bottom Right:* The Final Battle

flank, struck across the Rapido, this time north of Cassino. Its objectives were Cassino itself and the mountain overlooking it; once these had been taken, Alexander intended that Lieutenant General Sir Bernard Freyberg's New Zealand Corps, newly formed and added to Fifth Army's strength, should move into the Liri Valley and head for Rome.

The French colonial troops again did well, crossing the river safely to seize strongpoints east of Monte Cairo by 26 January. Unfortunately, they had by-passed enemy units on Monte Cifalco. On the 27th, these attacked the Frenchmen from the rear at the same time that other German formations engaged them head on, checking their advance and recapturing their foremost positions. Juin made several attempts to recover the lost ground over the next few days but without success and at heavy cost.

Meanwhile 34th US Division was making painful progress in the face of immense difficulties. It was attempting to cross the Rapido in the area where the broken dam had flooded the approaches to the river, and beyond it were the usual fixed defences, shielded by mines and barbed wire. It was not until 26 January that a small bridgehead could be established. Even then it took three more days before engineers could lay down artificial surfaces strong enough to carry tanks and a further two before the bridgehead was firmly secured.

On 1 February, 34th US Division, supported by elements of 36th US, struck southwards from the bridgehead. Over the next few days, in pouring rain, under heavy fire, the Americans strove nobly to reach Monte Cassino and its monastery, Cassino town and Route 6 beyond it. They were able to penetrate the outskirts of the town but could make no further progress. On 4 February, they captured Point 593, a rocky knoll forming the highest point of Snake's Head Ridge, the key enemy defensive position north-west of the monastery – only to lose it again to a counter-attack. By the 7th, they had been forced to call off their assaults; they made one last effort on the 11th in exceptionally vile weather, but it was halted as well. Two days later, when 34th US was relieved by 4th Indian Division from the New Zealand Corps, stretcher-bearers carried away not only the wounded but men so exhausted by their efforts and so numbed by the cold that they could no longer walk unaided.

The First Battle of Cassino, as it was later called, was over. The Second was not long delayed but it would be fought in quite different circumstances. On 31 January, Alexander visited Clark, who had established his Advanced Headquarters at Anzio, directing him to capture Cisterna, strengthen the area between this and the British salient pointing towards Campoleone, and improve communications throughout the beachhead to assist in repelling German assaults which Intelligence reports indicated were imminent. These were wise instructions but before anything could be done to carry them out, von Mackensen made his first moves to eliminate VI US Corps.

Late on 3 February, under cover of an artillery bombardment and in heavy rain which prevented the Allied airmen from intervening, the Germans attacked the British salient from both sides. On the 4th, they cut off the foremost unit, 3rd (British) Brigade, which fought its way out of the trap only at a cost of 1,400 men, 900 of them prisoners. Luckily, 168th (British) Brigade from 56th Division, which had just been transferred from the Garigliano front, helped to stabilize the position – if only temporarily.

There followed two days of heavy raids by the Luftwaffe; then the Germans renewed their attacks in the area of the salient on 7 February, concentrating on the hamlet of Carroceto and the agricultural centre at Aprilia, known as the Factory. After a grim struggle, with heavy casualties on both sides, the enemy secured the Factory by the afternoon of the 9th. Carroceto fell next morning, and 1st (British) Division, which had borne the brunt of the fighting, had to be withdrawn into the Corps reserve. 45th US Division began a series of counter-attacks, but despite covering fire from Allied artillery, Allied aircraft and the guns of Allied warships offshore, these had all failed by 13 February.

The Germans now began to build up their strength for further assaults, hampered but not halted by Allied air attacks. Alexander and Clark were well aware that these were coming since 'Ultra' was recording blood-curdling demands from Hitler that Anzio's defenders should either be slaughtered or else driven into the sea and drowned. It was clear to Alexander that instead of exerting pressure at Anzio to assist his main forces to break through the Gustav Line, he must attempt to break through the Gustav Line to assist the imperiled garrison at Anzio – and as soon as possible.

This attempt, the Second Battle of Cassino, was entrusted to Freyberg's New Zealand Corps, but was handicapped from the start by the urgency of Anzio's needs. There was very little time for original plans or proper preparations and Freyberg would receive limited support from the Allied Air Forces, the bulk of which had had to be diverted to the aid of VI US Corps. The intention was that 2nd New Zealand Division would advance down the railway line to enter Cassino town from the south-east. Meanwhile 4th Indian Division would assault the mountain from Snake's Head Ridge; having secured it, they would move down it to attack the town from the west.

4th Indian Division was commanded by Major General Francis Tuker, who would have preferred quite different tactics and who had already been understandably enraged by Intelligence failures which had resulted in his not having been advised that Point 593 had been recaptured by the Germans, and not having been given any information about the construction of the monastery, which he believed to be the key to the enemy's defences. It was certainly not the job of the Divisional Commander to obtain such details from Naples bookshops – as Tuker had had to do – though equally, it was not that of the corps, army or army group commanders either.

Tuker, however, was a singularly acerbic character, from whose caustic tongue no one was spared, and whose anger would later find vent in tirades against his superiors. He felt patronizingly sorry for Freyberg, 'but he should never have been put in command of a corps'; Clark he considered 'a flashy ignoramus'; but his particular resentment was reserved for Alexander: 'He is quite the least intelligent commander I have ever met in a high position . . . I found that I could not talk to him for more than five minutes, whereas I can talk for hours to intelligent men. Perhaps it is too harsh to say that he's bone from the neck up, but perhaps it isn't.'

Since men of the greatest intelligence and the widest interests, such as Churchill and Macmillan, found no difficulty in talking with Alexander, there must have been a different explanation as to why Tuker found this so hard. Possibly the real reason was that Alexander found him a bore. Tuker's greatest virtues were his admirable leadership of 4th Indian Division and his steadfast devotion to his soldiers, which they deservedly repaid. Yet this also had a negative aspect. Tuker's only interest was in his division and he seems to have been incapable of assessing a situation from any point of view apart from the effect that it would have on his own men.

Thus during the fighting in the Desert and Tunisia, Tuker gave little enough praise to formations other than 4th Indian, but its achievements he frequently exaggerated. During the struggle for the Gabes Gap, for instance, after his men had taken their objective, the Djebel Fatnassa, Tuker sent off a jubilant message that the way was clear for the British armour to break through, there was nothing to stop it and the end of the war in Tunisia was in sight. In reality, the line of advance was still blocked by another range of hills, the Oudane el Hachana, and even when this had been cleared, progress was opposed by anti-tank and field guns sited in protected positions, which were continuing to kill some of Tuker's own troops several hours later.

Tuker's reaction to this situation was that the British armour should have rushed the guns – not a practice recommended by past experience – but his attitude in February 1944 was rather different. He dreaded sending his division across difficult ground to attack heavily protected defences at Monte Cassino. He would have preferred a wide turning movement over the lower slopes of Monte Cairo, to cut off the defenders from behind and force their evacuation. Freyberg had at first approved this plan, but subsequently changed his mind and determined on the direct assaults previously described.

Tuker, whose temper had not been improved by his having fallen ill, never ceased to protest against this change, and when considering his assessments of his superiors and colleagues, it is important to realize that these depended entirely on whether or not they agreed with his views on this subject. Thus Juin, who supported the wide turning movement and wished French troops to join 4th Indian in attempting it, is called by Tuker 'probably the finest tactical commander in Italy'. As already seen, those who were not of the same mind, and the most senior of these was Alexander, are treated more harshly; they were 'guilty of military sins no less'.

Yet if the issue is examined objectively, it is possible at least to understand the reasoning of the 'military sinners'. The sweep envisaged by Tuker would give more room for manoeuvre and would fall on Germans of a less high calibre, but it would also have to cross a whole series of high ridges, be at the risk of attacks from behind like those Juin had experienced from Monte Cifalco, and necessitate a long supply line which would not have been easy to maintain; Clark, indeed, believed it could not possibly be maintained because there were simply not enough mules available to do so.

In addition, there was the question of the time it would take before such a movement could succeed, and whereas Tuker appears not to have been concerned about the fate of the men at Anzio, his superiors were – and rightly so. The needs of VI US Corps were urgent and although there was in fact an alternative route by means of which speedy assistance could be brought to them, this was only discovered later and by accident. In February 1944, it seemed that help could only be provided by breaking through the Liri Valley. Tuker would later declare that he could never understand the 'extraordinary obsession in British commanders' minds that they must challenge the enemy strength rather than play on his weakness'. This frankly was nonsense. The British commanders did not wish to challenge the enemy strength, they wished to challenge the enemy where they thought success would be most decisive, and unfortunately such vital points were bound to be strongly defended.

Of course we now know that Alexander and his commanders did not achieve success but at the time the chances of their doing so appeared high, especially to Clark and many other American officers. They pointed out that their own troops, who had had to secure crossings over the Rapido first, had come desperately close to gaining their objectives. Surely fresh units, without such preliminary difficulties and with several important positions already in their hands, should be able to capture the few hundred yards of ground still retained by the enemy. The Allied leaders did not appreciate the skill and determination of the defenders and it does seem regrettable that they rejected a further suggestion from Juin that diversionary attacks should be made against other parts of the Gustav Line to distract the Germans' attention, but it is a travesty of the facts to dismiss them as being criminally incompetent.

Not content with his subsequent denigration, Tuker – this time, it is interesting to note, without the support of Juin – took the first step leading to an event which would ultimately cause more criticism of Alexander than any other. Describing the Monte Cassino monastery as a 'fortress' and a 'thorn in our side', he insisted that his division could not undertake its planned assault until this had been 'directly dealt with by applying blockbuster bombs from the air'. He dismissed as irrelevant the question whether it was presently held by a German garrison, as even if it was not it would be available as a final place of refuge when the positions outside it were overrun: 'It is therefore also essential that the building should be so demolished as to prevent its effective occupation at that time.'

Tuker has received singularly little Christian forgiveness from the monastery authorities, but their accusations that his views, given with 'an air of infallibility', were 'ludicrous and ignorant', do have some point. For Tuker had confused the historic building with the mountain on which it stood. It was the latter which was the fortress and the thorn in the Allied side, not the former. Kesselring had given express orders that it should not be occupied by armed troops, and these orders had been echoed by von Senger und Etterlin, the Corps Commander with responsibility for the defences, who was a devout Catholic from Bavaria. It seems that the nearest German soldiers were stationed at least 300 yards from the monastery walls and they were prevented from entering the building by military police.

It is not unfair to add that the German leaders were perhaps thinking less about the monastery's sacred character than the fact that it was an obvious target and their men would be safer in shell-proof bunkers on the hill. The same motive prompted their failure to use the monastery as an observation post, though in any case the slope of the hill restricted the view from it and in reality the German positions outside it had a better field of vision.

Yet whatever the Germans' motives, it cannot be accepted that Tuker was right to suggest it was irrelevant whether or not they had occupied the monastery. If they had not, then bombing it would do no harm to military personnel or military installations, would give the Germans a splendid propaganda weapon and would allow them to take over the building with a clear conscience. What was irrelevant was Tuker's comment that they would do this anyway as a last resort. As Clark and Juin argued at the time, and von Senger und Etterlin confirmed was the case later, the ruins of the monastery, with no roof left to fall on top of its defenders, would make a far finer stronghold.

In Tuker's favour, it has been argued that he had anticipated that the remains of the monastery would promptly be seized by 4th Indian Division, providing an admirable defensive position from which to repel any counter-attacks. Tuker had certainly thought that the air-raid would immediately be followed by the ground assault, though this might well be difficult to achieve since the bombing would have to take place in one of the rare intervals of good weather, regardless of the state of 4th Indian's preparation. It will be recalled, however, that Tuker wished the monastery to be 'so demolished as to prevent its effective occupation' by the Germans. It is difficult to see how he expected air attacks to destroy such a strong building so completely, but since apparently he did, he cannot have anticipated that it could be effectively occupied by the Allies either.

Tuker personally would later argue that whatever he had or had not demanded, the monastery in any case 'was bound to be destroyed if a direct attack was delivered upon the hill', and therefore any blame should fall on the Germans for including it within their defences. Since the Germans could hardly be expected to abandon Monte Cassino, the key bastion of the Liri Valley, and the monastery happened to have been erected on top of it, it seems somewhat unfair to place responsibility on them, particularly considering that an assault had in fact already been made on the hill without the monastery being hit by more than a single stray shell.[4] It seems even more unfair that it is the man whom Tuker most fiercely criticized who is usually saddled with responsibility for Tuker's own errors of judgement.

Tuker's demands were naturally referred to his immediate superiors. Freyberg, ceaselessly badgered by Tuker from his sick bed, informed Clark that he agreed that the monastery should be made a target as soon as possible. Clark, as already noted, thought that bombing would increase rather than diminish its value as a fortification, but his Chief of Staff, Major General Alfred Gruenther, rang Harding to report Freyberg's advice and Clark's own views on the subject. Harding, who did believe that the monastery was being used for military purposes, said he would have to consult with Alexander.

No one, surely, could fail to have immense sympathy for Alexander, thus faced with the need to reach an emotive, far-reaching and obviously controversial decision. He had faith in Freyberg's opinions but equally he did not want to put Clark in a difficult position. He received no help from his Intelligence staff, who could provide no definite evidence either way as to whether the monastery was occupied by the enemy or not, and apparently an 'Ultra' interception which might have confirmed the truth was mistranslated. Yet such was Alexander's integrity and strength of character that he seems not to have hesitated for an instance.

Alexander's soldiers, almost without exception, were convinced that the monastery housed German observers at least. That it was a man-made structure, with windows as its 'eyes', made it more threatening than any natural feature, however formidable. Every man who saw it rearing above him felt exposed and vulnerable, and regarded it as an evil, malignant presence which he feared and hated. Unlike Tuker and like Clark, Alexander did consider that it was relevant whether the monastery was occupied or not and questioned whether bombing it might not do more harm than good, but, in the last resort, he believed that the effect this would have on his troops was more important than 'purely material reasons'. 'Every good commander,' he would later declare, 'must consider the morale and feelings of his fighting men.'

So Alexander made it clear to Clark that, in his opinion, the bombing of the monastery was justified, and the Fifth Army Commander reluctantly obeyed the wishes of his admired superior. Alexander had his own sincere regrets at the time, but, as he would state afterwards: 'A commander, if faced by a choice between risking a single soldier's life and destroying a work of art, even a religious symbol like Monte Cassino, can only make one decision.' The cheers of the watching troops as the monastery was pounded, would justify the attention he had paid to their 'morale and feelings'.

The air attacks took place on the morning of 15 February, which for once provided clear visibility. There were two main strikes, both by the US Army Air Force: the first by 135 Flying Fortresses from Foggia, dropping some 280 tons of bombs and some 60 tons of incendiaries from heights of between 15,000 and 18,000 feet; the second by forty-seven Mitchells and forty Marauders, dropping

283 100lb bombs from a lower level. These raids killed at least 100 refugees who had taken shelter in the monastery and reduced the building to a shattered ruin; it was promptly occupied by enemy soldiers who found, as Clark had feared, that it provided them with better defences than it would have done if it had been left intact.

It had been essential that the raids were made on the 15th, partly because a further period of stormy weather was forecast and partly because the air forces would soon be required elsewhere – it was known from 'Ultra' that the great German assault on Anzio was planned for the 16th. Freyberg had tried to arrange for 4th Indian Division to deliver its attack on the 15th, but Brigadier Dimoline, who had taken over from Tuker, felt that the main assault could not be launched until the night of the 16th/17th. Apparently he did not notify his battalion commanders of the time of the raids and some forward positions were hit by bombs which fell wide. Mercifully, the Division's casualties were small, if greater than those of the Germans who did not lose a man.

That evening, 4th Indian Division's 7 Brigade mounted a preliminary attack on Point 593, which, it will be recalled, was still in enemy hands. This was halted without difficulty, as was a heavier assault on the night of the 16th/17th. Yet another attempt was made on the following night, in still greater strength, with still greater losses, but with no greater success. 4th Indian could still not secure Point 593, let alone make meaningful progress towards the monastery.

The New Zealand Division's part in the Second Battle of Cassino began late on 17 February, when a Maori battalion advanced along the wrecked railway line, capturing its primary objective, Cassino station, by midnight. Behind it, sappers set to work to prepare crossings over the Rapido and to fill gaps in the railway embankment where bridges had been demolished, so as to turn the embankment into a route by which tanks and anti-tank guns could be brought forward. This had to be done during the hours of darkness, because with daylight the sappers would be in full view of German observation posts on Monte Cassino. Unfortunately, for all their efforts, they could not quite complete their task, and the Maoris were left isolated and unsupported.

It seems that the capture of the railway station greatly alarmed the Germans. When congratulated later by his Commander-in-

Chief for having regained this, von Vietinghoff admitted that he had not thought he would be able to do so – to which Kesselring replied, 'Neither did I!' In reality, the Maoris' situation was hopeless, and although the New Zealand artillery tried to shield them by laying down a continuous smokescreen, at about 1500 on 18 February, German tanks and infantry burst into the station from two directions and drove its defenders back across the Rapido.

So the attempt to assist Anzio by breaking through the Gustav Line had failed miserably, and meanwhile the ordeal of the bridgehead had already begun. The Germans had marshalled ten divisions to oppose an Allied strength of less than five. Their morale was high, for they had been given personal assurances by Hitler that everything had been done to guarantee success and that their inevitable victory would have decisive and far-reaching effects.

Consequently, it was with high hopes that von Mackensen began his offensive early on 16 February, under cover of raids by a reinforced Luftwaffe and the heaviest artillery bombardment the defenders of Anzio had suffered. With Kesselring's approval, von Mackensen had intended to attack over a wide area from the general direction of Carroceto and Aprilia, but Hitler had insisted that the assault should be concentrated on a narrow front around the Campoleone road. This turned out to be unwise, for it enabled the Allied artillery, together with the Allied Air Forces, now switched from the front at Cassino, to inflict heavy losses on the attackers. As a result, 45th US Division, which bore the brunt of the assault, was driven from several outposts, but preserved its main defensive line intact.

Meanwhile Alexander had been faced with another difficult administrative decision. It had become clear to him that Lucas, whatever else might be said in his favour, was not a positive or inspirational leader, and had lost the confidence of his divisional commanders. Alexander was always very reluctant to act against senior American officers, for the sake of inter-Allied relations, but he now felt compelled to warn Clark that changes would have to be made. Clark was not happy with the position either, but late on 16 February, he compromised: Lucas was given two deputies, one British and one American. The American was Truscott, and Clark clearly intended that he would, in effect, supervise Lucas and ultimately replace him – as he did on the 22nd. This might seem hard on Lucas, whose determination to ensure the security of his beach-head had almost certainly saved it from destruction, but even as only Deputy Corps Commander, Truscott was able to encourage VI US Corps in a way that Lucas had never managed.

It was just as well, for on the night of 16/17 February, the Germans forced a wedge into the heart of 45th US Division, and next day their armour and infantry drove the Americans back with heavy casualties. Their own losses, however, were even greater as fire from Allied guns onshore and on warships poured down upon them, and a stream of Flying Fortresses, Liberators, Mitchells, Marauders and Wellingtons struck at them constantly in the teeth of heavy and accurate AA fire.

Already von Mackensen had suffered well over 2,500 casualties, but his men persisted in their efforts. On the night of the 17th/18th, they repelled an American counter-attack, and in the morning, taking advantage of bad weather which restricted the Allied airmen to a few strikes by Warhawk fighter-bombers, they pushed forward to the Allies' final defensive perimeter, in much the same area as that secured by the original landings. All the rest of that day and the following night, 45th US and 1st (British) Divisions held out against desperate assaults. These came perilously close to success, but on the morning of the 19th, a tremendous artillery fire again fell on the enemy, the Allies mounted a counter-attack and suddenly the cumulative effects of their ordeals, their losses and their exhaustion became too much for the Germans. They fell back, and as the Allies followed up, numbers of them began to surrender.

It was not the end of the German effort. Their commanders, well aware of the importance which Hitler attached to the elimination of the beachhead, reformed and tried again on 29 February, this time from Cisterna against 3rd US Division. Little progress was made before 2 March, when bad weather which had hampered both sides lifted and nearly 250 Flying Fortresses and Liberators, and some 180 Lightnings and Thunderbolts, savaged the enemy. Two days later, Kesselring ordered that the attacks which had cost von Mackensen a further 3,500 casualties and thirty tanks, should be discontinued, Fourteenth Army went onto the defensive and its mobile divisions were pulled back into reserve.

The defeat had been decisive. Had the Germans destroyed VI US

Corps or forced it to evacuate Anzio, they might well have caused grave doubts as to the Western Allies' prospects in future amphibious landings, and inspired bitter recriminations about the value of the whole Italian campaign. Instead, it was German morale which had been badly damaged, all the more effectively because of Hitler's own close association with the plans. Never again would they go onto the offensive in Italy. But they would continue to defend stubbornly, and now that Anzio was safe, it was perhaps a pity that the need to pin down the enemy forces in Italy persuaded Alexander, against his own original inclinations, to agree to fighting one more winter battle in an attempt to secure Cassino.

This would again be the task of the New Zealand Corps. Freyberg intended that 2nd New Zealand Division should assault Cassino town, preceded by as heavy an aerial and artillery bombardment as was possible. A detachment would also take Point 193 to the north-west of the town, on which stood a ruined medieval fortification which gave the feature its name of Castle Hill. From this, 4th Indian Division's 5 Brigade would fight its way up a winding road leading to the rear of Monte Cassino by way of Point 435, which was given the macabre title of Hangman's Hill, because its crest displayed the remains of a pylon which had once supported cable cars and now bore a ghoulish resemblance to a gallows. Finally, 78th (British) Division and American tank units would cross the Rapido in the vicinity of San Angelo, in preparation for an advance down the Liri Valley.

At 0830 on 15 March, the first Allied aircraft arrived over Cassino and from then until about midday, wave after wave of heavy or medium bombers – some 500 in all, escorted by about 200 Lightnings and seventy-five Spitfires, and supplemented by Kittyhawk and Thunderbolt fighter-bombers striking at individual targets, dropped 1,250 tons of high-explosive on the town. Then the Allied gunners joined in and, it is reported that during the day, almost 200,000 shells were fired.

Cassino was reduced to rubble, but its heroic garrison, 1st Parachute Division, was not subdued. Some of the Germans were stationed just outside the town. Others took refuge in caves on the mountainside or in specially prepared steel shelters. Also, ironically, the destruction was too thorough. Piles of debris and huge craters, which were soon filled by heavy rainfall, slowed the New

Zealanders' advance and blocked their supporting tanks, giving the enemy a chance to recover. By evening, the attackers had captured about two-thirds of Cassino, but it was not until 17 March that they took the railway station on its south side and all attempts to drive the Germans from the western part of the town were thwarted. Alexander's deserved tribute to his foes – he did not think that any troops could have resisted successfully other than 'these Para boys' – perhaps provides justification for his having permitted the battle to have been fought.

On 15 March, the New Zealanders had also seized Castle Hill, but 5th Indian Brigade could push forward from this only slowly and with heavy losses. That night, a company of Gurkhas reached Hangman's Hill and on the following night the rest of their battalion joined them, but they could make no further progress and were isolated by German counter-attacks. The decisive moment came on 19 March. Freyberg had planned converging attacks, one from Hangman's Hill, the other from the positions just short of Snake's Head Ridge which had been held by 7th Indian Brigade since the Second Battle of Cassino. 7th Indian itself had not yet recovered sufficiently to mount such an assault, but Freyberg intended to spring a surprise by delivering it with light tanks which would move up to the front line over a rough track which his sappers had secretly prepared – a remarkable feat of security as well as of engineering.

Sadly, the Allies' run of ill-luck continued. On the 19th, the Germans delivered a series of raids on 5th Indian's main positions. These were beaten off but they forced the cancellation of the Brigade's own planned offensive and prevented more than a handful of reinforcements getting through to join the Gurkhas on Hangman's Hill, where they had to be kept supplied by parachute drops. The armour did go in but was met by artillery fire which destroyed six tanks and crippled sixteen more. Renewed attacks by the New Zealanders in Cassino itself also failed to make any progress.

Next day, Alexander received an angry signal from Churchill, demanding an explanation for the lack of progress. Freyberg was willing to try again but, with great moral courage, Alexander refused to ask the New Zealand Corps, which had already suffered some 4,000 casualties, to make further sacrifices. On the night of

24/25 March, under heavy artillery fire, the Gurkhas withdrew from Hangman's Hill.

Another attempt to take Cassino had failed. Rome seemed as far away as ever. Silence fell on the battlefield.

Notes:
1. Alexander did receive very detailed information from the 'Ultra' interceptions, but one often gets the impression that his Intelligence officers felt that as long as they had 'Ultra', there was little need to trouble about anything else.
2. It was perhaps significant, though, that while Lucas was very ready to accept pessimistic Intelligence which turned out to be unfounded, he rejected optimistic Intelligence which was quite correct. He had been advised that both 29th and 90th Panzer Grenadier Divisions had moved from the Anzio area to the Gustav Line but he strongly doubted this, even in the face of personal assurances from Alexander.
3. This last figure aroused the wrath of Churchill, who signalled sarcastically to Alexander: 'We must have a great superiority of chauffeurs.'
4. Tuker would also make great play with the atrocities the Nazis had committed against the Jews. Horrifying though these were, the destruction of a celebrated Catholic religious building hardly seems an appropriate retaliation.

Chapter 8

Diadem

It would not have been remarkable if the Allied soldiers in Italy, fighting in vile conditions, suffering heavy casualties, their best efforts constantly thwarted by the enemy and the elements, had lost all heart and hope, or, at best, become cynical and disillusioned. A few individuals, tried beyond endurance, did lapse into despair, but they formed a minute proportion of the whole. The overwhelming majority cursed but carried on.

There were several reasons for this, of which the chief was the men's own courage, discipline and fortitude. Yet an almost equally important factor was that they still retained their faith in the Higher Command, particularly in Alexander. This was partly because they liked and admired him, but mainly because they were well aware of his concern for their interest, as he had demonstrated, to his subsequent cost, by his decision to allow the bombing of the Monte Cassino monastery.

Throughout the days of deadlock, Alexander had continuously strengthened that confidence by his actions. It was perhaps typical of him that these were basically similar to the actions taken by other senior commanders at such times, but with little additional touches which were very much his own.

Thus Alexander was not the only senior commander who visited the front line, but he was one of the few who deliberately made himself conspicuous, wearing his usual immaculate uniform and his cap with its prominent red band – a somewhat risky procedure, since Alexander tended to go surprisingly far forward. On one occasion, when visiting 2nd New Zealand Division just prior to the Third Battle of Cassino, his party came under artillery fire which killed two New Zealand soldiers. It was also typical of Alexander that on such occasions he would recognize not only officers but other ranks who had served with him in the past, and would sit down with them to discuss former and present campaigns with every sign of interest and enjoyment.

Similarly, Alexander was not the only senior commander who went to see casualties in hospital, but Rupert Clarke tells us that he was 'particularly good' at this and relates how he delighted wounded soldiers from India by talking to them in Urdu. Alexander was not the only senior commander to praise and decorate deserving subordinates, but Clarke describes one special occasion on 3 April 1944, when Alexander presented Major William Sidney of the Grenadier Guards – who later became Baron De L'Isle and Dudley – with the Victoria Cross. It had proved difficult to obtain the ribbon for the decoration but Alexander's old chief, Lord Gort, himself a holder of the VC, had insisted on his own ribbon being used. Gort had a particular interest in the ceremony, because Sidney was his son-in-law – which was why Alexander, with typical consideration, had invited him to attend.

Major Sidney had earned the supreme award by 'superb courage and utter disregard of danger' on the night of 7/8 February, when, although twice wounded, he had single-handedly held off an attack on the Anzio bridgehead with a tommy-gun and hand grenades. Alexander could not claim to have performed a similar feat – it was scarcely part of the Army Group Commander's job, even if those who knew him were sure that he would have relished such a task. However, Anzio's peril did provide another example of Alexander's technique of raising morale by his calm assurance that everything would come right in the end.

The officer who tells the story is Major General Gerald Templer, who then commanded 56th (British) Division and had just taken over responsibility for 1st (British) Division as well when its former leader had been wounded by a shell splinter. Alexander had flown to an improvised landing ground in the bridgehead, jammed behind the pilot of a single-seat fighter. According to Templer: 'We sat and talked about this and that – mostly Ireland or Yorkshire. Several times I tried to steer the conversation round to my troubles and problems. Always he adroitly turned the conversation in some other direction.' Finally, to Templer's surprise, as it was early morning and Alexander drank sparingly at all times, he accepted a glass of gin. Having downed this, Alexander 'jumped up and said,

"Gerald, I must be off. I have done all I could to help you, haven't I?" I replied. "Yes, indeed, you have, Sir," and I meant it. We hadn't discussed one thing about the battle or any of my problems, but he had instilled hope and courage and determination into me at a moment when I wanted it badly.'[1]

By contrast, Alexander did have numerous discussions on how to break the deadlock with his staff, particularly with Harding, who had been a pupil of Montgomery at the Staff College, Camberley and shared with his former tutor, whom he much admired, great clarity of vision and a ruthless determination to carry through those courses of action which he believed to be correct. Like Montgomery, he also regarded it as vital to retain the initiative; he was therefore unhappy at the way the threat to Anzio and the need to 'keep the Germans on their heels' had meant that, in practice, Fifteenth Army Group had been forced to respond to the course of events, rather than dictating it.

On 22 February 1944, Alexander's staff, under Harding's direction, produced an Appreciation, intended as a guideline on how the Allies could both regain the initiative and ensure that the Germans kept the greatest possible number of divisions in Italy prior to the execution of OVERLORD. Harding entirely agreed with Alexander that this last task was Fifteenth Army Group's primary duty, but he felt that too much attention was being paid to the capture of Rome; the best way of achieving the desired result would be not just to capture Rome but at the same time to so maul the German formations in Italy that Hitler would have to send replacements if the whole Italian front were not to collapse.

Alexander accepted this advice and its implications. It would in fact be a considerable feat to capture Rome by merely driving back the Germans, let alone to maul them in the process, for his Intelligence had learned that Kesselring was preparing further defensive positions beyond the Gustav Line. Some 8 miles to the rear was the Hitler Line, which blocked the Liri Valley in case the Allies finally managed to capture Cassino. It consisted of concrete strongpoints, protected and joined up by anti-tank ditches, mines and barbed wire, and it included a number of tank turrets set on concrete bases. Their high-velocity 75mm guns would come as an unpleasant surprise, for their existence had not been discovered by Intelligence.

Kesselring had realized that if Alexander did break through the Gustav Line, or, even more, if he broke out from the Anzio beachhead, it would be necessary to pull back the German Tenth Army very quickly to prevent this from being cut off. He had therefore started work on the Caesar Line, which ran from just north of the beachhead, south of the Alban Hills to the town of Valmontone on Route 6, and through Avezzano on the east-west Route 5, to the Adriatic at Pescara. Work on this line had not progressed very far, but priority had been given to the positions which blocked the roads to Rome from both south and east.

In order to achieve their aim, therefore, it would be necessary for the Allies to attack in far greater strength than they had done hitherto; Harding estimated that they would need at least a local superiority of three to one in infantry. This in turn would mean that Alexander would have to receive sizeable reinforcements from other parts of the Mediterranean. It would mean that the Allied dispositions on the Gustav Line front would have to be altered so as to concentrate maximum effort on the main point of attack, which was once more to be the Liri Valley, supported by subsidiary actions on the Mediterranean coast and a breakout from Anzio. It would mean that the operation would have to await the better weather of spring, for it had already been found that only a limited number of attackers could be supplied and supported during an Italian winter. On the other hand, the delay would give tired units a chance to rest and refit and, as the skies cleared and the ground became more firm, so the Allies would be able to make more use of their armour, artillery and aircraft.

Harding's Appreciation was masterly and would form the basis for Operation DIADEM, Fifteenth Army Group's final triumphant Battle for Rome. As a result, there have been critics who have not hesitated to urge that Alexander was little more than a figurehead and it was Harding who was the Army Group's 'brains'. Most plans, however, evolve from discussions, to which many different men contribute. It seems fair, then, to look at the details of DIADEM and speculate – it can only be speculation – on the influence Alexander personally may have had on its evolution.

For a start, the basis of the DIADEM plan, namely that Fifteenth Army Group's attack on the Gustav Line should be assisted by forces landed at Anzio, had originally been suggested by Alexander before Harding had even joined him.[2] The concentration of maximum strength at the crucial point by the transfer of formations from one actual or proposed line of advance to another was also nothing new to Alexander, who had practised it in the past in Tunisia and during the landings in Sicily.

Since this regrouping would be bound to take time and the offensive would not commence until the spring anyway, it was decided to combine it with an adjustment of the current command structure so that, on the Gustav Line front at least, all American troops, or those who had been equipped by the Americans, such as the French, should come under Fifth Army control, while all units with British equipment should form part of Eighth Army. Again it seems reasonable to detect the influence of Alexander who, on taking over Eighteenth Army Group in North Africa, had insisted that the men from the different Allied nations should be allotted separate sectors.

It would also appear that the part that the Allied airmen would play in the offensive owed much to Alexander. It was agreed that every attempt should be made to bomb the German communications system, but this had been done previously when Alexander had been in command, both in North Africa and in the Italian campaigns of 1943. Much stress was laid on the value of the 'Rover David'/'Cab Rank' system, but this had been introduced and had been used by Alexander before Harding became his Chief of Staff.

Not that Harding did not leave his own mark on DIADEM. As a fine staff officer, it was he who coordinated the details of the plans and translated ideas into practicalities. Since he had arrived in Italy comparatively recently, he had not imbibed the obsession with Rome that had gripped all other major participants on both sides, including Alexander, and it was therefore he who emphasized the importance of savaging enemy formations. Again though, it is to Alexander's credit that he wholeheartedly embraced Harding's arguments. On 5 May, an Operation Order of Fifteenth Army Group declared that the object of DIADEM was 'To destroy the right wing of the German Tenth Army; to drive what remains of it and the German Fourteenth Army north of Rome; and to pursue the enemy to the Rimini-Pisa line inflicting maximum losses on him in the process'.

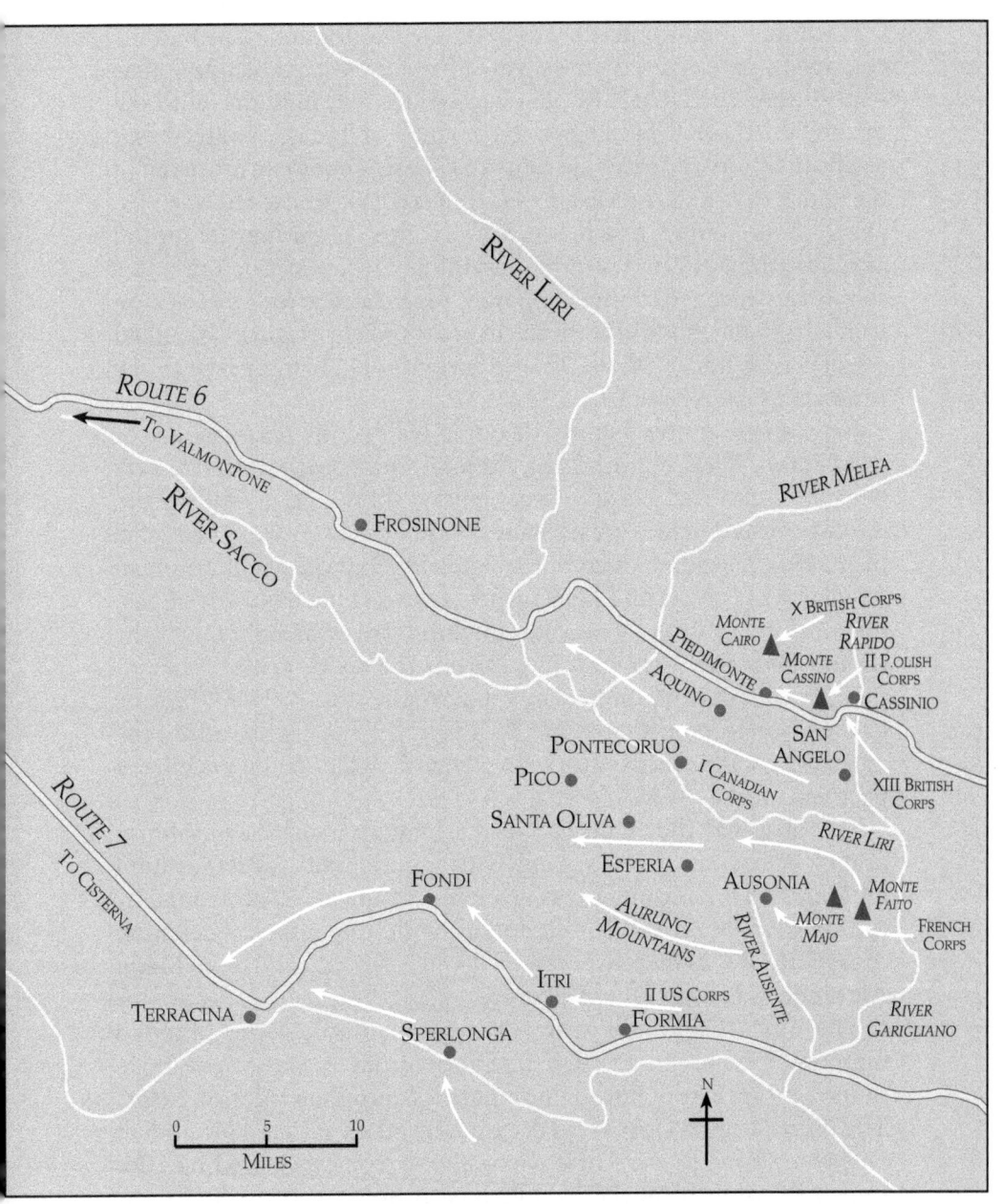

Map 10: Operation Diadem – The First Stages

Harding's final influence was that, like Montgomery, he had the courage to put forward views which he knew would be unpopular – inevitably, the DIADEM plan caused friction. In addition to the main OVERLORD landings in Normandy, it had been agreed that a subsidiary operation, code-named ANVIL, should be mounted in the South of France in May 1944. If DIADEM proceeded as envisaged, there would not be enough troops or enough shipping available for ANVIL. Harding accordingly recommended that this should be cancelled, though apparent preparations for an attack on southern France should continue in order to help disguise the Allied intentions in Italy. This was not a proposal likely to appeal to the American Chiefs of Staff.

Remembering how highly Alexander valued the maintenance of good inter-Allied relations, he probably had some secret regrets when he supported Harding's contention, knowing the difficulties it must cause. There were perhaps two main reasons why he stifled them. He believed, with complete sincerity, that the Mediterranean strategy was correct and foresaw benefits accruing from it well past the capture of Rome – as witness his anticipation of a pursuit to the Rimini-Pisa area – and to judge from the tone of his Order of the Day on 10 May, immediately before the start of DIADEM, he had complete confidence in the ability of his troops after the magnificent, if unsuccessful, efforts that they had made during the past few months.

The proposal did, indeed, cause a long and surprisingly bitter argument between London and Washington, and it was not until 24 March that Alexander was given the 'go ahead'. Unfortunately, the approval of DIADEM did not, after all, imply the cancellation of ANVIL. It was merely postponed and it would survive, to blight Alexander's prospects in the future.

The next five weeks saw Alexander complete the planned regrouping of his forces. Existing formations took up new positions; new formations were incorporated into the Order of Battle. The New Zealand Corps was disbanded and its battered 4th Indian Division retired to the Adriatic coast, where it was joined by 10th Indian Division from the Middle East to form V (British) Corps. Leese's remaining Eighth Army formations were transferred to a front 85 miles in length, in the area of Cassino – a move carried out openly in an attempt to double-bluff the Germans by suggesting that the Allies wished them to detect this activity and it was intended to mask Alexander's real point of attack.

In accordance with Alexander's wish to simplify the command structure, X (British) Corps left Fifth Army and the Garigliano sector, to take up station opposite Monte Cairo, securing Leese's right flank. 2nd New Zealand was the only division now on the strength of this corps, but it also controlled several independent brigades, including a Liberation Group of Italian personnel. The two divisions of II Polish Corps, commanded by Lieutenant General Wladyslaw Anders, which had just joined Eighth Army, took over the Allied positions on Snake's Head Ridge, in preparation for what, it was hoped, would be the final attempt to capture Monte Cassino.

Eighth Army's major assault would be delivered by the one armoured and three infantry divisions which made up Lieutenant General Sidney Kirkman's XIII Corps. Its task would be to cross the Rapido in the vicinity of San Angelo, outflanking Cassino town, the garrison of which would have to retreat to avoid being cut off, and link up with the Poles. Then, with the Poles on its right, it would advance down the Liri Valley to the Hitler Line, which it would overrun, with the assistance, if necessary, of an armoured and an infantry division provided by I Canadian Corps; this was another new arrival, as was the Army Reserve, 6th South African Armoured Division.

On the Fifth Army front, Keyes had two divisions in his II US Corps on the Mediterranean coast, but they too were recent arrivals and their line of attack along Route 7 was hemmed in by the Aurunci Mountains. It was thus very timely that the French Corps, because it used American equipment, had been transferred to the right flank of Fifth Army. Juin now commanded four divisions, plus the equivalent of a division of Goumiers, irregular troops recruited from the Berber tribes of the Atlas Mountains with French officers and NCOs. His men, particularly perhaps the Goumiers, were very experienced in mountain warfare and he urged that they be allowed to thrust through and to the north of the Aurunci range. Alexander and Clark agreed. It seems that they anticipated the French would advance side by side with II Corps, but Juin had greater ambitions. He envisaged a rapid breakthrough as far as a north–south road which ran west of the Aurunci from Route 7 to Route 6 by way of the towns of Itri and Pico. Its capture would threaten to cut off enemy forces still resisting further east and would outflank the main Hitler Line which ran from the village of Piedimonte on the southern slopes of Monte Cairo, through Pontecorvo, east of Pico, to end at Santa Oliva, south-east of Pico. Events would conspire to ensure a spectacular French success – a great stroke of luck for Fifteenth Army Group and its leader, but one which few will deny they had richly deserved.

As his Army Reserve, Clark had the experienced 36th US Infantry Division, with which he proposed to support II US Corps if the need arose. If not, it would be used to reinforce VI US Corps in Anzio. Even without this, Truscott's force had been built up to two British infantry divisions, and one US armoured and three US infantry divisions. Their task would be to complete the Allied victory by striking at the rear of the enemy at the decisive moment when Kesselring's reserves had been drawn into the fighting for the Gustav and Hitler Lines; by cutting Routes 6 and 7, they should trap at least the right wing of von Vietinghoff's Tenth Army.

Alexander was thus commanding British, American, Canadian, New Zealand, South African, Indian, French, Polish and Italian soldiers. It required considerable diplomacy to handle such diverse nationalities, each with its own special needs and characteristics, particularly since some of the best subordinate commanders, such as Anders, Juin and Freyberg, tended to be both temperamental and very conscious of the interests and prestige of their own contingents.

Alexander dealt with the problem in his distinctive gentle style. He would first listen carefully to a subordinate's views. This has led to critiscisms that he relied on others for ideas, having none of his own. Certainly Alexander would always welcome and adopt plans which fitted in with his overall schemes, but, equally, he was never afraid to make any corrections he thought were needed. He would do so, however, particularly in the case of officers of a different nationality, by comment and advice, so tactfully given that often the recipient would feel that the idea was really his own. If necessary, Alexander would follow up, not with express commands but with reasoned suggestions which were made with such charm and quiet authority that, in the period before DIADEM, they always carried the same weight as orders – with, sad to say, one vital exception.

As we have seen, Alexander believed that the attack from Anzio would prove the decisive stroke. Contrary to his usual practice, he therefore reserved for himself the decision as to when VI US Corps would participate in the battle.

During March and April, Truscott directed his staff to prepare four possible contingency plans. Of these, the most important were TURTLE, an attack on Campoleone, then to Albano on Route 7 and along this to Rome; and BUFFALO, an attack on Cisterna and then, passing between the Alban Hills and the Lepini Hills which lay to the south-east of them, to Valmontone on Route 6. It is clear, however, that Alexander considered that only BUFFALO would have worthwhile results. In a conference as early as 2 April, he told his senior subordinates, including Clark, that VI US Corps was to 'break out of the Anzio bridgehead and advance on Valmontone', cutting Tenth Army's line of communications along Route 6. The Fifteenth Army Group Operation Order of 5 May expressly confirmed this intention.

Also on 5 May, Alexander paid another visit to Anzio, where Truscott briefed him on the details of his alternative plans. Afterwards, as Truscott would later record: 'General Alexander, charming gentleman and magnificent soldier that he was, let me know very quietly and firmly that there was only one direction in which the attack should or would be launched, and that was from Cisterna to cut Highway 6 in the vicinity of Valmontone in the rear of the German main forces.'

Truscott, who shared this opinion, was delighted, and also touched by the way in which Alexander had shown his gratitude for the VI US Corps' plans. But when Clark was notified of this conversation, he was not pleased. He protested that he 'deeply resented' Alexander having issued instructions directly to his own Corps Commander and expressed a belief that Alexander and Harding were rigid in their 'pre-conceived ideas'. Alexander endeavoured to mollify him but made it clear that it was still his intention that VI US Corps would advance to Valmontone when he considered the time was right. Clark was not appeased. Next day, he expressly informed Truscott that 'the only important objective' was 'the capture of Rome'.

Lieutenant General Mark Wayne Clark was a forceful, determined, self-confident man, whose personal courage has already been noted. He was also extremely ambitious, and so far the campaigns in Italy had been a great disappointment to him, beginning with the near disaster at Salerno. Clark had received a good deal of criticism for his handling of the situation, particularly for his refusal to permit a preliminary naval bombardment, his inability to link up his two corps, and his scheme for the possible re-embarkation of one or other of them.[3] What he had found especially irksome, though, was the fact that credit for ultimate victory had been given to Alexander, to the approach of Eighth Army, and to the naval and air forces, rather than to himself.

Clark's part in the successful liberation of southern Italy had also been soured by the long delay before he could capture Naples and the heavy losses suffered by his Fifth Army as it fought its way up to the Gustav Line. In 1944, matters had gone from bad to worse with the failure of 36th US Division to cross the Rapido, which not only caused immense bitterness at the time, but led to subsequent investigations by Congress and the War Department, the failure of 34th US Division to take Monte Cassino, and the failure of VI US Corps to achieve more than a bloody stalemate at Anzio. Clark's relationships with many of his American subordinates deteriorated badly, his chief British subordinate, McCreery, subjected him to a series of carping complaints, and he had an unfortunate quarrel with Leese over the boundary to be set between their respective forces.

So, by the time DIADEM was being planned, Clark had acquired an almost desperate longing that his army, and thereby himself, should gain the glory of some spectacular achievement. And close at hand he could see the most glittering of prizes: the city that was not just the capital of Italy, not just the heart of the Catholic Church, but the source of Western civilization. Patton's obsessions with Palermo and Messina were as nothing compared to Clark's desire for Roma Aeterna and his anguish lest he somehow be cheated of the honour of its capture.

Had Clark been less obsessive, he would have realized that the success of DIADEM would guarantee him his claim to fame. Alexander had personally assured him and Harding's Appreciation had expressly stated that, after the junction of Fifteenth Army Group's main strength with VI US Corps from Anzio, Fifth and Eighth Armies would both assault the Caesar Line, but Clark would be 'directed on Rome', while Leese would move on Tivoli which lies to the east of Rome, bypassing the capital. The plans for exploitation after Rome's fall were naturally cast in somewhat general terms but they provided confirmation of this arrangement: Fifth Army would capture the harbour of Civitavecchia on the coast just beyond Rome and the airfields at Viterbo just north of the city, then advance to Leghorn, another Mediterranean port; Eighth Army would move on Florence in the centre of the peninsula and Ancona on the Adriatic coast.

Tragically, just as Patton had indulged in a meaningless 'race' for Messina because he felt that Montgomery's gift of both the east–west roads leading to it must be a clever trick, so nothing could convince Clark that Alexander's decision to direct VI US Corps towards Valmontone, rather than straight towards Rome along Route 7, was anything other than a devious scheme to give Eighth Army a better chance of getting to the capital first. Clark's protests to Alexander over his direct orders to Truscott foreshadowed the discords which would impair Alexander's victory just when it was on the verge of a triumphant conclusion.

At 2300 on 11 May, DIADEM began with an artillery bombardment by 2,000 guns, which may have reminded Alexander of El Alamein – but there had been other parallels with that battle which had occurred well before the barrage opened. At El Alamein, Eighth Army had deceived the enemy as to both the place and the time of the offensive, with the result that Rommel had been on leave and had had to be recalled in haste to confront an already menacing situation. Prior to DIADEM, Alexander had mounted a similar deception plan, which made clever use of past occurrences, and would be even more decisive in its results.

Alexander's main device was to give the impression that he was planning an amphibious landing north of Rome – an eventuality which, it was known, the Germans considered likely and which caused them the greatest concern. False wireless traffic and ostentatious rehearsals in the area of Naples and Salerno suggested that I Canadian Corps and 36th US Division had been detailed for such an operation. Alexander was soon delighted to learn from 'Ultra' interceptions that enemy Intelligence considered that future Allied moves would be a new amphibious landing, a breakout from Anzio, or another major assault on the Gustav Line – in that order of probability.

This advice left Kesselring with little choice but to position his mobile divisions so as to counter the most likely eventualities, and he kept the Hermann Göring and 29th Panzer Grenadier Divisions north of Rome to deal with the danger of a seaborne landing, while 26th Panzer and 90th Panzer Grenadier Divisions watched the Anzio bridgehead. Only 15th Panzer Grenadier Division was near the Gustav Line and the bulk of this was stationed near the coast in case Alexander's amphibious move turned out to be a short 'left hook' round the Line's Mediterranean flank. The German mis-apprehension had the further advantage that when DIADEM began, it would be considered only a holding attack. Moreover, the original Anzio landings had achieved complete surprise because Kesselring had already committed his reserves to the Gustav Line. Though he had then recovered with remarkable agility, the experi-ence had made him reluctant to send reinforcements to the Line until it became quite clear that it was here that the major threat lay.

Alexander was equally successful in deceiving his opponent as to the timing of his offensive. As was mentioned earlier, the move of the Eighth Army units from the Adriatic side of the peninsula was not disguised but they were sent to training areas, apparently resting and refitting, and only went up to the front immediately before DIADEM began. The transfer of the French to the Fifth Army area was similarly concealed, and the Germans believed that Juin had only one division in the Garigliano sector. Every attempt was made, by means of false signals and deliberately 'leaked' infor-mation, to suggest that the period for rest and re-equipment would not be completed before the end of May: for instance, Fifth and Eighth Armies issued detailed training programmes up to 21 May. Since the end of May would coincide with the date when the Russian 1944 summer offensive was anticipated, the Germans swallowed the bait. At the end of April, Hitler arranged an investi-ture, followed by an indoctrination course, and several senior commanders were called home from Italy to attend this. Others were allowed to go on leave. Kesselring remained at his post, but among those absent on 11 May were his Chief of Staff, Westphal, von Vietinghoff and a number of important figures from XIV Panzer Corps, including von Senger und Etterlin and his chief staff officer. Their absence was destined to have a crucial effect.

Not that this was apparent at first. The Polish attack began at

0100 on 12 May. Instead of a direct assault on the ruins of the monastery, Anders had planned a thrust over the ridges to the west of them, which would ultimately link up with XIII Corps, cutting Route 6 and isolating both the monastery and Cassino town. First though, Snake's Head Ridge would have to be secured and although the Poles had improved the tracks leading to their positions, enabling tanks to provide covering fire, they found the German defenders as stubborn as ever. The oft-disputed Point 593 fell on that first night but next day repeated German attacks, supported by heavy artillery fire, finally regained it. At 1400, having suffered very heavy losses, the Poles were forced to withdraw to their start line.

Leese, who arrived at the Polish Headquarters two hours later, was naturally very disappointed, having expected much from the attack, but he responded nobly. He consoled Anders and his staff, praised their men's courage, assured them that they had assisted events elsewhere by holding down crack German troops, and predicted that they would have learned from their mistakes and would certainly succeed when he gave the order to attack again.

Leese's reaction was the more commendable because in reality – if through no fault of the Poles – matters had not gone well for the main part of the Eighth Army offensive. XIII Corps was badly served by Intelligence which underestimated both the extent of the German defences and the fast flow of the river it had to cross – despite the fashion, mentioned earlier, of calling this the Rapido, instead of its true name of the Gari. Many of the assault boats were swept downstream and landed at unintended places. Confusion was made worse by an unusually thick mist which rose from the river and was increased by the German defensive fire. The moon was obscured, the attackers lost direction, and by first light XIII Corps had secured only two shallow bridgeheads.

Everything now depended on Kirkman being able to strengthen and secure those bridgeheads. South of San Angelo, where 8th Indian Division had crossed, the sappers managed to construct two 30-ton bridges during the night, and on 12 May, Canadian tanks were able to cross these and assist in holding off determined counter-attacks by armour and infantry. The Germans took no similar action against 4th (British) Division, established nearer

Cassino – which was very fortunate, since heavy fire, directed from observation posts on the mountain, prevented any bridges being erected in this area.

It was obvious that a resolute counter-attack here might prove disastrous for 4th (British) Division. Kirkman therefore gave orders that Major Robin Gabbett's engineers must build a bridge during the night of 12/13 May 'at all costs' – which expression, he made clear, must be taken literally. Although attempts were made to mask the work from enemy observers by the extensive use of smoke-screens, almost half of the 200 sappers employed had become casualties before the 'Amazon Bridge' had been completed at 0400 on the 13th. Their sacrifice had not been in vain. Reinforcements, including British tanks, hurriedly crossed and in the course of the 13th, the bridgeheads over the Rapido were secured and united.

On the Fifth Army front, II US Corps was opposed by the German 94th Infantry Division. This did not have a very high reputation, but it offered a determined defence, against which the two American divisions could only make slow progress. The French achieved the biggest success of the first night by capturing Monte Faito, one of the outlying peaks guarding Monte Majo, which formed the equivalent bastion on the south side of the Liri Valley to Monte Cassino on the north. French attacks elsewhere were less successful and the German 71st Infantry Division delivered a series of counter-attacks on the 12th which compelled Juin to go forward in person to direct his men's resistance. His calm resolution, so similar to that of Alexander, inspired the defenders to repulse all the enemy's efforts with heavy casualties.

Yet the most beneficial actions on 12 May were not carried out by the ground troops. Alexander, throughout his career, had greatly valued the cooperation of the Allied Air Forces, and his attitude was now richly repaid – 728 sorties by heavy bombers, 429 by medium bombers and 294 by fighter-bombers were flown on the 12th. This massive support inflicted heavy losses on the enemy, particularly the luckless 71st Infantry Division, but perhaps the most valuable strikes were those made on the Headquarters of both Tenth Army, which was particularly hard hit, and XIV Panzer Corps. The damage done to communication systems completed the lack of control caused by the absence of senior officers in Germany.

Deprived of the instructions of their experienced leaders, the staffs of von Vietinghoff and von Senger und Etterlin, and their divisional commanders on the Garigliano front, committed a number of fatal errors, though, in fairness to them, they were faced with odds of two divisions to one in the coastal area and the equivalent of five divisions to one in the French sector, all of these being backed by a heavy superiority in artillery and an overwhelming superiority in the air. In an attempt to stiffen resistance, they sent 15th Panzer Grenadier Division – already dispersed between the southern front and the Liri Valley – to support both 71st and 94th Divisions, thereby splitting it up into a number of small groups and leaving XIV Panzer Corps with nothing in reserve. Worse still, they were so disheartened by the casualties suffered by 71st Division, that when on 13 May the French resumed their attacks on the outlying bastions of Monte Majo, these met with steadily less resistance until, that afternoon, the capture of the main feature was opposed only by rearguards covering the division's retreat to Ausonia in the valley of the Ausente River which divides Monte Majo from the main bulk of the Aurunci Mountains.

As the exhausted 71st Division fell back, leaving 2,000 men behind as prisoners, the French followed up with exemplary swiftness. Taking full advantage of his superiority in numbers, Juin sent his 1st Motorised Division north of Monte Majo to strike along the south bank of the Liri, while his three other regular divisions swung south of Monte Majo to move up the Ausente Valley. Ausonia fell to the French on the 15th, and the position of 94th Division, thus outflanked and again under attack from the Americans, became an impossible one. It withdrew towards Formia with the loss of a further 1,000 prisoners.

With the two German divisions in the south falling back in different directions, Juin thrust his Goumiers between them into the Aurunci Mountains. These were almost undefended, for the Germans had not believed that they could be crossed by any substantial forces. Moreover, the breakdown in control and communications had become such that no proper reports on the situation reached the German High Command. 'It is an intolerable condition,' complained Kesselring on the 14th, 'when a division remains in the dark for one and a half days about the events in its own sector. It is equally intolerable for a division to be in fighting contact with the enemy for two days without knowing whom they are fighting. I demand a clear picture by noon.'

Kesselring's problems were increased by his belief that the entire assault on the Gustav Line was only a diversionary move to draw his attention away from the main Allied attack, which, the Germans were still convinced, would be delivered elsewhere. Nonetheless, he had already ordered 90th Panzer Grenadier Division to support his forces in the Line. The commander of this formation was another of those officers who had been called back to Germany, but its arrival finally checked the seemingly irresistible French. Juin's men captured Esperia at the head of the Ausente Valley on 17 May but when they attempted to proceed beyond it to outflank the Hitler Line at Pico, their advance guard was ambushed and compelled to fall back.

Further south, the Goumiers were also moving on Pico. Their supply line was now becoming tenuous but thirty-six medium bombers dropping 40 tons of supplies enabled them to cut the Pico–Itri road on the 17th, though they too were unable to get to Pico itself in the face of mounting resistance. On the coast, the Americans captured Formia on the 17th and Itri two days later, by which time the German 71st Division had all but disintegrated, and the 94th Division had been ordered to scatter and retire as best it might. 'I can tell you quite frankly,' snarled Kesselring to Major General Wentzell, Tenth Army's Chief of Staff, 'I can't call anything like that tactics.'

The defenders of the Cassino area were infinitely bolder. This was no surprise to Leese who had anticipated, with considerable accuracy, that even if Fifth Army was able to make rapid progress, Eighth Army would be bound to meet vicious opposition in this particular quarter, the retention of which had become of immense significance as a matter of morale. He sent his reserve infantry division, the 78th (British) over the Rapido on 14 May. A brigade of 6th British Armoured Division had already crossed on the previous day and on the 15th, I Canadian Corps followed suit. On 16 May, 4th (British) and 78th (British) pushed northward towards Route 6 and made sufficient progress to convince Leese that he should order a concerted attack by both XIII Corps and the Poles the following day.

By that time, the Germans had at last gained a clear picture of the task confronting them. Confirmation of the presence of the whole French force and the Canadian Corps among the attacking formations had finally dispelled the illusion that Alexander had planned an amphibious landing north of Rome. With his southern front in ruins, Kesselring accepted that it would be necessary to abandon Cassino town and mountain, and ordered a general with-drawal to the Hitler Line, but, optimistic as always, he felt that he had a good chance of holding this. All the same, its name was prudently changed to that of the Dora Line.

At 0700 on 17 May, Kirkman and Anders began their assaults. Both quickly learned that the German parachutists were deter-mined to hold their ground until the very last moment and inflict as much harm as they possibly could on their foes. All day the struggle continued. By nightfall, XIII Corps had cut Route 6 and during the hours of darkness the defenders of Cassino town reluc-tantly slipped away over the mountain slopes. Next morning, British troops entered its battered, devastated ruins, though not without further casualties to mines or booby traps.

On Monte Cassino, the fighting was more savage still. Since the failure of their first assault, the Poles had whittled down the numbers of their enemy by well-planned bombardments and frequent fighter-bomber strikes. They now attacked with typical headlong valour, again well supported by artillery and aircraft, but the resistance they met was as staunch as ever. Progress was desper-ately slow, but by evening, the hated Point 593 was firmly in Polish hands, and as night fell, the Germans finally abandoned their exposed salient. Even then rearguards on the south-western slopes of Monte Cassino kept up the fight until midday on the 18th. Previously, at 1020, a patrol from the 12th Podolski Lancers had entered the shattered monastery, captured its last garrison – thirty men, mostly wounded – and hoisted the Polish flag. Leese again hastened to visit Anders, armed with a gift of champagne.

Alexander had broken the Gustav Line and won the first part of his battle. He now prepared for the next stage, transferring 36th US Division from Keyes to Truscott and directing Clark to send VI US Corps against Valmontone on the night of 21/22 May, or the morning of the 22nd, whichever he preferred. This, as Alexander informed Churchill, was in order to 'get astride the enemy's communications to Rome'. Clark's first response was to express his shock that this decision had been made without reference to him. It was scarcely a valid complaint, for, as we saw earlier, Alexander had declared this intention before DIADEM had even begun, and it may be that Clark's reaction should have warned him that there would be difficulties ahead.

Alexander also advised Churchill of his proposals for taking the Hitler Line, as he continued to call it – an example which perhaps we may be allowed to follow for the sake of convenience. Leese was ordered to 'use the utmost energy to break through . . . before the Germans have time to settle down in it'. Meanwhile, the Poles were to advance towards Piedimonte to turn the Line from the north, and the French towards Pico to outflank it from the south. 'If these manoeuvres are successful,' Alexander announced, 'it will go a long way towards destroying the right wing of the German Tenth Army' – still, it will be noticed, his primary objective.

The manoeuvres would be successful, but not nearly as swiftly as Alexander had hoped. In the Liri Valley, the British and Canadians moved forward together and, desperately eager to regain the mobility which had been lost in the winter conditions, but had been promised to them when the better weather returned, they crowded too many transport vehicles onto the inadequate cart tracks that in most cases passed for roads, causing a great deal of congestion. The main blame though, must, once again, be attributed to inadequate Intelligence. The Liri Valley, which had been endlessly trumpeted as the 'Gateway to Rome', turned out to be a difficult route even in summer, being criss-crossed by numerous steep-sided streams or ditches, which had to be bridged before the advance could continue. Then, when the Hitler Line was reached on 19 May, the fixed tank turrets, of which no Intelligence reports had reached Eighth Army, inflicted heavy losses on Leese's armour and the hope that the Line could be taken 'on the run' quickly faded.

Leese now decided that a full-scale attack would have to be mounted, for which detailed plans would have to be drawn up, reconnaissance carried out, stocks of ammunition brought forward. A spell of bad weather, luckily only temporary, caused further delay. Leese has been condemned in some accounts for the cautious thoroughness of his preparations and for entrusting the task to the Canadian Corps alone, but there were, in fact, good reasons for his actions. The defences of the Hitler Line were strong and well planned and, contrary to the later assertions of Clark and Juin, German records make it clear that neither Kesselring nor von Vietinghoff had any intention of abandoning them unless and until they were compelled to do so. As for the use of a single corps, this enabled the attack to be supported by the artillery of both – a factor which would prove of vital importance – and Leese preferred to have the Canadians deliver the blow as a similar move by XIII Corps would have been made in full view of the German observation posts on Monte Cairo.

Juin, in fact, was generally critical of Eighth Army's rate of progress at this time, but he paid scant attention to the difficulties that Leese faced. Eighth Army had been and still was opposed by far stronger fixed defences than the French had encountered; it was hampered by superbly placed enemy observation posts which was not the case with the French; and it was engaged with far better German units than the French had been. Ironically, Juin now had to solve similar, if lesser, problems himself. There were prepared positions running from Santa Oliva at the south of the Hitler Line, through Pico to the sea at Terracina, but although these were collectively known as the Senger Line, they were widely separated and rather rudimentary. Kesselring had ordered 26th Panzer Division from the Anzio area to oppose the French at Pico, but von Mackensen had objected strongly. 26th Panzer finally moved forward later than intended and arrived in the Pico area in separate detachments over a fair period of time.

Even so, the better defences and the better defenders made all the difference. The French offensive opened on 20 May, but, despite the aid of Canadian artillery, and air attacks on the German tanks, progress was slow and costly. Juin did capture Pico in the late afternoon of 22 May, but 26th Panzer continued to hold out north of the town, and infantry units from the Adriatic coast were arriving to reinforce it. Alexander's hope that the French might outflank the Hitler Line from the south had been dashed. It was not to be outflanked from the north either. The Poles reached Piedimonte on 20 May, but could not take it until the 25th, and X Corps, on the Poles' right, only secured Monte Cairo on the 25th as well.

So it was up to the Canadians to break the Line. The infantry of their 1st Division, backed by tank units and a massive artillery bombardment, strove throughout 23 May to drive back its brave and capable defenders, who were also assisted by counter-attacks by their own armour. The Canadians suffered 900 casualties and heavy losses of tanks, but they were through the Hitler Line by about 1730, and before dark were firmly established on a ridge dominating the town of Pontecorvo, which the enemy evacuated next day.

Though Aquino to the north remained in German hands, and more rain buried the approaches to the front line under mud, 5th Canadian Armoured Division pressed forward through the breach in the Line. Not until 1030 on the 24th did the Germans offer much resistance, but then a new foe was encountered: the Panzer Mark V. The 'Panther', as this was called, though not as celebrated as the 'Tiger', was, in practice, a better design: with a 75mm gun, 80mm armour which was sloped to help deflect shell hits, and with a speed of 28 mph, it was an ideal mixture of firepower, protection and rapidity.[4] But the Canadians were not to be stopped and they destroyed three of their antagonists before moving on.

The next obstacle in the Canadians' path was a natural one – the Melfa River, a tributary of the Liri. By the end of the day, they had managed to establish a small bridgehead over it. This was fiercely counter-attacked by German tanks, but an infantry company from the Westminster Regiment, aided only by three light tanks from Strathcona's Horse, held out all evening and night, winning a Victoria Cross for its OC, Major Mahoney. On the 25th, the Canadians successfully crossed the Melfa in strength, while XIII (British) Corps, having captured Aquino, also moved up to the river, which it crossed that night. That same evening, Kesselring, with Hitler's grudging consent, ordered a controlled retirement to his last main defensive feature, the Caesar Line.

His decision was reinforced by events on the Fifth Army front, where the Americans had continued to make progress. On 20 May, II US Corps took Fondi on the so-called Senger Line. Next day, an American infantry battalion in DUKWs made a 'short hook' to Sperlonga, where it came ashore unopposed. Keyes then pushed on to Terracina on Route 7, but here II US Corps had to pass through a narrow gorge which offered the Germans a splendid defensive position. Moreover, on the 19th, Kesselring had ordered 29th Panzer Grenadier Division south to hold

Terracina and to block any attempt by Keyes to link up with the Anzio bridgehead.

Happily for the Allies, the German Supreme Commander was now afflicted by a problem with which Alexander was only too familiar: a difficult subordinate. Having given his orders, Kesselring had set out on a tour of the front. On his return to his Headquarters late on 20 May, he found that von Mackensen had refused to allow his last reserve division to be sent to the aid of Tenth Army. Kesselring did have one luxury denied to Alexander: none of his subordinates came from Allied nations whose feelings had to be pampered. He curtly repeated his commands and would later decide to dismiss von Mackensen. But the harm had already been done, for it proved too late for the wretched 29th Panzer Grenadier Division to prevent the Americans reaching high ground dominating the Terracina defile. As Kesselring would complain bitterly: 'An excellent defensive zone had been thrown away and the enemy handed an almost impregnable position.' The Germans did still resist in Terracina town, but were forced to withdraw on the night of 23/24 May.

Meanwhile, all was ready for the great breakout from Anzio. On 21 May, Alexander had changed the date of this to the 23rd, so as to coincide with Eighth Army's assault on the Hitler Line. Truscott had made exacting preparations for this moment. Emplacements had been dug for supporting artillery, thousands of rounds of ammunition brought forward, and careful note made of potential targets such as command posts. For days the Americans had bombarded enemy positions for about an hour ending at 0630, which had become a largely ignored routine. At night, American tanks would move up to fire at targets of opportunity, then fall back to the rear – except that increasing numbers remained, unnoticed, near the front, concealed under camouflage nets, their crews eating cold food so that no smoke would give away their locations.

On 23 May, all this care would be rewarded. There was the usual morning bombardment, which seemed heavier than expected but attracted little notice. When it ended, the Germans stood down, only to find a new barrage commencing and wave after wave of fighter-bombers appearing, to strike at objectives, such as artillery positions, beyond the front line. Then, while Truscott's two British divisions made diversionary attacks at the north of the perimeter,

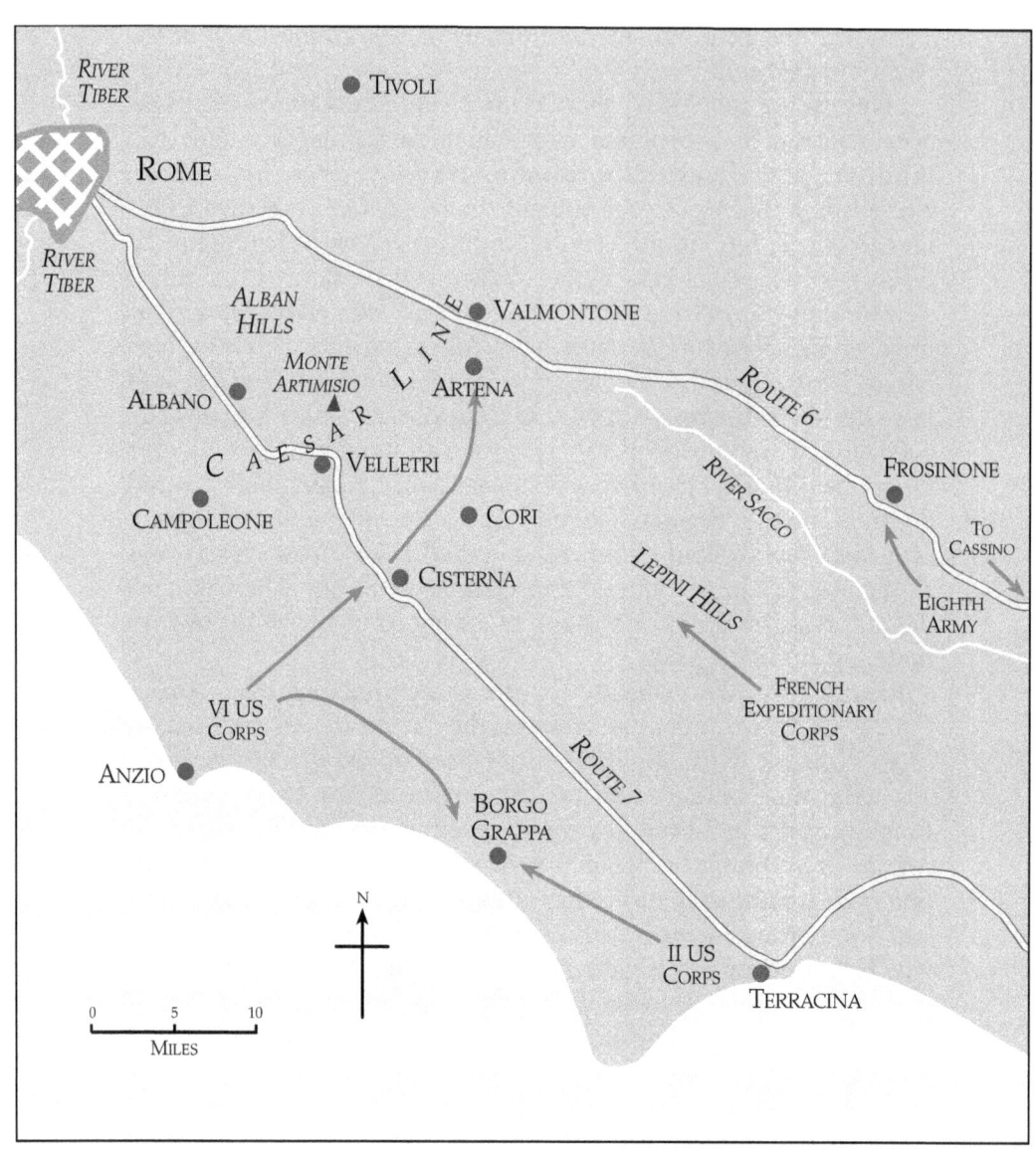

Map 11: Operation Diadem –The Break-Out From Anzio

the Americans delivered the major assault in the direction of Cisterna, the first stage of the planned Operation BUFFALO.

Surprise was complete, but the Germans fought with their usual ferocity. The Americans lost over 100 tanks or self-propelled guns and 3rd US Infantry Division alone had over 950 men killed, wounded or missing, yet the enemy suffered even more severely, losing over 1,500 prisoners. Savage struggles took place all through 24 May, as the Americans strove to capture Cisterna and pushed over Route 7 towards the town of Cori, between the Alban and the Lepini Hills and well on the way to Valmontone. Both Cisterna and Cori fell on the afternoon of the 25th, by which time American casualties had risen to nearly 2,900, some 500 of them fatal, and the prisoners they had taken had risen to well over 2,600. Earlier, at 0730, at a coastal village called Borgo Grappa, Truscott's advance guards had met the soldiers of II US Corps moving forward from Terracina. Clark's Fifth Army was reunited at last.

The German situation was now desperate. Kesselring sent reinforcments, including his last mobile reserve division, the Hermann Göring, to check Fifth Army's progress. In their frantic need for haste, they were compelled to move in daylight, they were detected from the air and every available fighter and fighter-bomber that the Allies possessed fell on this enticing target. By nightfall on 25 May, the area between Cori and Valmontone was a scrapyard of burned or wrecked tanks, guns, cars and lorries. Claims of 645 vehicles destroyed and 446 others damaged may have been exaggerated, but certainly not by much.

To the very last, Alexander had fulfilled his primary duty of preparing the way for OVERLORD. OKW had always hoped to use the Hermann Göring Division to oppose this – but in vain. Four extra divisions had been sent to Italy since DIADEM had commenced, as had a regiment of Tiger tanks from France. Now it seemed that Alexander would achieve the main aim of DIADEM as well. Contrary to what would be stated later, he never imagined that he would be able to trap the whole of Kesselring's forces, but he did believe, as he had declared back on 5 May, that he could 'destroy the right wing of the German Tenth Army'.

After the capture of Cori, 3rd US Infantry Division struck forward towards Valmontone, supported by the 1st Special Service Force, an American-Canadian unit which had been sent to Anzio in February, and by a mixed force of armour and infantry from 1st US Armoured Division under Colonel Hamilton Howze. Few German tanks were encountered, for as late as the evening of 27 May, the Hermann Göring Division could still muster only eighteen Panzer Mark IVs, of which about half were fit for action. Allied aircraft, however, as Howze reported, 'added further excitement by straffing the entire area without taint of discrimination'.

Route 6 appeared to be within easy reach. All that was needed, in the opinion of the 3rd US Division's commander, Major General O'Daniel, was his reinforcement by the main body of 1st US Armoured and by a fresh infantry division – of which Truscott had two available – and the German defences would be 'wide open to Valmontone'. Howze and his superior, the Commander of 1st US Armoured, Major General Harmon, entirely agreed, and Truscott himself, who, like Alexander, considered that the main purpose of the thrust from Anzio was to trap as many enemy soldiers as possible, was 'jubilant', confident that 'by the following morning we would be astride the German line of withdrawal through Valmontone'.

Truscott's jubilation was short-lived. In the late afternoon of 25 May, Brigadier General Brann, Clark's Head of Intelligence, arrived at his command post with express instructions that he should limit the troops making for Valmontone to 3rd US Infantry and 1st Special Service Force, and use the rest of VI US Corps to carry out Operation TURTLE, the advance down Route 7 to Rome. Truscott was 'dumbfounded'. He would later confirm his belief that, had not Clark 'changed the direction of my attack . . . the strategic objective of Anzio' – the destruction of the right wing of Tenth Army – 'would have been accomplished in full. To be first in Rome was poor compensation for this lost opportunity.' O'Daniel and Harmon would echo his doubts, while Howze would call Clark's commands 'one of the worst decisions I ever knew'. All protests, however, were in vain. Truscott had no choice but to obey clear orders.

Despite numerous attempts by Clark to rationalize his actions, his post-war statements and the entries he made in his diary at the time leave no doubt that his real reason was his obsession that 'the British have their eyes on Rome, notwithstanding Alexander's constant assurance to me that Rome is in the sector of the Fifth

Army' and that 'this great prize, the honour of taking Rome' must go to him and his Fifth Army, regardless of all other considerations. Clark would even declare that he told Alexander that if any forces from Eighth Army tried to advance on Rome, he would have his troops fire on them. Since there are no other reports of this conversation and no evidence whatever that it took place, and since such a threat would surely have tried even Alexander's legendary patience too far, it may be doubted that this was ever said, but that Clark should have as much as entertained this monstrous thought reveals only too well his utter lack of balance on this issue.

It also confirms that Clark's later excuses were just that and nothing more. He claimed that VI US Corps would not be strong enough to break through to Valmontone. That was certainly not an opinion that he gained from Truscott or his divisional commanders, who believed exactly the opposite. An advance to Route 6 would theoretically risk being attacked from the flank, but Kesselring had already committed his last mobile reserve division and the reports of Clark's subordinates, plus 'Ultra' interceptions, which clearly revealed the steadily weakening condition of both Tenth and Fourteenth Armies, showed that this was hardly likely in practice.

By far the most reasonable of Clark's excuses was that even if Route 6 was secured, Tenth Army would still be able to escape by two good roads and a number of small tracks leading northward, but these were often precipitous, ran through narrow defiles and were very vulnerable to attacks by the Allied Air Forces. Alexander had good reason therefore to believe that if Route 6 was blocked, the right wing of Tenth Army would be terribly mauled at the very least. It should be added that this belief was shared by the enemy. Von Vietinghoff would state that if Route 6 was lost, the 'bottling up' of the bulk of Tenth Army would have been 'unavoidable', while von Senger und Etterlin agreed that 'If the enemy should succeed in firmly securing the key position at Valmontone, the withdrawal of these forces would be jeopardised. The remaining available mountain roads east of the Via Casilina [Route 6] were now of doubtful and limited value in view of the enemy's overwhelming air superiority.' That strikes on these roads by heavy bombers had already caused a great deal of damage and persistent fighter-bomber attacks were being made on all moving targets only increased these officers' fears.

In the last resort, though, just as Truscott obeyed Clark's orders, albeit reluctantly, so Clark should have obeyed those of Alexander. He compounded his fault by not informing his superior of the action he had taken until 1115 on 26 May, and then leaving this to his Chief of Staff, Major General Gruenther. When Alexander expressed his hope that Clark would still 'continue to push towards Valmontone' as well as towards Rome, Gruenther assured him that Clark was advancing on both places and the move towards Valmontone was being made with 'powerful forces'.

Alexander remained outwardly calm, remarking that he was in favour of 'any line which the Army Commander believes will offer a chance to continue his present success'. Those who knew him well were not deceived. According to McCreery, who, it is only fair to point out, disliked and was disliked by Clark, this disobedience 'made Alexander livid and it has rankled with him ever since'. When Macmillan learned what had happened, he asked Alexander why he had not asserted his authority. 'Why do you talk nonsense?' Alexander snapped – it was the sole occasion on which Macmillan saw him lose his temper – 'How can I give orders?'

On the face of it, this question was an extraordinary one. Clearly the Fifteenth Army Group Commander could give any orders he wished. What Alexander in these particular circumstances presumably meant was: what was the point of overriding Clark and cancelling Operation TURTLE? By the time Alexander had had his conversation with Gruenther, VI US Corps had completed the highly complicated arrangements needed to change the direction of its major offensive and TURTLE had already begun. Meanwhile the 'powerful forces' which were continuing the advance to Valmontone, far from being reinforced as Clark's subordinates had urged, had been reduced in strength, the defenders were slowly increasing in number, and although Artena, only 3 miles from Route 6, fell on 27 May, O'Daniel was unable to proceed further. The opportunity had, in fact, been lost, and an attempt to change back the main line of advance would only have resulted in further delay and tremendous confusion.

Even more important to Alexander, by overruling both the wishes and the instructions of his chief American subordinate, he would have caused tremendous controversy, while had he further attempted to discipline Clark, who was extremely popular with most American servicemen, as many of his British officers wished, the damage done to Allied unity might have been irreparable. It seems quite likely that Clark had gambled on this for, though he respected Alexander as a soldier and acknowledged his experience in war, he believed that his chief was not firm enough, calling him, in moments of exasperation, 'a peanut and a feather duster'. It is easy to suggest that this episode confirmed Clark's opinion. Alternatively, it might be thought to confirm Alexander's complete unselfishness, in that he was prepared to swallow his righteous anger for the sake of the common good.

In furtherance of that common good, Alexander made no formal complaint, either at the time or in his Official Despatch; instead he praised Fifth Army's forcefulness, and he tried to appease Churchill who was urging that 'the glory of this battle, already great, will be measured not by the capture of Rome or juncture with the bridge-head but by the number of divisions cut off.' He expressed his real feelings, however, in his *Memoirs* which, unsatisfactory and disappointing as they are, may perhaps be allowed the last word on this vexed question:

> When the final battle for Rome was launched, the role of the Anzio forces was to break out and at Valmontone get across the German main line of supply to their troops in Cassino. But for some inexplicable reason General Clark's Anglo-American forces never reached their objectives, though according to my information later, there was nothing to prevent their being gained. Instead, Mark Clark switched his point of attack north to the Alban Hills in the direction of Rome. If he had succeeded in carrying out my plan the disaster to the enemy would have been much greater; indeed most of the German forces would have been destroyed. True, the battle ended in a decisive victory for us, but it was not as complete as might have been. I had always assured General Clark in conversation that Rome would be entered by his army; and I can only assume that the immediate lure of Rome for its publicity value persuaded him to switch the direction of his advance.

The crowning irony of this affair is that by not allowing VI US Corps to proceed to Valmontone in full strength, Clark not only prevented it from inflicting at least greater harm on Tenth Army, but, so Truscott believed, actively delayed the capture of Rome. Had Valmontone been seized and Truscott then moved down the line of Route 6, he would have struck the Caesar Line at its weakest point before the defences could have been organized and, in the words of his Chief of Staff, Colonel Carleton: 'It was highly possible that we might turn the entire German position.' According to Major General Harmon, if his 1st US Armoured Division had been sent down Route 6, it could and should have 'been in Rome in an hour and a half'.

As it was, it seemed likely for a time that the Allies had forfeited all chance of an early capture of Rome as well as of destroying the right wing of Tenth Army, and would be faced with another long struggle to break a strongly defended German Line. The main body of VI US Corps, advancing to the south of Route 7, had, in fact, been directed against the Caesar Line's strongest defences, and although bitter fighting continued unabated for another four days, dusk on 30 May saw little gains made and heavy losses of tanks and men, including Lieutenant Allen Brown, Marshall's stepson, shot dead by a sniper when standing up in the turret of his Sherman tank.

Meanwhile, behind Truscott's back, von Vietinghoff was withdrawing his battered Tenth Army as fast as possible north-eastward out of the trap and towards the safety of the Caesar Line. Eighth Army might still have been able to have mauled and perhaps cut off at least part of von Vietinghoff's command had it pressed on rapidly to the important road junction at Frosinone on Route 6, but, sadly, that did not happen either.

Eighth Army had had a frustrating time since crossing the Melfa River. The valleys of the Liri and its tributary the Sacco, through which Route 6 ran, and which Intelligence reports before DIADEM had so seductively called the 'Gateway to Rome', were, in reality, totally unsuitable for speedy exploitation. Route 6 itself had been thoroughly blocked by mines, demolitions and over-enthusiastic Allied bombing. The other roads were very narrow, with steep banks, on which small rearguards could easily present endless difficulties. Eighth Army approached in full strength, only to find itself

advancing on a 'one-tank' front. It also added to its own difficulties by ignoring the advice of Alexander's brilliant Chief
Administrative Officer, Major General Robertson, that all reserve
transport should be kept off the roads; as a result, traffic congestion became an often appalling problem.

On Eighth Army's left, Juin's French Corps was making better
progress through the Lepini Hills and south of the Liri and Sacco.
This was inevitable, for it was in this area that the Germans were
withdrawing as rapidly as possible to escape being surrounded,
whereas the advances of Eighth Army and of the Americans
towards Valmontone formed the jaws of the trap, so naturally met
with far stronger opposition. Clark and Juin took little account of
this and urged that the boundary between the Fifth and Eighth
Armies should be altered, and that the French should swing
towards and over Route 6, taking the Germans fighting Leese in
flank and rear. Alexander declined this suggestion and, in consequence, he has been much criticized for his supposed lack of
boldness.

Alexander's decision, however, had, as so often, to take into
account many more factors than his subordinates had to
consider. He was prepared to agree that if Valmontone fell
quickly, Juin could be given the use of Route 6, and Leese
directed further north. But Valmontone did not fall and so
unlikely did it seem that it would fall in the reasonably near
future that Clark decided that he must regroup his forces: he
would bring II US Corps up on Truscott's right and transfer 3rd
US Infantry to it. This would give Keyes three divisions with
which to make a new attempt to cut Route 6 – but it seemed clear
to everyone that there must a further delay for reorganization
before this attempt could even begin.

In addition, as we have seen, all indications were that the fight
for the Caesar Line was likely to be a stern one. Alexander therefore felt that he would need the assistance of Eighth Army if he was
to break through. He was advised by Robertson that, in that case,
Leese must have Route 6 for his main supply line, and if the French
crossed it, there would be an even more 'terrific traffic snarl'. This
Alexander was not prepared to accept, and it may help to justify
his decision if it is noted that by 31 May, when the Canadians
finally captured Frosinone, Valmontone was still held by the

enemy, and the French advance, at last faced with firm opposition, had noticeably slowed.

Fifteenth Army Group prepared to face another grim and lengthy struggle to overcome the Caesar Line. However, at this point, Alexander and his men enjoyed another stroke of good fortune – which curiously echoed that on an earlier occasion – thanks this time to Major General Fred Walker, whose 36th US Infantry Division had been placed on the right flank of VI US Corps to provide a link between Truscott and Keyes.

Confronted with a particularly stubborn German garrison which blocked Route 7 at Velletri, south-east of the Alban Hills, Walker had sent reconnaissance patrols to probe the defences of Monte Artemisio, a 3,000-foot high peak which dominated the little town. This should have proved a formidable obstacle, for the Hermann Göring Division had requested Fourteenth Army to supply reinforcements to hold it, and Kesselring had expressly ordered that this should be done. Yet, astonishingly, von Mackensen and his staff, perhaps confused by the rapidly changing series of events, had ignored pleas and command alike.

To Walker's delighted surprise, therefore, he learned that Monte Artemisio, like the Aurunci Mountains before it, was virtually undefended. He promptly proposed an attack upon it, and received the enthusiastic approval of Clark and Truscott.

During the night of 30/31 May, the infantrymen of 36th US Division silently made their way up the mountain, which they captured by dawn. Behind them, Colonel Stovell's Divisional Engineer Regiment began to turn a steep cart track into a passable route for tanks and transport. Von Mackensen repeated the errors made at the time of the French advance through the Aurunci by not reporting what had happened until late on 31 May. Kesselring's fury at his Fourteenth Army Commander's latest folly was such that von Mackensen escaped dismissal only by hastily resigning; he was succeeded by General Joachim Lemelsen.

Kesselring's reaction was understandable, for Walker had torn a great gap in the Caesar Line. Not only could he swing behind Velletri, which fell of 1 June, but observers on Monte Artemisio could direct artillery fire onto the enemy positions blocking both Keyes and Truscott. The latter would describe it as 'the turning point in our drive to the northwest'. Valmontone was at long last secured on 2 June and the tired but triumphant Americans surged forward, II US Corps down Route 6, VI US Corps down Route 7. Kesselring, accepting defeat, requested permission to declare Rome an open city and evacuate it without fighting. Though Mussolini added to the hatred in which he was held by urging that the capital be defended street by street, Hitler was not prepared to accept the sort of odium that had been heaped on the Allies over the destruction of the Monte Cassino monastery. Rome, he stated, was 'a place of culture' which must be preserved: 'in no circumstances' should it become a battlefield.

So the Germans began a general withdrawal. Tenth Army fell back to the east of the capital, suffering severely from Allied air attacks in the process. Fourteenth Army, its retreat covered by anti-aircraft gunners using their weapons in the familiar anti-tank role, retired through and to the west of the capital, though 2,000 men were trapped near the mouth of the Tiber and forced to surrender. The bridges within Rome were left intact but others over the Tiber outside the city were blown up to delay the Allied pursuit. In the late afternoon of 4 May, both US corps entered Rome, then moved through it to follow up their defeated enemy.

At 0800 on 5 June, Mark Clark made an entry as dramatic as that of Patton into Messina. Juin, Keyes and Truscott posed with him, red with embarrassment. Later on the same day, Alexander quietly toured round the sights of the Eternal City in a jeep which he drove himself. He had timed his victory to perfection. On 6 June, British, American and Canadian soldiers stormed ashore on the beaches of Normandy.

Notes:

1. Quoted in *Templer: Tiger of Malaya* by John Cloake. Templer gained his nickname when, as High Commissioner and Commander-in-Chief, he successfully quelled a Communist terror campaign in Malaya in 1952–4. He later became a field marshal and Chief of the Imperial General Staff.

2. It may be added that Harding would have preferred that the first assault in DIADEM should be made from Anzio, but Alexander over-ruled him. This was partly because Alexander knew from 'Ultra' interceptions that the Germans believed an attack from Anzio was more likely, but mainly because he felt it would be more effective to strike at Tenth Army's lines of communication at a time when von Vietinghoff was under maximum pressure on his southern front.

3. Even Clark's successful use of 82nd Airborne Division as a rein-
    forcement had aroused somewhat unfair criticism, on the grounds
    that he should have arranged this earlier.
4. The Canadians had had an advance warning of the Panther's effec-
    tiveness: the fitted tank turrets in the Hitler Line were Panther turrets
    with the Panther's 75mm gun.

Chapter 9

The Road from Rome

For the armies in Italy, the rest was anti-climax. Churchill sums up the situation perfectly when he describes how on 6 June he addressed the members of the House of Commons on the capture of Rome, 'keeping them on tenterhooks for a little', before relenting and giving them the news that they really wanted to hear: the Normandy landings had achieved tactical surprise and had begun well. The campaign in Italy had become a 'sideshow'.

It was never so regarded by Alexander, however. He was convinced that he and his men would soon enjoy further rewards for all their past efforts. 'Morale is irresistably high as a result of recent successes,' he declared. He knew that the Germans had suffered severely, their mobile divisions having lost a large proportion of their tanks, their infantry divisions desperately needing time to rest and reform. He lamented that 'If only the country were more open, we would make hay of the lot.' He ordered Clark and Leese to take 'extreme risks' in following up the retreating enemy as quickly as possible.

At first all went well. Fifth Army took the port of Civitavecchia on 7 June, and the important group of aerodromes around Viterbo two days later. On its right, Eighth Army thrust up the valley of the Tiber, and 6th South African Armoured Division seized another valuable airfield at Orvieto on the 14th. On the Adriatic coast, the enemy fell back from the area around Pescara and Chieti where their resistance had once blocked Alexander's first attempt to get to Rome. In the Mediterranean, French forces landed on the island of Elba on 17 June, capturing it together with 1,800 prisoners on the 19th, though at a cost of 1,000 casualties.

Alexander had directed Fifth Army towards Pisa and Lucca, and Eighth Army towards Florence and Arezzo. All these cities lay

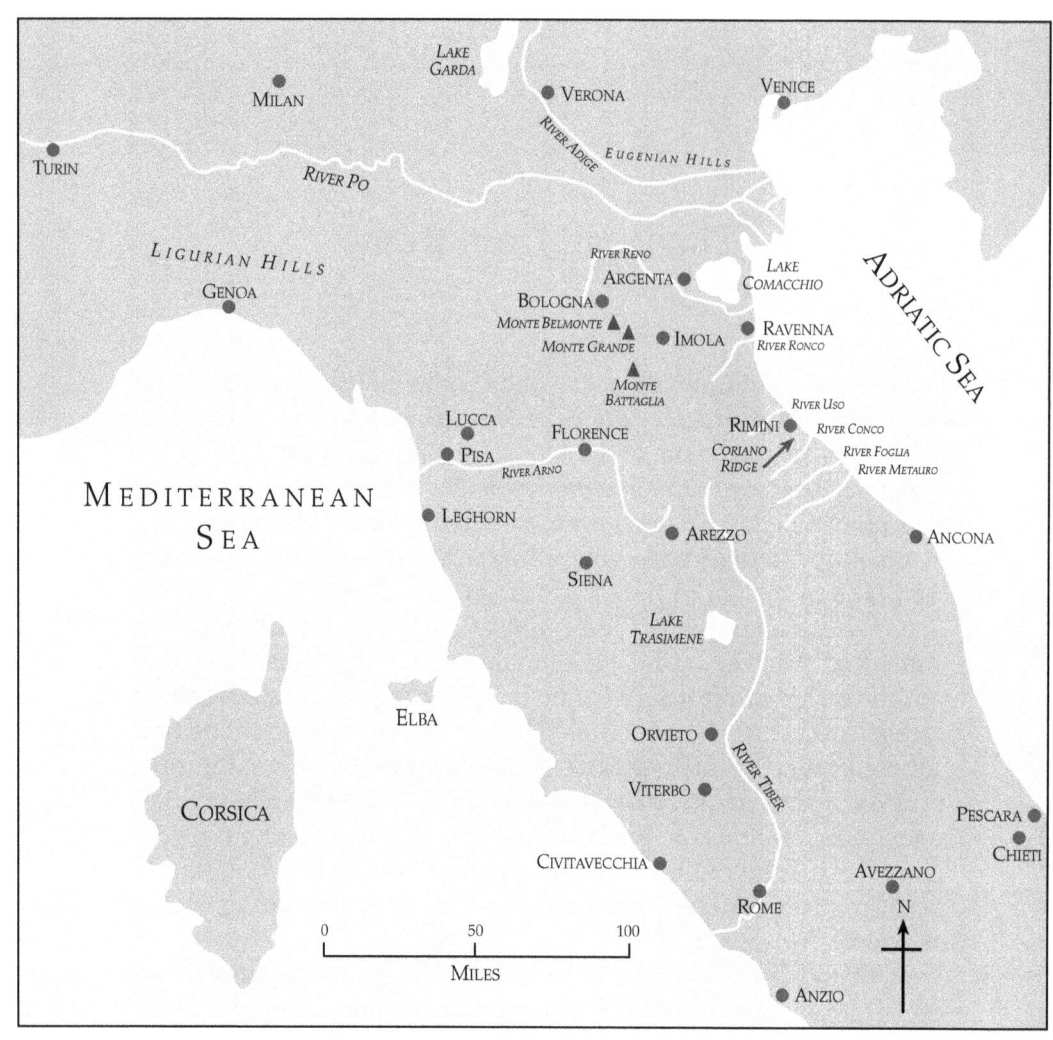

Map 12: Northern Italy

south of Kesselring's next major defensive position, the Gothic Line, 200 miles long, running across the Apennines from north of Pisa to south of Rimini, and guarding the valley of the River Po. Alexander believed that he would be able to achieve his initial objectives by the end of July, enabling him to attack the Line by 15 August. In view of the enemy's weakness in men and equipment, he was confident that he could break through this, and that he would then have little difficulty in advancing into north-east Italy and through the 'Ljubljana Gap' into Austria. He was sure that 'Neither the Apennines nor even the Alps should prove a serious obstacle' to his men's 'enthusiasm and skill'. All that could stop them reaching Vienna was a diversion to Italy of eight or more fresh German divisions, which would, of course, be immensely beneficial to Allied operations on other fronts.

Strategically, this was an enticing prospect, but it may be that Alexander was so entranced by its possibilities that he rather ignored the tactical and topographical difficulties which stood in the way of its fulfilment. Certainly his suggestion of advancing as far as Vienna in 1944 was considered impracticable by the professional head of the British Army. Though Captain Liddell Hart states that 'the plan appealed to Churchill and the British Chiefs of Staff, particularly Alan Brooke', in fact Brooke, in the course of a long argument with the Prime Minister on 23 June, declared bluntly that what Alexander was really proposing was that 'we should embark on a campaign through the Alps in winter'. He did not consider this an eventuality to be welcomed, or one that was likely to achieve satisfactory results.

Lest it be felt that Alexander was out of touch with reality, it should be said that his plan was strongly supported not only by Churchill but by Harding, Clark, Leese and Macmillan. Moreover, while, in retrospect, we may agree with Brooke that the plan's final stage was incapable of realization, it would still have been a tremendous achievement if the Allies had been able to break into the Po Valley. This would have deprived the Germans of the industrial towns of northern Italy and brought Allied ground and air forces dangerously close to Germany's southern borders. It might have mauled Kesselring's battered divisions sufficiently to have deprived Hitler of their services. And in any case, it would surely have diverted German attention and German troops to Italy, just at the moment, as it transpired, that desperate resistance was checking both the Western Allies and the Russians on the borders of the Fatherland.

Whether Alexander would have been able to reach the Po Valley had his well-balanced and experienced 'team' been left intact is obviously a matter of speculation. At the very least, though, it may be claimed that this was a distinct possibility – Alexander's Chief of Staff and both his Army Commanders would all later declare that they had no doubt whatever that it was as certain as anything in war can be. Yet sadly, at a crucial moment, Fifteenth Army Group was drastically weakened and all chances of success were imperilled.

The reason for this was Alexander's usual bane – politics. It will be recalled that he had only been able to execute DIADEM by getting Operation ANVIL, the planned Allied landing in the South of France, postponed. As soon as DIADEM was over, the Americans renewed their demands for ANVIL to be launched. Since the troops required to carry it out would have to come from Fifteenth Army Group, Alexander was naturally bitterly opposed to this scheme, but Roosevelt and Marshall remained adamant.[1] Arguments continued throughout June, but on the 23rd, Eisenhower intervened, urging that ANVIL was necessary in order to ensure the defeat of the enemy opposing him in Normandy. On 2 July, the British Chiefs of Staff bowed to their Ally's wishes. Alexander was formally advised three days later.

Already, preliminary steps had been taken in case ANVIL was decided upon. The headquarters of VI US Corps and three veteran US divisions – 3rd, 36th and 45th – were pulled into reserve during June, to be followed by two French divisions. The directive of 5 July confirmed that all these would be allocated to ANVIL, as would the rest of the French Expeditionary Corps. Though IV US Corps, the Headquarters of which had arrived in Italy some three months earlier, now joined II US Corps in Fifth Army's Order of Battle, they together controlled a total of only five divisions. In addition, one-third of Fifth Army's artillery strength left and the number of men under Clark's command fell from 249,000 to 153,000. Several American specialist units, such as construction battalions, which had served Eighth as well as Fifth Army, were also lost to Alexander. So was 70 per cent of Clark's supporting air

arm. So were the landing craft needed to carry the ANVIL formations, and their absence meant that there would be no point in
Alexander contemplating any new seaborne assaults in Italy for
some time to come.

Operation ANVIL – or, to be more exact, Operation
DRAGOON, for it had been so renamed – took place on 15
August. That it was a complete success, forced the surrender of
50,000 enemy soldiers who were cut off in south-western France,
and gave Eisenhower the reinforcements which would ultimately
make his advance into Germany irresistable, might seem to provide
ample compensation for the harm it inflicted on the Allied cause in
Italy. It is doubtful, however, if Alexander was consoled, for he was
well aware that that harm went far beyond the reduction in his
manpower and equipment.

When Alexander had opposed the resurrection of ANVIL, he had
emphasized how important it was that his men should feel that
their actions in Italy had real value. He feared that a major transfer
of forces out of Italy would indicate that this front had become of
only secondary importance – and he was right. The effect on the
French prior to their departure was particularly adverse. Juin,
formerly so staunch, showed no further interest in putting pressure
on the Germans retiring before him. By mid-July, Alexander,
through Clark, was almost pleading with him to allow the enemy
no relaxation, only for Juin to retort that the need to prepare for
operations elsewhere necessitated his going onto the defensive.
Even in Eighth Army, morale declined. Subsequent visits to Italy by
Churchill, Brooke and George VI, and the King's knighting of
Harding, Leese and McCreery could not entirely efface this impression. Fifteenth Army Group had temporarily lost its enthusiasm.

Moreover, all this happened just as the Allied momentum
began to falter. As was mentioned earlier, Kesselring had received
four new divisions and other reinforcements during the course
of DIADEM. Now Hitler sent him a further four divisions, all of
them, incidentally, either from or earmarked for the Russian front,
together with the equivalent of three more divisions of inferior
quality from Germany, the men of which were used to replace the
casualties in his existing formations. In return, he lost the Hermann
Göring Division, which went to Russia, and he would shortly have
to send two Panzer Grenadier Divisions to North-West Europe, but

clearly his net strength was appreciably increased. The only reinforcements that would reach Alexander in the near future were two
inexperienced formations, the American 92nd Negro Division and
the 1st Brazilian Expeditionary Division, the latter led by the
magnificently named Major General Joao Batista Mascarenhos de
Moraes.[2]

At this distance of time, it is difficult to begrudge Kesselring his
good fortune, for, despite his defeat and the Allied capture of
Rome, he remained as resilient as ever. Hitler had ordered him to
halt the Allies on the Gothic Line and he had promised he would
do so. He intended to fall back to this as slowly as possible, delaying
his pursuers on a series of advanced positions which, although
usually referred to as 'lines', were, in reality, a series of strongpoints
blocking the easiest routes northward.

At first the Allies had faced only small rearguards and as many
obstructions as the enemy sappers had had time to create. Every
bridge was demolished as a matter of course and roads and railway
lines torn up by explosions or blocked by rubble from wrecked
buildings or by trees felled across them. On 20 June, the advance
reached the first of Kesselring's preliminary defences, some 80
miles north of Rome, which the Germans called the Albert Line
after their Commander-in-Chief, and the Allies the Trasimene
Line since it was centred upon the lake of that name which had
once been the scene of perhaps the most famous ambush in history.
A series of violent thunderstorms greatly hampered their attacks
and it was not until the early hours of 30 June that the Germans
fell back – and then only to the next defensive position.

This was the Arezzo Line, so named from the town just to the
north of its centre. The Allies came up to this on 5 July, but it was
not until the 15th that they were able to persuade the enemy to
abandon it. Thereafter they continued to advance slowly. Arezzo
was captured by the British on 16 July, the port of Ancona on the
Adriatic by the Poles on the 18th, and Leghorn on the west coast
by the Americans on the 19th. By 4 August, the Germans had
retired over the Arno and Metauro Rivers, which formed their last
defences before the Gothic Line. The suburbs of Florence south of
the Arno were entered by 6th South African Armoured Division
but it found that the bridges over the river had all been blown up,
apart from the historic Ponte Vecchio which was blocked by demol-

itions at both ends. The Germans continued to occupy the rest of the city, though, in accordance with the wishes of both Alexander and Kesselring, the two sides tried their best to inflict as little damage on it as was possible.

Alexander now prepared to assault the Gothic Line. Despite the reduction in his strength, the directive of 5 July had still expected him to advance to and subsequently beyond the River Po. Alexander considered this 'somewhat optimistic' but, as Churchill, who visited him in mid-August, relates, he 'maintained his soldierly cheerfulness'. This was quite an achievement, for Alexander was naturally indignant and disappointed by the relegation of Italy to, in Churchill's words, 'a mere secondary part', and he was once again confronted by an impressive natural and man-made obstacle.

The Gothic Line was another typically efficient German defensive position, consisting of a chain of connected strongpoints – bunkers, pillboxes, artillery and machine-gun posts – up to 10 miles wide. These were protected by steel and concrete, vast lengths of barbed wire, endless rows of mines and literally miles of anti-tank ditches. There was even a new threat. The enemy had again fitted tank turrets into the Line, but this time not just Panther turrets – thirty Tiger turrets with their massive 88mm guns had been installed. In addition, as usual, the German engineers had taken full advantage of the country's natural features.

Between the Gustav and the Gothic Lines, the Apennines run up the centre and east of the peninsula, but beyond Florence the mountains swing away north-westward towards the Ligurian Hills north of Genoa, close to the Mediterranean coast. The Gothic Line followed this great bend. An attempt to break through it in the west, where the attackers would be hemmed in between the mountains and the sea, was not an encouraging proposition. By contrast, the coastal plain on the Adriatic side now began to widen, but beyond the River Foglia, which formed the eastern section of the Line, there flowed a series of other rivers, all of which would have to be crossed and over which, no doubt, new bridges would have to be erected to replace those demolished by the defenders. And between these, low ridges ran down from the Apennines to the sea, providing further natural lines of defence. Remembering the problems that had arisen in a similar situation at the time of the Battle of the River Sangro, Eighth Army's staff officers were reluctant to repeat that experience, while Kesselring also awaited any assault on his eastern flank 'with a certain confidence'.

Accordingly, Alexander and Harding had originally intended that Fifteenth Army Group should break through the Gothic Line in its centre, aiming for Bologna. A successful offensive here would split the defenders in two and enable Alexander to advance towards either southern France or Austria as seemed most advantageous. The disadvantage of this move was that it would be delivered in the heart of the Apennines, but there were a number of good mountain roads leading northwards towards the Po Valley which the attackers would be able to follow.

Unfortunately, when Alexander had approved this scheme, he had envisaged his French forces playing the same role that they had carried out so effectively in the Aurunci Mountains during DIADEM: they would clear the high ground on either side of the roads. When these mountain-warfare specialists were diverted to the South of France, the prospect of a direct assault towards Bologna became much less desirable, especially since it had been learned that the Germans were strengthening their defences in this area.

It appeared particularly unattractive to Lieutenant General Sidney Kirkman, commander of XIII Corps. On 3 August, he had a long conversation with Leese, during which he expressed his concerns about the existing plan. Kirkman advocated that, instead of Eighth Army trying to force its way to Bologna side by side with Fifth Army, it should transfer its main strength to the east and endeavour to break through the Gothic Line along the Adriatic coast. After the two generals had studied the terrain ahead of them from an observation post in a church tower, Leese expressed his agreement with this proposal. Next day, he met Alexander and Harding on Orvieto airfield and urged them to change their plans accordingly.

Leese would later declare: 'It was always a great privilege to serve under General Alexander as he was always so ready to hear your views and to discuss future plans with one.' On this occasion he probably found it a pleasure as well as a privilege, for Alexander liked his ideas immediately, realizing that they would enable him to use his two armies in combination, striking blows on either flank or on both simultaneously as opportunity offered. After further consultations with Harding, Leese, Clark and Kirkman, Alexander decided that Eighth Army would deliver the main offensive – code-named Operation OLIVE – on the Adriatic coast on 25 August. Then, on a date that he would determine, but at least five days later, by which time the enemy strength north of Florence should have been reduced by the need to transfer troops to engage Eighth Army, II US Corps would attack towards Bologna through the centre of the Gothic Line.

This task would not be an easy one, for the departure of French and American forces to southern France had left Fifth Army dangerously weak. Leese therefore suggested that Kirkman's XIII Corps, the Eighth Army formation nearest to the Americans, should be put under Clark's command. Alexander again approved and Kirkman was ordered to support Keyes with 6th (British) Armoured and two infantry divisions, while 6th South African Armoured Division was transferred directly to IV US Corps which would keep up a diversionary pressure along the Mediterranean coast.

It is worth emphasizing Leese's offer, for Harding, perhaps disappointed that his own ideas had been overruled, would later suggest that the prime motive of Leese and Kirkman was to put distance between themselves and Clark, whom they disliked. Since one result of the change of plans was to place Kirkman directly under Clark, and his diary confirms that he was well aware of the possibility, this seems most unlikely, at least in his case. Leese did consider that to have Fifth and Eighth Armies separated was an additional advantage: he had not forgotten the troubles over inter-army boundaries, not only during DIADEM but as far back as Sicily, and was anxious to avoid them in the future. He had also been offended by Clark's vainglorious utterances after the fall of Rome, which had entirely omitted any mention of the contribution made by Eighth Army, and by the way in which he (Leese) had been cold-shouldered by Clark and Juin at a celebration arranged by the latter. However, Leese was very forgiving and, as well as his offer of XIII Corps, his private correspondence at this time, showing that he sympathized with Clark over the weakening of Fifth Army and acknowledging Clark's 'experience and energy', suggests that their differences had already been forgotten.[3]

In any case, Leese's main motive was his genuine belief that the suggested move would prove decisive. His enthusiasm was contagious and served to revive his men's flagging morale – it would later be said that he had promised that Eighth Army would reach Bologna in two days, Venice in four, and Vienna in seven. Since Leese was well aware, from the conferences that had been held, that the Eighth and Fifth Army thrusts would be interdependent and the latter would not even start for some days after his own offensive, and since in his address to his senior officers on 23 August, he stressed that the coming battle would not be an easy one, such reports – which were only made long afterwards – do sound somewhat unlikely. They may, however, perhaps reflect the eagerness and optimism that Leese had managed to generate in Eighth Army at this time.

It also seems that, while Leese realized the difficulties involved in breaking the Gothic Line and in crossing the numerous rivers which lay beyond it, he did indeed feel that, as soon as he could reach open country, where the Allied superiority in tanks and guns would be fully effective, the German armies in Italy would be broken and it would then still be possible to advance on Vienna. This of course, was the hope that had originally been entertained by Alexander, and it appears that between them they succeeded in convincing Harding, who on 21 August wrote to Leese that his offensive could prove 'one of the culminating decisive battles of the war'. Whatever may be thought of the practicality of a march on Vienna, it should be recorded that Alexander and his Army Commander would turn out to be quite correct in their assessment of the results of engaging the enemy in the open. Unhappily, this would not happen for many a weary month.

There were two main reasons for this. For a start, Alexander's men would have to advance considerably farther than was realized before they gained ground suitable for their armour. Intelligence reports had indicated that once Eighth Army had passed Rimini, it would reach an area of low, level ground, known as the Romagna Plain, which would provide good 'tank going'. In reality, this area was covered by numerous deep rivers and irrigation ditches, none of which would be easy to cross. Worse still, the land, though now given over to agriculture, had in the past been reclaimed from marshes, so quickly became waterlogged after rain.

Then again, it would prove more difficult than anticipated to get as far as Rimini in the first place. Kesselring could be relied upon to resist with his usual resourcefulness, and he had a marvellous line of communications – Route 9, the Via Emilia – running behind and parallel to the Gothic Line, enabling him to transfer troops quickly to counter Alexander's pressure on any part of his defences. The gift of XIII Corps, though inevitable, obviously reduced Leese's strength. And the one great detrimental effect of the change of plans had been the loss of precious time. It will be recalled that Alexander had formerly hoped to attack the Gothic Line on 15 August. A postponement of ten days may seem a small matter, but every one that passed increased the risk of the Allies being hampered by bad weather, should this set in early – as an unkind fate had decreed it would.

As so often in Italy, it all began well. The transfer of Eighth Army to the eastern flank had to be carried out secretly at night in transport which could show no lights. Yet brilliant staff work ensured that the soldiers, together with 1,000 guns, 1,200 tanks and about 60,000 other vehicles were succesfully redeployed. Moreover, the Germans remained totally unaware of what had happened; their attention was concentrated on the South of France, for Kesselring feared that the landing forces there would wheel north-eastward into Italy to take his command in the flank and rear.

On the night of 25/26 August, Wellingtons and Liberators heavily bombed Ravenna, the Germans' main supply base behind the eastern part of the Gothic Line, and, an hour before midnight, Operation OLIVE began. Surprise was total. It will be remembered that the front had stabilized on the River Metauro, some 12 miles south of the main enemy defences. It so happened that the Germans were withdrawing troops from their advanced posts to the Line at the very moment that Eighth Army crossed the Metauro. In the confusion, it was not at first realized that a major Allied offensive was taking place. By 29 August, Eighth Army had reached the Foglia River, marking the boundary of the Gothic Line. Next morning, while Boston and Baltimore light bombers of the Desert Air Force probed ahead, looking for enemy transport or gun positions, Kittyhawk fighter-bombers performed the unusual task of blasting a clear passage through the minefields for tanks and infantry. The Foglia was duly crossed and the forward positions of the Gothic Line were seized, in many cases before they could be manned by the defenders allotted to them.

Although by this time the Germans had appreciated the true situation and were rushing reinforcements to the threatened area, they were too late. Savage fighting raged over the next three days, but by the evening of 2 September, the enemy had fallen back, leaving some 20 miles of the Gothic Line in Eighth Army's hands. That same night, the Canadians seized a bridgehead over the next major obstacle, the River Conco. Meanwhile, Kesselring, wisely deciding that he must shorten his defensive front, had ordered his advanced forces facing Fifth Army to retire to the Gothic Line. Clark followed up, occupying Lucca on 6 September. Even the visit of Churchill proved less of a distraction than might have been the case. Alexander took him up near the front line – dangerously near some felt, but the old warrior was, of course, delighted to be close to the fighting and to hear enemy rifle and machine-gun fire.

Alexander was equally delighted, but in his case with the progress his men had made. But now the tide began to turn against him. There remained only one major obstacle between Eighth Army and Rimini, the Coriano Ridge which, with its southward extension, the Gemmano Ridge, enabled German artillery to dominate Leese's line of advance. Lieutenant General Charles Keightley, the young, ardent commander of V Corps, which was Eighth Army's strongest formation, had made preparations for his 1st (British) Armoured Division to force its way over the ridge early on 4 September. Unfortunately his four infantry divisions were, understandably, beginning to tire, and did not achieve the necessary preliminary gains until the afternoon. To make matters worse, the tracks leading to the ridge were rapidly deteriorating and a large proportion of 1st Armoured's tanks suffered mechanical failure before they could so much as reach their start line.

As a result, Keightley's armour could not attack until 1545, and then in much diminished strength. The German anti-tank guns repelled their every attempt. During the night, 29th Panzer Grenadier and 162nd Infantry Divisions, transferred by Kesselring from the Fifth Army front, arrived to support 26th Panzer and the three infantry divisions which were already facing Eighth Army. Next day, Keightley could still make no progress, and on 6 September, the elements intervened. Two days of heavy rain bogged down the armour, turned the approach roads into the well-remembered and much-hated mud tracks, and persuaded Leese that there would have to be a pause while preparations were made for a new full-scale assault.

Alexander, who visited Leese on 7 September, accepted the delay, but, alarmed at the prospect of further bad weather, urged that this be reduced as far as possible; he also felt, with some reason, that the Germans' reserves must by now have been committed to the Adriatic coast, so it was time to order Clark to commence the Fifth Army offensive. It was agreed that Leese would attack first on the night of 12/13 September, and next day, II US Corps and XIII (British) Corps would advance against the Gothic Line, with Bologna as their ultimate objective.

Eighth Army's attack began just before midnight, with a bombardment by 1,000 guns. On the 13th, 1st (British) Armoured Division, with Gurkha infantrymen riding on the backs of its tanks, cleared the Coriano Ridge, thereby outflanking the Gemmano Ridge as well; it was taken without difficulty next day, by which time its defenders were already evacuating it. For Kesselring, this was 'terrible news', but his ally, the weather, remained loyal to him. As 1st Armoured's tanks moved forward from Coriano, they were bogged down by watercourses, trivial a week earlier, but now raging torrents. And although von Vietinghoff told his chief that Tenth Army had no reserves left, in practice, on the 14th, 356th Infantry Division began to arrive to help shore up the broken front.

Fifth Army had begun its offensive on 13 September, as planned. For four days, a desperate struggle rocked backwards and forwards, while above the fighting, American light bombers pounded the enemy's lines of communication and supply dumps, and Thunderbolt fighter-bombers struck at gun sites and troop concentrations. Finally on 17 September, Keyes and Kirkman between them broke into the Gothic Line's defences, but it was not until the 21st, that these were finally secured, and Keyes could send forward 88th US Division, which he had kept back in reserve. Since the direct route to Bologna was heavily guarded, this division was directed on the town of Imola, south-east of Bologna on Route 9. On 27 September, the Americans captured Monte Battaglia, only 12 miles from their objective, but a series of fierce counter-attacks and worsening weather prevented further progress.

Eighth Army's fortunes were similar. On 17 September, the redoubtable 90th Panzer Grenadier Division was added to the list of its opponents, but the British and Canadians pressed on doggedly. Under cover of attacks by strafing Spitfires and Kittyhawk fighter-bombers, they at last captured Rimini on 21 September, and on 26 September, they crossed the River Uso, which, long ago, had been known as the Rubicon, and had marked the boundary of Italy. Then their advance too ground to a halt in drenching rain.

Operation OLIVE was over. Eighth Army had conquered the Gothic Line and reached Rimini; it had savaged the German formations facing it and taken 8,000 prisoners. These achievements, though, had been paid for at a cost of 14,000 men killed, wounded and missing, the strength of the infantry units had fallen dangerously low and there were no reinforcements available to replace the casualties. 1st (British) Armoured Division had lost 250 tanks in action, plus 230 more as a result of mechanical problems; those that remained were distributed among other armoured formations – but what made these losses so hard to bear was the discovery that the Intelligence predictions that beyond Rimini Eighth Army would find good 'tank going' were entirely incorrect.

Despite this disappointment, Alexander believed that the offensive could still obtain far-reaching results. It was an opinion shared by his 'opposite number'. 'I have the terrible feeling that the whole thing is beginning to slide,' Kesselring told his staff. Leese left Eighth Army on 1 October, having been promoted to overall command of the Allied Land Forces in South-East Asia, but McCreery, who succeeded him, resumed Eighth Army's drive forward, northwards towards Ravenna, and north-westwards along Route 9 towards Imola and a junction with Clark.

It quickly became clear that Alexander's hopes and Kesselring's fears were alike unjustified. The torrential rains continued. On 26 October, for instance, an Eighth Army bridgehead across the River Ronco was left isolated when bridges spanning other rivers along its supply route were washed away. The enemy promptly counter-attacked and the bridgehead was destroyed; it would be another five days before McCreery was able to regain the Ronco's far bank. In November, the weather became worse still and a number of lorry drivers drowned when their vehicles were caught in flash floods.

Eighth Army's miserable pilgrimage continued into the New Year, with ever-greater suffering and ever-diminishing rewards. Ravenna was eventually entered by the Canadians on 4 December, but Imola remained well out of McCreery's reach.

Alexander had already concluded that the best prospects for success were to be found on the Fifth Army front. In early October, he sent 78th (British) Division, which had just returned from a period of rest and refitting in the Middle East and which had originally been intended for Eighth Army, to XIII Corps instead. This enabled Kirkman to resume the pressure against Imola, while Keyes made directly for Bologna with II US Corps. On 20 October, the Americans captured Monte Grande, and three days later, Monte Belmonte, successes which brought them within 5 miles of Route 9 and about 9 miles from Bologna. Yet by the end of the month, Clark had suffered 20,000 casualties since his original offensive had begun, and he too had no reinforcements on hand with which to make good his losses. With the prize so nearly in his grasp, he was forced to go onto the defensive.

Alexander remained optimistic that Clark would soon be able to resume his advance, particularly if pressure by Eighth Army could compel von Vietinghoff – who had taken over temporary command of all German forces in Italy[4] – to divert more of the divisions facing Fifth Army to his eastern flank. Sadly, this never happened, and on 26 December, the extent of the Allies' exhaustion became very apparent when a counter-attack was made in the Mediterranean sector, mainly by Italian troops who had stayed loyal to Mussolini. They proved fully capable of driving back the 92nd Negro Division, and though 8th Indian Division quickly restored the situation and regained the ground lost, Alexander took the hint. He was not prepared to embark on another winter campaign. There would be no further offensives until spring.

It was high time this decision was taken. The men of Fifteenth Army Group were by now becoming thoroughly disheartened, and not only by their failure to make further progress. Troubles in Greece, which will be mentioned shortly, had led to the transfer there of 4th Indian Division, followed later by X Corps with two further divisions. In the New Year, the Canadian Corps with one armoured and one infantry division also left – to join the forces in North-Western Europe – as did two American fighter groups.

No wonder, then, that the troops had begun to revert to their former attitude: to feel that they were considered of little importance in the highest political and military councils, and that all attention and all concern was directed towards the armies of Eisenhower and the Russians who, between them, would crush the Germans in any case, whatever happened in Italy. It was understandable that to many, it appeared stupid and pointless to risk death or mutilation in such circumstances, and there was a sharp increase in the numbers of deserters, not to the enemy, but to seek shelter among the usually sympathetic Italian civil population. Had Alexander's soldiers faced the additional prospect of a campaign amid the icy winds, rain and snow of the Italian winter, morale might well have come close to collapse. As it was, the vast majority of them rested, re-equipped, and were prepared to try again in the spring.

While the fighting in Italy lapsed into an aggrieved stalemate, there was much movement in the ranks of the higher commanders, caused principally by the death of Field Marshal Sir John Dill, Brooke's predecessor as CIGS, but now Head of the British Military Mission in Washington. Alexander's nominal superior, Wilson, was promoted and took Dill's place. Alexander himself beame a field marshal on 27 November – the appointment being back-dated to the time of the capture of Rome – and the Supreme Commander, Mediterranean on 12 December. Clark, whose intransigence at the time of DIADEM had been tactfully forgiven by Alexander, became head of Fifteenth Army Group, and Truscott Fifth Army Commander. Finally, on 6 March 1945, Harding replaced Kirkman, who had fallen ill, in command of XIII Corps, being succeeded as Alexander's Chief of Staff by Lieutenant General Sir William Morgan.

His change of status made little difference to Alexander's control of his armies. Churchill had always directed that Wilson should deal only with political and administrative matters, leaving Alexander in complete charge of the campaigns in Italy. It was not a position fully accepted by Wilson, who had, on occasion, attempted to intervene, but without much effect. Alexander, though always a model of courtesy, had corresponded directly with Churchill and Brooke, and advised Wilson of his plans, as he later declared, merely 'out of politeness'. By contrast, when Alexander became Supreme Commander, Mediterranean, he continued to direct the Allied strategy, though always in close and tactful liaison with Clark. He also, it may be added, continued to stay in close touch with his fighting soldiers. The Supreme Commander's official Headquarters was at Caserta, near Naples, but Alexander spent most of his time at his Tactical Headquarters near Siena, from which he was constantly making personal visits to the forward troops.

What his new post did do was to give Alexander additional and highly unwelcome responsibilities. On 11 December, the day before his official appointment, Alexander, accompanied by Macmillan, arrived in Athens. By the end of August, the German forces stationed in Greece had begun to withdraw in order to avoid being cut off by the Russian advance into the Balkans. British troops, under Lieutenant General Scobie, had moved into Greece in the wake of the retreating enemy, and on 15 October had entered Athens, only to be involved in clashes between Communist guerillas, to whom the Germans had supplied arms in return for immunity from interference during their retirement, and the Greek pro-Royalist Government. By early December, they were caught in the crossfire of a Greek civil war.

Alexander was then attending conferences in London, but the War Cabinet quickly dispatched him to Greece, giving him full authority to restore order. On reaching Athens, he signalled to Churchill that the military situation was worse than had been believed: the British forces were virtually besieged in the centre of the city. He promptly took control, arranged the transfer of reinforcements from Italy and, as so often before, heartened everyone with his air of complete confidence and his insistence on examining the main scenes of the fighting in person, regardless of the risks involved.

Alexander's other responsibilities necessitated his speedy return to Italy on 12 December, but he kept in close touch with Macmillan, who remained in Athens, and with the British Ambassador, Mr (later Sir) Reginald Leeper. By 18 December, the British position was secure, but three days later, Alexander reported to Churchill his concern that there might be a continuing drain to Greece of his forces in Italy and his opinion that, in any event, 'the Greek problem cannot be solved by military measures'.

The answer to the Greek dilemma, in the view of Alexander, Macmillan and Leeper, was to entrust all power to Archbishop Damaskinos, who alone had the confidence of all contending parties. Churchill was not convinced, but after considering Alexander's signal, he decided to fly to Greece to examine the situation for himself. Alexander also returned to Greece in a destroyer, arriving on the morning of Christmas Day. That afternoon, he, Macmillan and Leeper briefed Churchill on his arrival at Kalamaki airfield. In the evening, Churchill met and was suitably impressed by Damaskinos, and next day, the various Greek factions agreed that King George II, who was then in London, should be requested to appoint the Archbishop as Regent. Churchill then returned home and persuaded the exiled monarch to give his formal acceptance on 30 December. The Communist agitation was by no means ended and in 1947 would flare up in a bitter two-year conflict, but Alexander had gained his immediate aims. The current fighting, which had cost over 1,500 British casualties, ended on 15 January 1945, and he was able to arrange the return of X Corps in time to take part in his final campaign in Italy.

For this final campaign, the Chiefs of Staff favoured no more than 'limited offensive action' which would 'contain the German forces now in Italy and prevent their withdrawal to other fronts'. But Alexander had different ideas. 'I considered,' he would afterwards write, 'I might yet be able to do something more drastic.' He determined to attempt the destruction of the enemy forces in Italy by trapping them south of the Po with a great encircling movement carried out by both Fifth and Eighth Armies, and he won over Clark, McCreery and Truscott to an enthusiastic consent.

What was really remarkable, though, was the eager response of the men of Fifth and Eighth Armies. It is worth exploring the reason for this astonishing revival of their morale. The coming of spring undoubtedly cheered them, as it does everybody, but this was a minor factor. We are told that McCreery made a great contribution, but it seems permissible to doubt this. The same sources confirm that, although direct and forceful with his superiors and equals, and rightly respected by his officers, McCreery was surprisingly diffident with his soldiers, by whom he was not well known; moreover, that he merely repeated the old assurance of final victory which, even the least cynical must have reflected, had been promised before. Successes on other fronts where Eisenhower's men had swept up to and over the Rhine, and where the Russians had come within 50 miles of Berlin – and, incidentally, would take Vienna on 13 April – played their part, but, as was seen earlier, there was some risk that these could have an adverse effect, by convincing Alexander's troops that the war would be won anyway, without the need for any action on their part.

It would appear, therefore, that the major credit for the transformation should go to Alexander, whose orders and whose whole attitude made it clear that, in his view, Fifteenth Army Group did have a vitally important role to play. The feeling that this engendered was strengthened by the arrival in Italy of specialized equipment: 'Fantails' – huge landing vehicles, fitted with tracks, which could carry infantry through shallow flooded areas; 'Kangaroos' – Sherman tanks minus their turrets, also used to transport infantry; 'Crocodiles' – Churchill tanks carrying flame-throwers; 'DDs' – Duplex Drive amphibious tanks. All these had long been employed on more favoured fronts, and their presence seemed to confirm that Italy was no longer regarded as an area of secondary importance.

If Alexander's obvious belief in the value of the coming encounter uplifted his men, his faith in the outcome was equally heartening to his officers. In the past, Alexander had been adept at displaying a confidence which he had sometimes not really felt; now his confidence was unbounded and he had good reason for it.

The travails of the previous autumn had not attained the results for which Alexander had hoped but they had helped to prepare the way for his eventual triumph. In mid-February, the 10th US Mountain Division, another recent arrival in Italy, had captured a number of high points south-west of Bologna, the possession of which would assist a Fifth Army breakout to the River Po. Eighth Army was also reasonably close to the Po Valley. It could reach this by continuing its advance along Route 9 towards Bologna, though this was obstructed by four more rivers. Better still, it could strike up Route 16, crossing the Bastia Bridge over the River Reno, of which all the northward-flowing rivers were tributaries, then moving on through the narrow Argenta Gap between Lake Comacchio and an area of land which the Germans had deliberately flooded.

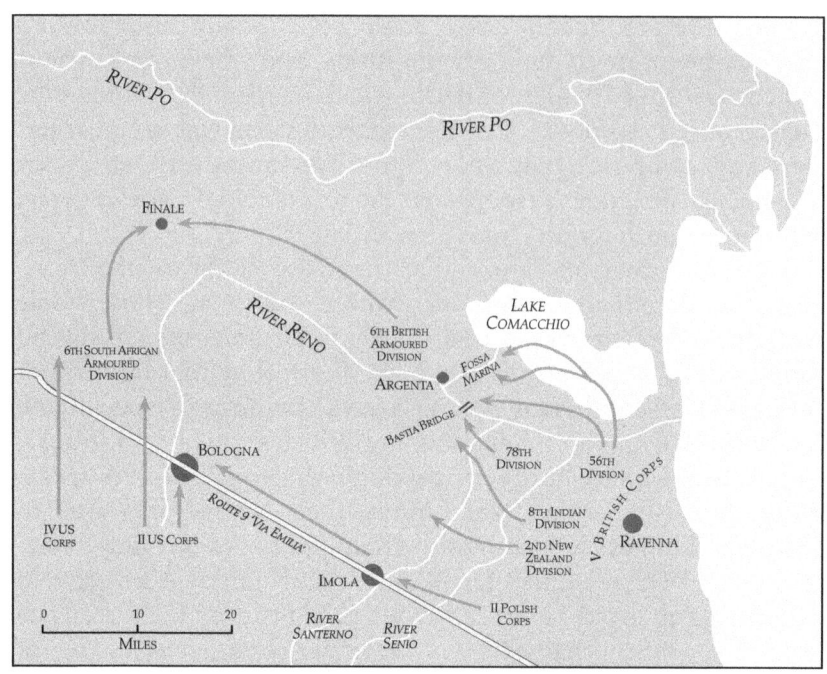

Map 13: Alexander's Final Offensive

Neither Allied Army had an easy initial task, but once the Po Valley had been reached, both would enjoy those conditions of which they had been dreaming for so long. At last the natural features would not all favour the defenders. At last the attackers would be operating in a terrain least likely to be affected by bad weather and most conducive to the best possible use of their immensely superior strength in armour, artillery and aircraft.

And how superior was the Allied strength was well known to Alexander and his senior subordinates. During the winter, Kesselring had been forced to part with one armoured and three infantry divisions, but it is usually claimed that at the start of the final Allied offensive, there were twenty-three German divisions, plus the equivalent of four more of Italians loyal to Mussolini, opposing Alexander's seventeen. These figures though, need a great deal of qualification, for there were a number of other factors which are rarely taken into account.

For instance, not only did most of Alexander's divisions contain considerably more troops than did the German ones, but he also controlled six independent armoured brigades and four independent infantry brigades, which gave him the equivalent of at least three more divisions. The Italians were now playing a full part in the Allied Order of Battle, and as well as manning two of the independent infantry brigades, they had formed six separate smaller combat groups. On a count of heads, Alexander had a total of 606,000 men under his command, not to mention 60,000 Italian partisans who were active behind the German lines, forcing them to divert their efforts from their more important tasks. The Axis numbers amounted to just under 600,000 men, of which only 491,000 were German, 45,000 of which were anti-aircraft personnel.

In equipment, the balance vastly favoured the Allies. They had a superiority of two to one in artillery pieces and of three to one in armour, quite apart from the fact that all the German mobile units were desperately short of fuel. They had the new specialized vehicles – the 'funnies', as they were called. As for their aerial dominance, suffice it to say that when the Eighth Army offensive opened on 9 April, it was supported by 825 heavy bombers which dropped 175,000 fragmentation bombs on defensive positions, 234 medium bombers which dropped 24,000 20-pound incendiaries on gun positions, and 740 fighter-bombers which delivered a series of strikes on forward troops and such targets as headquarters and command posts.

Alexander's confidence must have been still further increased by his knowledge that on 8 March, General Karl Wolff, the supreme head of the SS in Italy, had met with Allen Dulles, the chief of the American Office of Strategic Services in Switzerland, in order to discuss the possible surrender of German forces in Italy. Alexander took no personal part in the negotiations, though he did later send Intelligence officers to talk with Wolff; nor could he be certain that the negotiations would bear fruit. Nonetheless, the very fact that they had been opened by the most powerful enemy officer in Italy, apart from the Commander-in-Chief, showed that many responsible Germans realized that their situation was perilous in the extreme.

The senior German military commanders were, indeed, aware that their only chance of effective resistance lay in repeating their previous tactics by falling back in good order through a series of intermediate positions, of which the most important were first the

Reno, then the Po, until they reached their major defensive system. This was the Venetian Line, which conceded the north-west of Italy to the Allies, but blocked their line of advance into Austria. It ran from the Alps near the Swiss border, to meet the deep, wide and fast-flowing Adige, Italy's largest river apart from the Po, near Verona; after which it followed the Eugenian Hills, just north of that river, to the Adriatic, which the Adige enters between the estuary of the Po and the city of Venice.

Unfortunately for the defenders, Hitler was not prepared to contemplate such a major withdrawal, or even a limited tactical one which might disrupt the Allied offensive. Perhaps, therefore, the greatest of all Allied advantages was that on 8 March, Kesselring had been called to Berlin, where he was told by Hitler that he was to leave Italy and become the new C-in-C, West, opposing Eisenhower. In the past, Kesselring had ordered evacuations first and advised OKW afterwards, and even at this late date he was sufficiently independent of mind and sufficiently trusted by the Führer to make it probable that he would risk ignoring the orders to stand his ground as soon as it was obviously dangerous to do so. Von Vietinghoff, who succeeded him, would also eventually order a retreat, but only after it was far too late to have any hope of averting disaster.

At 1400 on 9 April, Alexander's last offensive – code-named Operation GRAPESHOT – began with those massive strikes by the Allied Air Forces already described. These prepared the way for Eighth Army to break over the River Senio, which then formed the front line. When the fighter-bombers came in for the final time at 1920, they made only a 'dummy run' to keep the defenders' heads down, and at the same moment, the infantry advanced, supported by over 1,000 artillery pieces and by the new flame-throwing tanks.

The Germans had been aware that the attack was coming, although the main thrust was not delivered along Route 9 as expected but well to the north of this. The strength of the aerial and artillery support had not been anticipated either. Keightley's V Corps had been entrusted with the main assault, with the Polish Corps on its left, and X and XIII Corps – the latter now back under Eighth Army's control – holding positions in the mountains between the Poles and the Americans. 8th Indian and 2nd New

Zealand Divisions crossed the Senio with minimal casualties, took 1,300 prisoners, and pressed on to the next river, the Santerno; the Poles, who had met heavier resistance, advanced only a little less rapidly. On the morning of 11 April, the two V Corps divisions crossed the Santerno under another barrage by guns, bombers and the terrifying flame-throwers, and the leading formations of the Polish Corps had followed suit by the 12th.

Attention now turned to the Route 16 line of advance. Another of Keightley's divisions, 78th (British), also crossed the Santerno, then swung northwards to head for the Bastia Bridge. Meanwhile, one brigade of his 56th (British) Division struck across the lower reaches of the Reno, and a second one was carried over the flooded areas along the shores of Lake Comacchio in the new 'Fantails' of 9th (British) Armoured Brigade. By 12 April, 56th Division's two brigades had joined forces and by the evening of the 13th, its third brigade had made a wider sweep over the lake in the 'Fantails', to put further pressure on the defenders of Bastia from the flank and rear. It was, however, to 78th Division, carried in the new 'Kangaroos' – which proved invaluable in reducing casualties – that the bridge fell on 14 April, before it could be more than partially demolished.

Both 56th and 78th Division then combined to move up to a canal, called the Fossa Marina, which provided the main defensive line in front of Argenta. Ferocious fighting lasted throughout 16 April, but on the 17th, assisted by heavy air attacks, the British were able to secure bridgeheads on the canal's far bank. Argenta was taken next day, and by the 20th, V Corps was through the 'Gap', while 6th (British) Armoured Division had been brought up from Eighth Army Reserve to exploit success in the open country beyond.

Alexander had intended that Fifth Army should join in the offensive on 12 April, the delay ensuring that the enemy would be looking elsewhere when Truscott attacked, and that Eighth and Fifth Armies in turn could both enjoy the support of the maximum number of aircraft. Another spell of bad weather had resulted in a postponement, but, mercifully, this was of brief duration. At 0945 on the 14th, raids by 500 warplanes preceded the American assault, and next day, 1,500 tons of bombs were dropped on the units directly opposing the attackers, while 800 tons more fell on targets farther behind the enemy lines.

Truscott's initial objectives were Bologna and Route 9, the Via Emilia. II US Corps, which at this time controlled 6th South African Armoured as well as three American infantry divisions, moved on the city from the south and south-west. At the same time, the Polish Corps, 8th Indian and 2nd New Zealand Divisions from V Corps, and XIII Corps, which in practice now contained only 10th Indian Division, all attacked towards Bologna from the south-east. On the left flank of II US Corps, 1st US Armoured Division, the Brazilian Division and 10th US Mountain Division, which together made up IV US Corps, also pushed forward.

It was 10th US Mountain Division, fighting in the conditions for which it had been specifically trained, that made the most rapid progress. By 17 April, it had broken through the enemy defences. 90th Panzer Grenadier Division tried to intervene, only to lose most of its tanks in a savage clash with 1st US Armoured. By the evening of 20 April, 10th US Mountain had cut Route 9 north-west of Bologna and 6th South African Armoured and 88th US Infantry Divisions from II US Corps had cut it just to the west of Bologna. The city was entered by both the Americans from the west and the Poles from the east the following day.

Also on 20 April, von Vietinghoff nervously informed Hitler that he had had to order a retreat to the Po to save his forces from being destroyed – though it was already almost certain that they would be destroyed in any case. The ceaseless Allied air raids had wrecked the enemy lines of communication and, according to von Senger und Etterlin, had 'made the fuel and ammunition situation very critical'. Strafing fighters and fighter-bombers, which could be called upon at a moment's notice through the 'Rover David'/'Cab Rank' system, attacked all forms of transport. Rocket-firing Hurricanes were directed against enemy tanks. The 'very presence over the battlefield' of the Allied airmen, lamented von Vietinghoff, 'paralysed movement'.

Conversely, the Allied armoured formations at last had the advantage of freedom of movement. They proved more cautious than had been hoped, but there was no possibility that the German mobile divisions, by now having to abandon their own tanks because of a lack of fuel, could stop them. 6th South African Armoured pushed north, then north-east from Bologna; 6th

(British) Armoured north-west from Argenta. Enemy units south of their lines of advance were compelled to destroy petrol and ammunition dumps, before beginning a desperate withdrawal, but on 23 April, the two armoured divisions met at a village with the singularly apt name of Finale, trapping and forcing the surrender of great numbers of Germans, including the 1st and 4th Parachute Divisions.

Those enemy troops who had not been cut off fell back in confusion to the River Po only to find that the Allied Air Forces had got there first. Bridges and ferries had been destroyed, and the only Germans who were able to escape had to swim to safety, leaving behind their guns, tanks, transport and other equipment. 'North of the river,' reports von Senger und Etterlin, 'we were no longer an army.'

Further resistance was impossible and during 24 and 25 April, Fifth and Eighth Army crossed the Po, while the Germans, closely pursued and harried from the air, fled to the Adige, where again they escaped only at the cost of abandoning any remaining equipment. Both Allied armies crossed the river on the 27th. Two days earlier, there had been a general uprising on the part of the Italian partisans, and such important cities as Milan, Turin and Venice were already firmly in their hands by the time the Allied soldiers reached them.

General Wolff's desire to bring about a surrender was now belatedly fulfilled and, on 28 April, his representatives and those of von Vietinghoff arrived at Alexander's Headquarters at Caserta. At 1400 next day, they signed the document authorizing the unconditional surrender of all German troops in Italy; this took effect on 2 May, when nearly a million men laid down their arms. Alexander was not present at the signing, being represented by his Chief of Staff, Lieutenant General Morgan and, with that perversity that so often dogged his career, his tremendous achievement attracted much less attention than it deserved, being quickly overshadowed by still greater capitulations elsewhere.

It was also on 28 May that a Communist murder squad shot Mussolini, his brave and beautiful mistress Clara Petacchi, who tried desperately to shield him, and fifteen others guilty of such 'crimes' as being the dictator's secretary or his personal pilot. The bodies were then mutilated by a mob and put on display in a garage forecourt. It was a sordid end to the great saga of Italy's liberation, but worse was to follow.

Taking advantage of the German invasion of Russia, 40,000 Cossacks – men, women and children – had migrated to northern Italy. Here they were joined by compatriots who had moved to western Europe after the Russian revolution, and many of the men subsequently served in the German armed forces. They were all now rounded up and forcibly returned to Russia, where they were slaughtered without mercy. Some 30,000 Yugoslavs, mainly Croats, both soldiers and civilians, who had opposed the Communist faction there, were similarly handed over and later killed or left to die in prison. It is impossible to read about these actions and the lies and broken promises that accompanied them without revulsion, but it is grossly unjust that Alexander has some-times been held responsible; nor was he the man to be appeased by attempts to transfer the blame onto the equally innocent Macmillan. The whole business had, in fact, been arranged months before at the Yalta Conference in February, and the guilt must lie with those who knew so little about the Communist regimes that they admired and trusted them.

It seems even more unjust that such tragic events have still further overshadowed and soured Alexander's triumph. But then Alexander was never greatly concerned whether he received his full measure of praise and recognition or not. As Churchill had long ago realized, for Alexander 'duty was a full satisfaction in itself, especially if it seemed perilous and hard'.

Notes:
1. It should be pointed out that America's political and military leaders genuinely, if mistakenly, believed that Alexander would still have sufficient forces left to drive the Germans out of Italy in any case. Marshall, indeed, thought at this time that Kesselring would volun-tarily withdraw to the line of the Alps.

2. Brazil had declared war on Germany (and Italy) on 22 August 1942, following repeated attacks by U-boats on Brazilian merchant ships. During Alexander's first visit to the Brazilian Division, its Headquarters was shelled and one unlucky sentry was killed. Alexander, of course, remained completely unperturbed, his calm bearing providing just that boost to morale which the newcomers needed.

3. Equally, Clark would later praise Leese as 'a magnificent soldier', 'a fine officer' and 'a good strategist', and report that 'we got along beautifully'. It should be added that the two men remained in friendly contact with each other after the war.
4. Kesselring had suffered a fractured skull when his car was struck by the barrel of a mobile gun emerging from a side turning on the night of 25/26 October. He resumed his post in mid-January 1945.

Conclusion

On 1 October 1945, when Alexander relinquished his command, it would appear that he did so more with relief than with regret. As early as September 1944, Macmillan had noticed that Alexander looked 'rather tired, even strained', and had felt that 'these continuous five years of command, almost always in conditions of great anxiety, have left their mark on him.' Alexander never lost his overriding sense of duty or his determination to complete the liberation of Italy, and Nigel Nicolson records that, when he visited the Headquarters of 1st Guards Brigade, of which Nicolson was Intelligence Officer, again in late 1944, he stated that Fifteenth Army Group must and would continue its advance. Yet he added, almost to himself, 'I'll be glad when it's all over. I suppose they'll want me to govern some Dominion or other. But all I shall want to do is to paint and fish.'

Alexander did, indeed, serve as Governor-General of a Dominion, as the self-governing parts of the British Commonwealth were then called, and of the largest of them, Canada, from 1946 to 1952. It was a position which required him to make few decisions, but he gained widespread praise for his tact and diplomacy, and both he and his wife won all hearts by their genuine and obvious interest in the country and its people. In late 1951, Churchill returned to office as Prime Minister, and in March 1952, he called on Alexander to support him by becoming his Minister of Defence. Alexander agreed, out of loyalty to his former chief, but, although his action earned him his earldom, he was neither successful nor happy in his role, loathed political intrigue, and gladly went into retirement in October 1954. The following year, he received an appointment which was far more to his taste: President of the MCC. It was typical of Alexander that during his year of office, it was said that he made everyone he met feel important, because to him they were.

Alexander did manage to find plenty of time to paint, especially when on holiday with his close friend and ardent admirer, the artist Edward Seago, who considered that painting probably gave Alexander 'some of the happiest hours of his life'. A collection of Alexander's paintings, with an introduction by Seago, was published in 1973. It would doubtless have pleased Alexander greatly but, sadly, he did not see it, for he had died on 16 June 1969, at the age of seventy-seven.

In his introduction, Seago commented that he was particularly struck by 'the sense of enthusiasm and enjoyment' that was so obvious in Alexander's paintings. No evidence of similar feelings could be found in Alexander's *Memoirs*, which appeared in 1962. Although they had been promoted with the promise that they would provide the final judgement on numerous aspects of the Second World War, they not only did nothing of the kind, but in Nicolson's opinion, indicated that Alexander 'had not really wanted to take the trouble'. In fact, they reflected the impression that Alexander often gave, of regarding his own immense achievements as rather uninteresting and unremarkable.

Modesty of this kind can have, and in Alexander's case, did have regrettable consequences. Others took him at his word and also began to find his achievements less interesting and less remarkable than they had appeared at first glance. Their attitude was aided by the fact that Alexander was singularly unlucky in the timing of his successes. Apart from the surrender of the Axis forces in Tunisia, most of these did not make the impact that they deserved, because they were quickly followed and overshadowed by greater events: the capture of Sicily by the Italian surrender; the capture of Rome by the D-Day landings; the final victory in Italy by the end of the war in Europe. In addition, Alexander's accomplishment of diverting to, or holding in Italy substantial forces that the Germans could better have employed elsewhere, was not one that could be proclaimed at the time, and would probably have aroused little enthusiasm if it had been.

For some commentators, it then proved a short step from indifference and underestimation to belittlement. Worse still, they did not have to look far to find corroboration from seemingly impeccable sources. It is reported that one senior officer, who had quarrelled with Montgomery, refused to comment further on the subject because he had found that 'those who criticise Monty loudest' were 'so uniformly second-rate' that he did not wish to be associated with them. Unfortunately, it is not possible to dismiss all of Alexander's critics so easily.

Even Brooke, though warmly supporting him when he was the object of undeserved abuse from Churchill, was not an unquestioning admirer of Alexander, whom he felt possessed only some of the qualities needed by a commander. Yet it was Brooke who had been prepared to entrust Alexander with the forlorn hope of Burma, the control of the Middle East at the moment of its greatest peril, the task of ending the alarming confusion in Tunisia and the duty of leading multi-national forces of varied quality through all the dangers and difficulties of the Italian campaigns. It seems fair to claim, therefore, that he accepted that Alexander's virtues far outweighed his alleged deficiencies.

In any case, Brooke's criticisms were cautious and restrained. The same cannot be said of the criticisms of other important and undoubtedly able commanders, and when those who later examined Alexander's career read that he was 'a mountebank' (Cunningham), 'bone from the neck up' (Tuker), who did not have 'the faintest idea of what was going on' (Slim), and 'cut a sorry figure at all times' (Patton), who can blame them for being dismissive? These and similar attacks have already been quoted as and when they arose and, it is hoped, have already been explained and answered. Suffice it, then, to repeat that they occurred mainly because his detractors either did not understand Alexander's character or did not appreciate the nature and extent of Alexander's responsibilities.

It was perhaps not surprising that Alexander's personality remained a mystery to many. His experience, his reputation, his aristocratic background, his political connections, even his unfailingly immaculate appearance, all tended to make him seem a little distant, a little different, a little detached from those who would otherwise have been considered his peers. Moreover he valued and guarded his privacy. Officers who served closely with him over long periods of time, such as McCreery and Harding, still found, in the latter's words, that 'he was a character whom it was extremely difficult to know.'

Some of his virtues, of course, were so obvious that none of his detractors have ever attempted to deny them. All accepted that, as Clark put it, 'Alex was a gentleman in every meaning of the word.' All acknowledged his charm, his unselfishness and his complete honesty. All admired his inspirational courage – except perhaps Slim, who preferred to call this 'foolhardy' – and his sense of duty. But they were forceful, forthright individuals, who were not particularly impressed by his modesty and who did not think to look for the motives which lay behind the cool, confident poise with which he confronted every situation.

In these attitudes and omissions lay the source of the trouble. As we have seen repeatedly, Alexander felt it his duty never to appear ruffled or upset or worried, but to maintain his composure at all times and radiate a confidence which he did not necessarily feel. By doing so, he achieved wonders for morale, but he led those who found it less easy to hide their disquiet to the erroneous conclusion that he had not appreciated how difficult and dangerous the situation really was.

This determination always to appear optimistic, when coupled with Alexander's innate courtesy, led to another cause of error. When a definite decision had been reached by his superiors, Alexander would never reveal any doubts which he might have – and sometimes did have. One reason why he was Churchill's favourite general was his steadfast loyalty. Again, though, it did mean that others who had justifiable concerns were apt, on occasions, to conclude that Alexander's own judgement was at fault.

At the same time, it must be said that his courtesy, and perhaps his modesty, were responsible for one of Alexander's genuine faults. He would often not argue strongly enough in favour of courses of action in which he personally believed. Examples which might be given include: his lack of persistence in advocating a landing on the Italian mainland during the course of the Sicilian campaign; his refraining from exploding Eisenhower's unrealistic projects at a time when Italy was on the point of surrender; his neglecting to give direct orders to Clark and Lucas to take forceful, if limited, action after the landings at Anzio; and his reluctance to make it very clear to Clark at the outset of DIADEM that when the breakout from Anzio took place, it must be directed towards Valmontone and no variation from this requirement was to be permitted.

Another aspect of the same fault was that, while Alexander could be blunt when he felt this to be essential, such as in his assessment of his American troops after he had taken control of Eighteenth Army Group, he tried, whenever possible, to avoid hurting or offending anyone. Hence his agreement to Auchinleck's selfish and dangerous desire to postpone the date of the handover of the Middle East and Eighth Army Commands, his preference that it should be the Americans who decided whether senior American officers, whom he personally believed to be inadequate, should be superceded, and his reluctance to replace members of his own Administrative staff when they failed him badly.

It could be argued that a further fault, arising from the same traits, was Alexander's tendency to request the opinions of others, rather than laying down clear, decisive objectives and leaving his staff to do no more than work out the details. Certainly more demanding and perhaps more strong-willed officers considered this a fault and Brooke, in a moment of exasperation, complained that Alexander 'had no ideas of his own and always sought someone to lean on'. Yet the only occasion when Alexander might be said to have abrogated responsibility was when he allowed the planners of Force 141 to determine the basic structure of Operation HUSKEY, the invasion of Sicily – and at that time he was distracted by the needs of the complicated situation in Tunisia. Moreover, when Montgomery took charge of the plans, altering most of them, Alexander backed him completely – it is worth recalling that Alexander almost always did back the 'winning horse'; and also that, whoever had had the ideas, it was Alexander who would shoulder the blame in the event of failure.

His willingness to listen and his desire to reach decisions by consent if possible, did, in fact, serve Alexander well in his various posts of Commander-in-Chief, Middle East, Deputy to Eisenhower in North Africa, Eighteenth Army Group Commander, Fifteenth Army Group Commander and finally Supreme Commander, Mediterranean. In all of these, his duty and his aim was to ensure that the Allied land, naval and air forces were a united team, that the best possible relationship was established with Britain's great

American ally, whose leaders, as he knew, were not particularly eager for commitments in the Mediterranean, and that the diverse conglomerate of formations under his command all pulled together for the common good.

It cannot be repeated too often that all Alexander's actions, both in North Africa and in Italy, were guided by these principles. It can be claimed that some, such as his allowing Patton to drive for Palermo, had an adverse effect on the purely military situation, while others, such as his failure to discipline Clark for his disobedience in the last stages of DIADEM, might be interpreted as signs of weakness – but then it is necessary to consider the possible consequences had Alexander acted otherwise. Those able officers who condemned his conduct were perfectly sincere but their viewpoints were limited. They were concerned with the interests of their country, service, army, corps or division. None of them remembered that Alexander had much wider responsibilities and had to take a much wider view: he had to consider the Allied cause as a whole.

Nor can it be repeated too often that Alexander succeeded in performing his duty and attaining his aim. It is a major misfortune that all these criticisms and arguments have tended to mask the number and extent of Alexander's achievements. Before reviewing these, however, it seems desirable to correct another misapprehension. General Sir William Jackson in *Alexander of Tunis as Military Commander*, assesses Alexander as 'a sound but uninspired strategist and an intuitive tactician'; while Nigel Nicolson declares more forcefully that 'As a tactician he [Alexander] had no rival but as a strategist he lacked profound foresight.' It is suggested, with some trepidation, the exact opposite was really the case.

In the most simple terms, the military tactician plans and fights battles, directing his soldiers in action and, during the Second World War, coordinating their efforts with those of their supporting airmen. The military strategist decides ultimate objectives and thereby, in effect, determines not how but where battles are fought. It is difficult to consider Alexander a tactician without rival when he was rarely called upon to be a tactician at all. His tactics during the retreat to Dunkirk were sensible but scarcely inspired and cannot be said to have risen as high as, let alone higher than those demonstrated by Brooke or Montgomery. Admirable as was his conduct during the evacuation itself, this was a display of intuitive leadership, not of intuitive tactics. And prior to the fall of Rangoon, his only really valuable action in Burma was his strategic decision to get his soldiers out of the jaws of a fast-closing trap while there was still time.

Thereafter, Alexander left the tactics to his Corps Commander in Burma and his Army and Corps Commanders in the Middle East, North Africa and Italy, and rarely added to their difficulties by interfering with them. Sensible, generous and usually beneficial though this forbearance might be, it must be conceded that Alexander occasionally carried the principle too far. In Burma, Slim was permitted to continue with his futile and dangerous counter-attacks for much too long before Alexander stepped in with another strategic decision – to withdraw his men altogether from what had become an impossible situation. In Italy, Alexander's American subordinates were sometimes not given the firm directions that would have been desirable. In the Middle East, accepting that time was desperately short, his own responsibilities were immense and he was well aware of his trusted lieutenant's professional ability, it still seems surprising that Alexander did not know what Montgomery's plans were for fighting the crucial Battle of Alam Halfa.

On the other hand, Alexander was a very fine strategist, and even when his hopes were not fulfilled, this was rarely the result of any lack of strategic foresight. If anything, he was sometimes too far-sighted and he found some strategic projects, such as the landing at Anzio or the proposed advance through northern Italy and Austria to Vienna, so obviously attractive in principle that he overlooked, in his eagerness, the short-term tactical problems that they entailed.

In most cases though, Alexander's strategy was very successful and this was all the more to his credit because, during the Second World War, the tasks of the military strategist had increased enormously; in earlier years, he had been concerned mainly with the movement of his forces: when, by what route and with what ultimate objective they should advance; if they should retreat and how they could best do so safely should this prove necessary. Coupled with and greatly influencing these questions was the need to establish secure supply lines, so that his troops could receive the equipment they would need and reinforcements could be sent to them with the minimum of delay.

That Alexander was well aware of these matters and more than capable of taking the necessary decisions goes without saying; that his decisions were usually the right ones can be judged from the results that he and his men achieved. Yet, because warfare had become so complicated and the Second World War in particular was fought over such a vast area, Alexander, from the moment that he became Commander-in-Chief, Middle East, had to be concerned not only with the campaigns which he was fighting but also the requirements of other operational areas; not only with military matters but also with naval and air force affairs.

Fortunately, Alexander's breadth of vision enabled him to resolve such issues almost instinctively. On arrival in the Middle East, for instance, he immediately understood the crucial importance of Malta as a base from which the enemy's seaborne supplies could be disrupted, and hence the need to gain the Martuba airfields so that fighter cover could be provided for the convoys sustaining the island. He saw at once that the most important prizes in southern Italy were Naples, as a port to which his own supplies could be brought, and Foggia, from the landing grounds of which Allied airmen could strike at targets in south-central Europe long before any soldiers could reach them. Above all, he recognized the need for his thankless and often criticized task of maintaining pressure on the Gustav Line in appallingly difficult conditions so as to compel the Germans to retain forces in Italy which might have proved decisive on other fronts.

Throughout the war, Alexander also had to adjust his strategy so as to respect and comply with the wishes and prejudices of Britain's Allies. He had realized the need for this early, as a result of the problems he had encountered with the French at Dunkirk and with the Chinese in Burma. In consequence, he had quickly become a diplomatist as well as a soldier, on whose determination to strengthen Allied unity we have so often had occasion to remark. That determination would cause most of the adverse comments that have been directed against him, but it won the admiration of Churchill and Macmillan, while Eisenhower, whose responsibilities and difficulties were similar, would declare that: 'I regarded

Alexander as Britain's outstanding soldier in the field of strategy.' It was also one of the main reasons why, first in Tunisia and later in Italy, he was able to hold together multi-national armies in the face of disappointments and setbacks, and lead them to victory over very tough and well-commanded enemies, fighting, in Italy at least, in ideal defensive country.

The other main reason was that he was himself a natural leader and his influence over his soldiers and the confidence that he inspired in them was increased because they not only respected but trusted him. This trust in turn arose from their knowledge that, for all the great commands that he held, and all the great affairs with which he had to deal, he never lost his interest in them or his concern for their welfare. It is notable that the only times he was prepared to risk a rift in inter-Allied or inter-Service unity came when he was sure that the needs of his men demanded this.

It was on the twin bases of his skill as a strategist and his effectiveness as a leader that Alexander's successes were achieved. As has been seen, his career divides into two parts. During the years when first the Allies were experiencing a whole series of defeats and then the issue was trembling in the balance, Alexander made his name by rescuing or rallying defeated armies – at Dunkirk, in Burma, in the Middle East, in North Africa. There is no need to elaborate on these episodes again here, but the sheer number of them should be emphasized: no one else could equal or even approach such a record.

In the last two cases, the armies in question were not only rallied but, given confidence in place of doubt and direction in place of uncertainty, they responded by embarking on successful offensives. Perhaps, however, the most notable contribution which Alexander made to the Allied advance to final victory – and certainly the largest in point of time – was his liberation of Italy, first from her own domestic tyrant, then from her German army of occupation. These campaigns have also been described in detail, but it seems important to add a rider on one particular aspect of them, for it was in Italy that Alexander, because he regarded the needs of his soldiers as transcending all other considerations, authorized the action for which he has been the most roundly condemned.

The destruction of the monastery at Monte Cassino is probably the best-known event in the Italian campaigns – and it is grossly unjust that this should be the case. War, by definition, brings death and devastation, and the fighting in Italy saw far more horrible incidents than the bombing of a historic sacred building: the atrocities which the Germans and the Italian partisans committed against each other; the shooting of Italian prisoners in Sicily as the result of Patton's ill-considered instructions; the conduct of the French colonial troops, the Goumiers, whose reputation was so sinister that it can only be hoped that this was grossly exaggerated. Nor is it often recalled that the monastery's main treasures had been removed earlier and the building itself would be rebuilt and reconsecrated in 1964. Yet the real reason why it may be claimed that its fate has been unfairly emphasized is that this was a very marked exception to the spirit in which Alexander normally conducted his campaigns.

'What a pity it is to maul this beautiful country,' Alexander had remarked to Nigel Nicolson, and he made every effort to maul it as little as possible. Saint Benedict's monastery may have been sacrificed but Alexander steadfastly rejected bellicose suggestions from Churchill, among others, that Rome should be bombed. When his troops were halted on the Arno, he personally gave orders that Florence was not to be bombed or shelled. He considered it a matter of pride, as he told Macmillan, that he had saved cities such as Pisa, Siena and Perugia, as well as Rome and Florence, from all except minor damage.

By limiting the harm done to cities, Alexander automatically saved many of their inhabitants from death or injury. He liked the Italians and tried hard to protect them from the miseries inherent in the conflict. Even in Sicily, at a time when a state of war still existed between his country and theirs, Alexander did what he could to assist the civilian population, aiding refugees, returning any lorries that had been requisitioned as soon as possible and ensuring an income for large numbers of them by employing them to repair roads and harbours.

Alexander can scarcely have had much affection for the Germans, but, just as he had never made the same mistake as Wavell and Slim by underestimating the Japanese, so he respected his enemies in Italy. He did not hesitate, for example, to acknowledge the quality of the 'Para boys' who had thwarted his every effort to break through at Cassino. He directed his operations, so far as was within his power, in strict accordance with the laws and customs of warfare, and it is reported that German prisoners were astonished, and presumably relieved, at the good treatment they received. In consequence, the most determined actions were fought fiercely but fairly and both sides, for instance, allowed medical personnel to carry out their work of mercy without let or hindrance.

The most generous of Alexander's acts, however, was reserved until after the war. In 1947, a British military tribunal declared that his most dangerous opponent, Field Marshal Kesselring, was responsible for the killing of Italian hostages in retaliation for a partisan bomb attack, and sentenced him to be shot. The verdict horrified most independent observers who felt that no consideration had been given to the fact that the real responsibility had been that of SS officers who were, at most, only nominally under Kesselring's command. Alexander protested strongly against the sentence. So also did Churchill and Leese, but it was mainly as the result of Alexander's intervention that Kesselring's penalty was commuted to twenty years imprisonment, and he was released, officially on grounds of ill-health, in 1952.

His absence of hatred or malice provides the final evidence that Alexander brought a humane spirit even to the often horrible war in Italy; that he came not as a conqueror but as a liberator. Not that anyone who knew him could ever have doubted this. Alexander's character was a complex one but the last word on it can safely be left to Field Marshal Montgomery, who had an uncanny knack of simplifying issues and whose judgement is the more significant in that it was made at the exact moment when he was most displeased with his superior's decisions in Sicily and plans for future operations on the Italian mainland. 'Alexander,' he noted in his diary, 'is the nicest chap I have ever known.'

Bibliography

Alexander, Field Marshal the Earl, 'The African Campaign from El Alamein to Tunis', *London Gazette*, 1948.

Alexander, Field Marshal the Earl, *The Alexander Memoirs*, Cassell, 1962.

Alexander, Field Marshal the Earl, 'The Allied Armies in Italy', *London Gazette*, 1950.

Alexander, Field Marshal the Earl, 'The Conquest of Sicily', *London Gazette*, 1948.

Arnold-Foster, Mark, *The World at War*, Collins, 1973.

Blaxland, Gregory, *Alexander's Generals*, Kimber, 1979.

Bryant, Sir Arthur, *The Turn of the Tide 1939–1943*, Collins, 1959.

Bryant, Sir Arthur, *Triumph in the West 1943–1946*, Collins, 1959.

Carell, Paul, *The Foxes of the Desert: The Story of the Afrika Korps*, Macdonald, 1960.

Carew Tim, *The Longest Retreat: The Burma Campaign 1942*, Hamish Hamilton, 1969.

Carver, Field Marshal Lord, *Dilemmas of the Desert War: A New Look at the Libyan Campaign 1940–1942*, Batsford, 1986.

Carver, Field Marshal Lord, *El Alamein*, Batsford, 1962.

Carver, Field Marshal Lord, *Harding of Petherton*, Weidenfeld & Nicolson, 1978.

Carver, Field Marshal Lord, *The Imperial War Museum Book of the War in Italy 1943-1945*, Sidgwick & Jackson, 2001.

Carver, Field Marshal Lord, *Out of Step* (Memoirs), Hutchinson, 1989.

Churchill, Sir Winston, *The Second World War*, vol. IV, *The Hinge of Fate*, Cassell, 1951; vol. V, *Closing the Ring*, Cassell, 1952; vol. VI, *Triumph and Tragedy*, Cassell, 1954.

Clark, General Mark, *Calculated Risk*, George G. Harrap & Co, 1951.

Clarke, Sir Rupert, *With Alex at War: From the Irrawaddy to the Po 1941–1945*, Leo Cooper, 2000.

Cloake, John, *Templer: Tiger of Malaya*, George G. Harrap & Co., 1985.

Collier, Richard, *The Sands of Dunkirk*, Collins, 1961.

Connell, John, *Auchinleck*, Cassell, 1959.

Connell, John and Roberts, Brigadier Michael, *Wavell: Supreme Commander*, Collins, 1969.

de Guingand, Major General Sir Francis, *Generals at War*, Hodder & Stoughton, 1964.

de Guingand, Major General Sir Francis, *Operation Victory*, Hodder & Stoughton, 1947.

d'Este, Carlo, *Bitter Victory*, Collins, 1988.

d'Este, Carlo, *Fatal Decision*, Harper Collins, 1991.

Ellis, John, *Cassino: The Hollow Victory*, Andre Deutsch, 1984.

Follain, John, *Mussolini's Island*, Hodder & Stoughton, 2005.

Fraser, General Sir David, *Alanbrooke*, Collins, 1982.

Fraser, General Sir David, *And We Shall Shock Them: The British Army in the Second World War*, Hodder & Stoughton, 1983.

Fuller, Major General J.F.C., *The Second World War 1939–1945*, Eyre & Spottiswoode, 1948 (Revised Edition 1954).

Gribble, Philip, *Off the Cuff*, J.M. Dent & Sons, 1964.

Hamilton, Nigel, *Monty: The Battles of Field Marshal Bernard Law Montgomery*, Hodder & Stoughton, 1994.

Hamilton, Nigel, *Monty: The Making of a General 1887–1942*, Hamish Hamilton, 1981.

Hamilton, Nigel, *Monty: Master of the Battlefield 1942–1944*, Hamish Hamilton, 1983.

Harpur, Bryan, *The Impossible Victory*, Kimber, 1980.

Hibbert, Christopher, *Anzio: The Bid for Rome*, Macdonald, 1970.

Hinsley, F.H. with Thomas, E.E., Ransom, C.F.G. and Knight, R.C., *British Intelligence in the Second World War: Its Influence on Strategy and Operations*, vol. II, HMSO, 1981.

Holland, James, *Together We Stand*, HarperCollins, 2005.

Horrocks, Lieutenant General Sir Brian, *A Full Life*, Collins, 1960.

Jackson, Robert, *Dunkirk*, Arthur Barker, 1976.

Jackson, General Sir William, *Alexander of Tunis as Military Commander*, Batsford, 1971.

Jackson, General Sir William, *The Battle for Italy*, Batsford, 1967.

Jackson, General Sir William, *The Battle for Rome*, Batsford 1969.

Jackson, General Sir William, *The North African Campaign 1940–43*, Batsford, 1975.

Kesselring, Field Marshal Albert, *Memoirs*, Kimber, 1963.

Kippenberger, Major General Sir Howard, *Infantry Brigadier*, Oxford University Press, 1949.

Lewin, Ronald, *Ultra Goes to War: The Secret Story*, Hutchinson, 1978.

Liddell Hart, Captain B.H., *History of the Second World War*, Cassell, 1970.

Llewellyn, Harry, *Passports to Life: Journeys into Many Worlds*, Hutchinson, 1980.

Lucas Phillips, Brigadier C.E., *Alamein*, Heinemann, 1962.

Lunt, Major General James, *A Hell of a Licking: The Retreat from Burma 1941–2*, Collins, 1986.

Macintyre, Captain Donald, *The Battle for the Mediterranean*, Batsford 1964.

Macmillan, Harold, *The Blast of War*, Macmillan, 1967.

Majdalany, Fred, *Cassino: Portrait of a Battle*, Longmans, Green & Co, 1957.

Molony, Brigadier, C.J.C., *The Mediterranean and Middle East*, vol. V: *The Campaign in Sicily 1943 and the Campaign in Italy, 3rd September 1943 to 31st March 1944*, HMSO, 1973.

Molony, Brigadier, C.J.C. and Jackson, General Sir William with Gleave, Group Captain T.P., *The Mediterranean and Middle East*, vol. VI, *Victory in the Mediterranean*, HMSO, 1973.

Montgomery, Field Marshal the Viscount, *El Alamein to the River Sangro*, Hutchinson, 1948.

Montgomery, Field Marshal the Viscount, *Memoirs*, Collins, 1958.

Moorehead, Alan, *Eclipse*, Hamish Hamilton, 1967.

Moorehead, Alan, *The Desert War: The North African Campaign 1940–1943*, Hamish Hamilton, 1965.

Nicolson, Nigel, *Alex: The Life of Field Marshal Earl Alexander of Tunis*, Weidenfeld & Nicolson, 1973.

Pack, Captain, S.C.W., *Operation Husky: The Allied Invasion of Sicily*, David & Charles, 1977.

Parker, Matthew, *Monte Cassino*, Headline, 2003.

Playfair, Major General I.S.O. with Flynn, Captain F.C., Molony, Brigadier C.J.C. and Gleave, Group Captain T.P., *The Mediterranean and Middle East*, vol. III, *British Fortunes Reach their Lowest Ebb*, HMSO, 1960.

Playfair, Major General I.S.O. and Molony, Brigadier C.J.C. with Flynn, Captain F.C. and Gleave, Group Captain T.P., *The Mediterranean and Middle East*, vol. IV, *The Destruction of the Axis Forces in Africa*, HMSO, 1966.

Richards, Denis and Saunders, Hilary St G., *Royal Air Force 1939–1945*, vol II, *The Fight Avails*, HMSO, 1954.

Richardson, General Sir Charles, *Flashback: A Soldier's Story*, Kimber, 1985.

Richardson, General Sir Charles, *From Churchill's Secret Circle to the*

BBC: The Biography of Lieutenant General Sir Ian Jacob, Brasseys (UK), 1991.

Roberts, Major General G.P.B., *From the Desert to the Baltic*, Kimber, 1987.

Rooney, David, *Wingate and the Chindits: Redressing the Balance*, Arms & Armour, 1994.

Roskill, Captain, S.W., *The War at Sea 1939–1945*, vol. II, *The Period of Balance*, HMSO, 1956; vol. III, *The Offensive*, Part I, *1st June 1943-31st May 1944*, HMSO, 1960.

Ryder, Rowland, *Oliver Leese*, Hamish Hamilton, 1987.

Saunders, Hilary St G., *Royal Air Force 1939–1945*, vol III, *The Fight is Won*, HMSO, 1954.

Sayer, Ian and Botting, Douglas, *Hitler's Last General: The Case Against Wilhelm Mohnke*, Transworld Publishers/Bantam Press, 1989.

Seaton, Albert, *The Fall of Fortress Europe 1943–1945*, Batsford, 1981.

Senger und Etterlin, General F. von, *Neither Fear nor Hope*, Macdonald, 1963.

Slim, Field Marshal the Viscount, *Defeat into Victory*, Cassell, 1956.

Smith, Brigadier E.D., *Battle for Burma*, Batsford, 1979.

Stewart, Adrian, *The Early Battles of Eighth Army*, Leo Cooper, 2002.

Stewart, Adrian, *Eighth Army's Greatest Victories*, Leo Cooper, 1999.

Trevelyan, Raleigh, *Rome '44*, Secker & Warburg, 1981.

Tuker, Major General Sir Francis, *Approach to Battle*, Cassell, 1963.

Turnbull, Patrick, *Dunkirk: Anatomy of Disaster*, Batsford, 1978.

Verney, Peter, *Anzio 1944: An Unexpected Fury*, Batsford, 1978.

Whiting, Charles, *Slaughter over Sicily*, Leo Cooper, 1992.

Willmott, H.P., *Empires in the Balance: Japanese and Allied Pacific Strategies to April 1942*, Orbis Publishing Limited, 1982.

War Diaries of the various Theatre Headquarters, armies, corps, divisions and brigades: Public Records Office, Kew.

Index

General Index

Note: All service personnel
are given the ranks they held
at the time of the incidents
described.

Aa Canal, 15
Abbeville, 11
Abrial, Admiral J., 20–2
Adige River, 236, 239
Adrano, 114, 116, 119–20
Agheila, El, 79–80
Agrigento, 115
Aircraft Types – Allied:
Albemarle (Armstrong
    Whitworth), 111, 114
Baltimore (Martin), 96, 225
Beaufighter (Bristol), 25
Blenheim (Bristol), 33
Boston, (Douglas), 96, 225
Dakota (Douglas), 26, 111,
    114
Flying Fortress (Boeing),
    146, 175, 178
Halifax (Handley Page),
    111, 114
Hurricane (Hawker), 23,
    30, 33, 86–7, 93, 96–7,
    111, 238
Kittyhawk (Curtiss), 89, 93,
    96–7, 142, 179, 225,
    228
Liberator (Consolidated),
    25, 178, 225
Lightning (Lockheed), 141,
    143, 178–9
Marauder (Martin), 175,
    178
Mitchell (North American),
    96, 175, 178
Mustang (North American),
    141
Spitfire (Supermarine),

95–6, 112, 141, 143,
    179, 228
Thunderbolt (Republic),
    178–9, 227
Tomahawk (Curtiss), 30, 33
Warhawk (Curtiss), 96–7,
    143, 178
Wellington (Vickers), 111,
    123, 178, 225
Aircraft Types – Axis
Dornier Do 217, 145
Junkers Ju 52, 76, 97
Junkers Ju 87, 11
Mitsubishi Zero, 38
Nakajima Ki 27, ('Nate'),
    38
Nakajima Ki 43, ('Oscar'),
    38
Air Forces – Allied, 19, 30,
    32–3, 65, 86–7, 95–7,
    111, 114, 123, 129, 141,
    143, 146, 157, 169,
    175–9, 196, 198, 205,
    207–8, 213, 225, 227–8,
    235–9
(See also separate entry:
    Desert Air Force)
Squadrons:
    No. 6 RAF, 93, 96; No.
    45 RAF, 33; No. 72
    RAF, 112; No. 225
    RAF, 87; No. 241
    RAF, 87; No. 250
    RAF, 93; No. 260
    RAF, 93; No. 601
    RAF, 23; No. 2
    SAAF, 97; No. 5
    SAAF, 97
Air Forces – Axis, 7–9, 11,
    15–16, 19, 20, 32–3,
    38–9, 44–5, 51, 76–9,
    83, 96–7, 105, 112–14,
    124–5, 144–5, 147, 165,
    170, 177–9, 210
Akyab, 32–3

Alamein El, 52, 59, 63, 66,
    68, 80, 90
Alamein El, Battle of, 67–71,
    74–5, 193
Alam Halfa Ridge, 67–8
Alam Halfa, Battle of, 62,
    67–8, 84, 248
Alban Hills, 162–4, 185,
    191, 205, 209, 212
Albano, 191
Albert Canal, 7
Alexander, Major General,
    later Field Marshal Sir
    H.R.L.G.:
Character and Personality,
    1– 2, 12, 13, 17, 18, 22,
    35, 39, 40, 49, 54–5,
    61–2, 64, 78, 81, 84,
    88–9, 100, 108, 119,
    136, 143–4, 153, 164,
    182–3, 190, 209, 233,
    240, 242–52
Pre-War Career, 2, 3
In Dunkirk Campaign, 3,
    10–23, 55, 66, 72, 84,
    247–50
In Burma Campaign, 3,
    25–6, 29–43, 45–9, 51,
    72, 84, 244, 248–50
In Desert Campaign, 3, 50,
    54, 58, 60–2, 64–70,
    72, 75–8, 153, 244,
    248–50
In Tunisian Campaign, 3,
    49, 69–70, 81–2,
    84–101, 107, 117, 119,
    153, 243–4, 246–8, 250
In Sicily Campaign, 105–11,
    115–19, 121, 123, 125,
    243, 245–6, 251–2
Plans Italian Campaigns,
    131–9, 245, 252
In Southern Italian
    Campaign, 134–6,
    141–54, 249

In 1943/44 Winter
    Campaign, 156–75,
    177, 179–84, 249
In Rome Campaign,
    184–94, 196, 199–201,
    203–9, 211–13, 243,
    247
In Later Italian Campaigns,
    215–37, 239–40,
    242–43, 248
In Italian Campaigns
    Generally, 2–3, 243–52
In Greek Campaign, 231–2
Post-War Career, 242–3,
    252
Achievements, 22, 39–40,
    47, 54, 62, 100–1, 145,
    242–52
Alexandria, 59, 66
Algiers, 74, 82, 89, 108, 110,
    123, 126
Allanmyo 35–6, 42
Allen, Major General T., 92,
    94
Allfrey, Lieutenant General
    C., 140
Alp Mountains, 217, 236
Ambrosio, General V., 136
Ancona, 193, 220
Anders, General W., 189–90,
    195, 199
Anderson, Lieutenant
    General Sir K., 75–8, 82,
    85, 90
Anstice, Brigadier J., 28
Anzio, 148, 158–66, 169–70,
    172, 176–9, 181, 183–6,
    190–4, 203–6, 209, 213,
    245–6, 248
Apennine Mountains, 139,
    146–8, 217, 221–2
Aprilia, 169, 177
Aquino, 202
Ardennes, 9, 11
Arezzo, 215, 220
Argenta, 237–9
Argenta Gap, 233, 237
Armies – Allied and Axis, see
    separate Index
Arnim, General J. von, 79,
    83–4, 86–7, 92, 94, 99,
    100
Arno River, 220, 251
Arras, 14
Artena, 208
Auchinleck, General Sir C.,
    51–4, 56–9, 61–3, 65–7,
    72, 78, 80, 84, 144, 246
Augusta, 112–14, 118
Arunci Mountains, 158, 189,
    197, 212, 222

Ausente River and Valley,
    197–8
Ausonia, 197
Austria, 136, 146, 217, 222,
    236, 248
Avezzano, 148, 185

Baade, Colonel E., 113, 122
Badoglio, Marshal P., 124–5,
    129, 136–9
Bald Hill, see Djebel Adjred
Bare Ridge, 68
Bari, 140, 145, 148
Barker, Lieutenant General
    M., 11, 13, 18–19, 22
Bastia, 233, 237
Beja, 87
Belgium, Campaign in, 7–12
Ben Gardene, 85
Bernhardt Line, 147–8
Biferno River, 147
Bizerta, 78, 97–8, 100
Bock, General F. von, 7–10,
    15–16
Bologna, 222–4, 227, 229,
    233, 238
Bone, 76
Borgo Grappa, 205
Bougie, 75
Boulogne, 15–16
Bourke, Brigadier, J., 40
Bradley, Major General O.,
    92, 98–100, 106, 109,
    114–15, 117–18
Brann, Brigadier General D.,
    162, 206
Brauchitsch, General H. von,
    9
Brereton, Major General L.,
    65
Brindisi, 140
Broadhurst, Air Vice
    Marshal H., 95–6, 99
Brooke, Lieutenant General,
    later Field Marshal Sir
    A., 11–13, 16, 18, 23,
    25, 49–50, 53–5, 57, 61,
    65, 78, 81–2, 84, 88,
    109, 119, 128, 135, 139,
    152–3, 217, 219, 230,
    244, 246, 248
Brown, Lieutenant A., 210
Buerat, 80
Burma, Campaign in, 24–48,
    51, 118, 141, 244,
    248–50

'Cab Rank', 157, 186, 238
Caesar Line, 185, 192, 202,
    210–12

Cairo, 25–26, 50, 53–5,
    59–63, 66, 68, 72
Calabrian Peninsula, 134
Calais, 15–16
Campoleone, 164–6, 169,
    177, 191
Cape Bon, 100
Carboni, General G., 137–8
Carleton, Colonel D., 210
Carroceto, 169, 177
Casablanca, 74, 89
Casablanca Conference, 81,
    124
Caserta, 231, 239
Casey, R., 64, 70
Cassibile, 119, 125
Cassino, 148, 155, 157, 159,
    162, 168, 170, 176–7,
    179–181, 184, 188–9,
    195–6, 198–9, 209, 251
Cassino, Battles of, 168–70,
    176–7, 179–83, 189,
    195, 198–9
Castellano, General G., 125
Castle Hill, see Point 193
Catania, 113–14, 119, 121–2
Catanzaro, 134
Centuripe, 120
Chiang, Kai-shek, 34–5, 43
Chieti, 148, 150, 215
Chindwin River, 45–7
Chott el Fedjadj (Salt
    Marsh), 90
Churchill, W.S., 1–3, 7, 18,
    21–3, 25, 33, 45, 48–51,
    53–5, 57, 61–2, 65,
    69–70, 72, 74, 76–8,
    81–2, 109–10, 128, 131,
    152–3, 158, 162, 164–6,
    170, 180–1, 199–200,
    209, 215–17, 219, 221,
    226, 230–2, 240, 242,
    244–5, 249, 251–2
Cisterna, 164–6, 169, 178,
    191, 205
Civitavecchia, 193, 215
Clark, Lieutenant General,
    later General M.W.,
    131–2, 136, 140–7, 151,
    157–8, 160–6, 169–70,
    172–7, 189–93,
    199–201, 205–19, 223,
    226–32, 241, 245, 247
Clarke, Major Sir R., 25, 35,
    50, 55, 61, 65, 68, 89,
    152, 183
Commachio, Lake, 233, 237
Compton, Captain J., 117
Conco River, 226
Coningham, Air Marshal A.,
    96

Corbett, Lieutenant General T., 54, 57
Cori, 205
Coriano Ridge, 226–7
Corsica, 125, 129
Crotone, 142
Cunningham, Admiral Sir A., 107–10, 121–3, 125, 133, 141, 143, 145, 244
Cyrenaica, 50, 86, 154

Daba El, 71
Darlan, Admiral J.F., 75, 101
Dawley, Major General E., 140, 144
De Guingand, Brigadier, later Major General Sir F., 57–8, 60, 63, 65–6, 70, 86, 134, 142
Dempsey, Lieutenant General M., 106, 133, 152
Desert Air Force, 57–8, 63, 67, 93–7, 142, 150, 157, 225
Dill, Field Marshal Sir J., 230
Dimoline, Brigadier H., 176
Dittaino River, 113
Djebel Adjred, 78, 99
Djebel el Almara, 79, 99
Djebel Azag, 78, 99
Djebel Fatnassa, 171
Djebel Tebaga, 91, 93
Djebel Tahent, 99
Dorman-Smith, Major General E., 57–9, 65, 67–8, 72, 84
Dorman-Smith, Governor Sir R., 28–30
Dorsale, Eastern (Hills), 79, 96
Dorsale, Western (Hills), 79, 84, 86
Dunkirk, 3, 11–22, 107, 141, 247–50
Dunphie, Brigadier C., 85, 89
Dyle River, 7–8, 10–12

Eden, A., 20–3
Egypt, 50, 52, 55, 63, 65, 149, 154
Eisenhower, Lieutenant General, later General D., 49, 74, 78–9, 81–2, 88–9, 91–2, 96, 98–9, 105, 108–10, 117, 123, 125, 129–33, 135–7, 141, 143–4, 152, 218–19, 230, 233, 236, 245–6, 249
Elba, 215

Enna, 114–15
Esperia, 198
Etna, Mount, 106, 114, 119

Factory, The, see Aprilia
Faid, 79, 83
Finale, 239
Florence, 193, 215, 220–1, 223, 251
Foggia, 129, 146, 149, 152, 175, 249
Foglia River, 221, 225
Fondi, 202
Fondouk, 79, 83, 96
Formia, 197–8
Fossa Marina (Canal) 237
Franklyn, Major General H., 13–14
Frascati, 138
Fredendall, Major General L., 88–9
Freyberg, Major General, later Lieutenant General Sir B., 88–9, 93, 95, 168, 170–1, 174–6, 179–80, 190
Frosinone, 210–11

Gabbett, Major R., 196
Gabes, 90, 94–5
Gabes Gap, 90–2, 94, 96–7, 171
Gaeta, Gulf of, 141
Gafsa, 83, 92
Gairdner, Major General C., 107
Gari River, 155, 195
Garigliano River, 146, 155, 158–9, 169, 189, 194, 197
Gela, 112
Gela, Gulf of, 108, 111
Gemmano Ridge, 226–7
Gibralter, 50, 74
Göring, Field Marshal, H., 9, 15, 19
Gort, Lieutenant General Lord, 7, 14, 16, 18–22, 183
Gott, Lieutenant General W., 55
Gothic Line, 217, 220–8
Graham, Lieutenant Colonel M., 60
Greece, 110, 126, 229, 231
Green Hill, see Djebel Azag
Gruenther, Major General A., 174, 208
Guderian, General H., 9, 11, 15–16
Guettar El, 92, 94–6

Gustav Line, 146–8, 151, 154–60, 163–6, 169, 172, 181, 184–6, 190, 192–4, 198–9, 221, 249
Guzzoni, General A., 105, 113

Halder, General F., 9–10, 15
Hammam El, 68
Hangman's Hill, see Point 435
Harding, Major General, later Lieutenant General A.F.:
At GHQ, Middle East, 59–60, 62–3, 66
As Alexander's Chief of Staff, 152, 174, 184–8, 191–2, 213, 217–19, 222–4, 230, 244
Harmon, Major General E., 206, 210
Harwood, Admiral Sir H., 64
Haysom, Wing Commander D., 157
Hitler, Adolf, 8–10, 15–16, 51–2, 74–6, 86–7, 92, 113, 120, 123–4, 126, 131, 136–7, 139, 146, 149, 154, 156, 163, 165–6, 169, 177–9, 184, 194, 202, 213, 217, 219, 220, 236, 238
Hitler Line, 184, 189–90, 198–203, 214
Holland, Campaign in, 7, 9–10
Homs, 80
Hope, Flight Lieutenant Sir A., 23
Horrocks, Lieutenant General Sir B., 93, 95, 99
Howze, Colonel H., 206
Hube, General H., 113, 120, 123
Hunt's Gap, 87
Hutton, Lieutenant General T., 24–5, 28–9

Iida, Lieutenant General S., 26–9, 32, 42
Imola, 227, 229
Imphal, 37, 45–7
Irrawaddy River, 28, 30, 35, 42–43, 45
Itri, 190, 198

Jacob, Colonel Sir I., 36, 55–7, 61, 72

Juin, General A., 89, 157,
    159, 168, 171–3,
    189–90, 194, 196–8,
    201, 211, 213, 219, 223

Kaing, 47
Kairouan 79, 97
Kalewa, 46–7
Karachoum, 79
Kasserine, 85–6, 93
Keightley, Lieutenant
    General C., 226, 236–7
Keith, Flying Officer G., 112
Kesselring, General, later
    Field Marshal A.,
    Character, 78
    In Campaign in Low
        Countries, 7, 9, 19
    Direct Attacks on Malta,
        51–2,
    In Tunisian Campaign, 74,
        76–80, 83–4, 86–7, 92,
        96, 98
    In Sicily Campaign, 105,
        109–10, 113–14, 120,
        123
    Relationship with Italians,
        124, 136
    In Italian Campaigns,
        137–9, 141–2, 145–7,
        149–50, 156–9, 163,
        165, 173, 176–8,
        184–5, 190, 194,
        197–9, 201–5, 207,
        212–13, 217, 219–22,
        225–8, 234–6, 240–1
    Trial of, 252
Keyes, Major General G.,
    151, 158, 189, 199,
    202–3, 211–13, 223,
    227, 229
Kirkman, Lieutenant General
    S., 189, 195–6, 199,
    222–3, 227, 229–30
Kohima, 36–7
Ksar Rhilane, 93, 95

Leclerc, General P., 93
Leeper, Sir R., 231–2
Leese, Lieutenant General Sir
    O.:
    In Tunisian Campaign, 90,
        93–4
    In Sicily Campaign, 106,
        108, 115–16
    In Italian Campaign, 152,
        188–9, 192, 195,
        198–201, 211, 215–19,
        222–5, 227–8, 241
    Post-War, 252
Leghorn, 193, 220

Le Kef, 84–5, 90
Lemelsen, General J., 212
Leonforte, 113–15
Lepini Hills, 191, 205, 211
Libya, 50–1
Li Colli Ridge, 148, 150
Lille, 13, 16
Liri River and Valley, 148,
    151, 155, 158–60, 168,
    172, 174, 179, 184–5,
    189, 196–7, 200, 202,
    210–11
Ljubljana Gap, 217
Longstop Hill, see Djebel el
    Almara
Lucas, Major General J.,
    144, 162–6, 177–8, 181,
    245
Lucca, 215, 226

Mackensen, General E. von,
    149, 166, 169, 177–8
Macmillan, H., 88, 98, 125,
    170, 192, 208, 217,
    231–2, 240, 242, 249,
    251
Magwe, 28–9, 32–3
Mahoney, Major J., 202
Maknassy, 79, 83, 93–4
Malta, 51–2, 69–70, 72, 76,
    97, 110–11, 123, 125,
    145, 249
Mandalay, 24, 36, 45–6
Manstein, General E. von,
    8–10
Mareth Line, 85, 91–2
Mareth Line, Battle of, 93–6
Marshall, General G., 81,
    109, 128, 131, 210, 218,
    240
Martuba, 52, 69, 72, 249
Matmata Hills, 91, 93
McCreery, Major General
    R.,
    As Alexander's Chief of
        Staff, 54, 70, 82, 133,
        244
    In Italian Campaigns, 140,
        143, 158–60, 208, 219,
        228–9, 232
Medenine, 85, 87
Medjerda River and Valley,
    78, 99
Melfa River, 202, 210
Mersa Matruh, 72
Messe, General, later Field
    Marshal G., 87, 91–2,
    96, 100
Messina, 51, 106, 109, 113,
    115–16, 118–22, 192–3,
    213

Messina, Straits of, 105,
    109–10, 113, 123, 131,
    133, 136
Metauro River, 220, 225
Meuse River, 8–9, 11
Mingaladon, 33
Minha, 43
Moletta River, 165
Monte Amaro, 155
Monte Artemisio, 212
Monte Battaglia, 227
Monte Belmonte, 229
Monte Cairo, 155, 168, 171,
    189, 201
Monte Cassino, 155, 160,
    168, 171, 173–6, 179,
    182, 189, 192, 196, 199,
    213, 250
Monte Cifalco, 168, 172
Monte Comino, 147, 151
Monte Corvino, 140–1
Monte Faito, 196
Monte Grande, 229
Monte Majo, 196–7
Montgomery, Major
    General, later Field
    Marshal B.L.:
    Character, 12–13, 18–19,
        184, 188, 252
    In Dunkirk Campaign,
        12–13, 16, 18–19, 248
    In Desert Campaign, 55,
        60–71, 76–8, 80–1, 84,
        143, 248
    In Tunisian Campaign,
        86–7, 92, 94–6, 98–9
    In Sicily Campaign, 106–9,
        112–16, 118–19, 121,
        193, 246
    In Italian Campaign, 131,
        133–6, 141–2, 150–1
    Appointed Land Forces
        Commander for
        OVERLORD, 152–3
    Relationship with
        Alexander, 18, 22, 70,
        76–8, 81, 86, 98–100,
        116, 119, 135–6,
        152–3, 244, 246, 252
Monywa, 46
Morgan, Brigadier, later
    Lieutenant General Sir
    W., 11, 230, 239
Moro River, 148, 150, 154,
    234
Morocco, 2, 74, 153
Morshead, Major General L.,
    64
Mountbatten, Vice Admiral
    Lord L., 25, 105

Mussolini, Benito, 24, 113, 118–19, 124, 129–31, 136, 213, 229, 239
Mussolini Canal, 165
Myittha River, 46

Naples, 129–32, 134, 140–2, 146, 152, 170, 192–3, 231, 249
Nile Delta, 59, 63
Nile River, 60
Normandy, Battle of, 188, 213, 215, 218, 243
Nye, Lieutenant General Sir A., 110

O'Daniel, Major General J., 206, 208
Operational Code Names – Allied:
ANVIL, 188, 218–19
AVALANCHE, 131–2, 135, 140–1, 145
BAYTOWN, 131–5
BUFFALO, 191, 205
DIADEM, 185–8, 190, 192–4, 200, 205, 210, 213, 218, 222–3, 230, 245, 247
DRAGOON, 219
GIANT, 153
GIANT II, 132, 137
GRAPESHOT, 236
HUSKEY, 105–6, 110, 113, 124, 129, 135, 246
OLIVE, 223, 225, 228
OVERLORD, 128–31, 149, 152–3, 184, 188, 205
SHINGLE, 148–9, 151, 158, 160–3
SLAPSTICK, 132
SUPERCHARGE, 70–1
TORCH, 49–50, 69–70, 72, 74–5
Operational Code Names – Axis:
ACHSE (AXIS), 136, 139
SICHELSCHNITT (SICKLE CUT), 7
Oran, 74
Orsogna, 150–1, 154–5
Ortona, 150–1
Orvieto, 215, 222
Oudane el Hachana (Hills), 171

Pachino Peninsula, 107, 112
Paestum, 143
Palermo, 107, 109, 118, 192, 247

Patton, Major General, later Lieutenant General G.:
In Tunisian Campaign, 89, 91–2, 94–6, 98
In Sicily Campaign: 106–7, 109, 112, 114, 116–22, 136, 144, 192–3, 213, 244, 247, 251
Comments on Operation SHINGLE, 162
Pegu, 28–31
Penney, Major General W., 163
Pescara, 138, 148, 150, 185, 213
Petralia, 115
Pico, 190, 198, 200–1
Piedimonte, 190, 200–1
Pin Chaung, 43–4
Pisa, 186–8, 215–17, 251
Po River and Valley, 217–18, 221–2, 232–4, 236, 238–9
Point 102, 68
Point 193, 179–80
Point 435, 179–81
Point 593, 168, 170, 176, 195, 199
Pontecorvo, 202
Ponte Grande, 111
Ponte Olivo, 108
Ponte Sele, 142
Ponte Vecchio, 220
Popoli, 148
Porto Empedolce, 115, 118
Primo Sole, 114
Prome, 36, 41
Pyinmana, 42–3

Qattara Depression, 52, 90

Ramsay, Admiral Sir B., 20, 107
Randazzo, 199–21
Rangoon, 24–33, 41, 47, 248
Rapido River, 155, 158–60, 168, 172, 176–7, 179, 189, 192, 195–6, 198
Ravenna, 225, 228–9
Reggio, 134–5
Reno river, 233, 236–7
Richardson, Major General A., 133, 152
Richardson, Lieutenant Colonel, later Brigadier C., 57, 59, 86, 143–4
Rimini, 186–8, 217, 224–6, 228
Roberts, Lieutenant Colonel G.P.B., 56–7

Robertson, Major General B., 157, 211
Romagna Plain, 224
Rome:
As an Allied Objective, 131–2, 137–9, 145–6, 148, 151, 154–6, 158, 162–3, 168, 181, 184–5, 251
Battle for, 185–212
Capture of, 213, 215, 220, 223, 230, 243
Rommel, Major General, later Field Marshal E.:
At Arras, 14–15
In Desert Campaign, 21, 51–3, 58–9, 62–3, 66–7, 71, 76, 80, 150, 193
In Tunisian Campaign, 83–7, 92, 100
In Italian Campaign, 136–7, 139, 142, 145, 149
Ronco River, 238
Roosevelt, F.D., 81, 124, 218
Route 5, 148, 185
Route 6, 155, 162–3, 168, 185, 189–91, 195, 198–9, 206–8, 210–11, 213
Route 7, 155, 162–4, 189–91, 193, 202, 205–6, 210, 212–13
Route 9, 225, 227–9, 233, 236, 238
Route 16, 233, 237
Route 81, 150
Route 113, 115, 119
Route 120, 115, 119
Route 124, 115
'Rover David', 157, 186, 238
Rundstedt, General G. von, 8–9, 11, 15
Ruweisat Ridge, 67–8

Sacco River, 210–11
Salerno, 136, 139–42, 145–6, 151, 162, 165, 192–3
Salerno, Gulf of, 131–2, 134–5, 140–2, 146
Sakurai, Lieutenant General S., 29, 31–2, 42, 45
San Angelo, 159, 179, 189, 195
San Fratello, 120
Sangro River, 146–8, 150, 154, 221
San Stefano, 113, 118, 120
Santa Oliva, 190, 201
Santerno River, 237

Sardinia, 74, 110, 125, 129, 137
Sbeitla, 83
Sbiba, 85
Scaletta, 122
Scheldt River, 7
Scott, Major General B., 43–4
Seago, E., 243
Sedan, 9
Sele River, 140, 142
Senger und Etterlin, Lieutenant General F. von, 159, 173, 194, 197, 207, 238–9
Senger Line, 201–2
Senio River, 236–7
Sfax, 79, 81, 92, 97
Shan States, 33, 35
Shwegyin, 46–7
Sicily, 51–2, 74, 82, 105–26, 129, 133–4, 136–7, 144, 151, 154, 163, 186, 223, 243, 245–6, 251–2
Sidi Bou Zid, 83
Sidi Nsir, 87
Sidney, Major W., 183
Siena, 231, 251
Simeto River, 113–14
Sittang River, 26, 29, 35, 43, 45
Slim, Lieutenant General W., 36–48, 244–5, 248, 251
Smith, Major General, later Lieutenant General W. Beddell, 108–9, 125
Snake's Head Ridge, 168, 170, 180, 189, 195
Somme River, 15
Sousse, 92, 97
Sperlonga, 202
Sperre General H., 8
Stalingrad, Battle of 76, 82, 100
Stevens–Guile, Captain G., 13
Stilwell, Major General J., 34–5, 37, 41–3, 45, 47, 89
Strong, Brigadier K., 125
Student, General, K., 137, 139, 142
Suez, 52, 59, 67
Sun, Lieutenant General L–J., 44–5
Syracuse, 107, 111–14, 118–19

Takeuchi, Lieutenant General Y., 29
Takonobu, Major S., 31–2

Tanks – Allied:
Churchill 'Crocodile', 233, 236–7
Duplex Drive (Amphibious), 233
Grant, 56
Sherman, 69, 210
Sherman 'Kangeroo', 233, 237
Valentine, 85
Tanks – Axis:
Mark IV Special, 53, 141, 206
Mark V 'Panther', 202, 214, 221
Mark VI 'Tiger', 78, 84, 87, 112, 202, 205, 221
Taormina, 121
Taranto, 131–2, 140–1
Tarhuna, 80
Taukyan, 30–2
Taungdwingyi, 43–5
Taylor, Major General M., 137–8
Tebaga Gap, 91, 95–6
Tebessa, 84–5
Tebourba, 78–9
Tedder, Air Chief Marshal Sir A., 64, 107–9, 123, 125, 142–3, 152
Templer, Major General G., 183–4, 213
Tennant, Captain W., 20–2
Termoli, 147
Terracina, 201–5
Thala, 85, 89
Tharrawaddy, 31–2
Tiber river, 132, 213, 215
Tivoli, 192
Tobruk, 21, 51–2, 56, 62, 80
Toungoo, 35, 41
Trasimene, Lake, 220
'Trident' Conference, 128–9
Trigno River, 147
Tripoli, 51, 74, 76–8, 80–1, 83, 86, 93, 152
Tripolitania, 78–9, 154
Troina, 119–20
Truscott, Major General L., 118, 163, 177–8, 190–1, 193, 199, 203–8, 210–12, 230, 232, 237–8
Tuker, Major General F., 170–6, 181, 244
Tunis, 76–8, 92, 97, 100, 116, 118, 123, 133
Tunisia, 49, 69–70, 76–9, 81–100, 105, 107, 153–4, 171, 186, 243–4, 246, 250

Twingon, 44

'Ultra' Intelligence, 37, 52, 62, 71, 73, 80, 83, 86, 92, 132, 169, 175–6, 181, 193, 207, 213
'Unconditional Surrender' Policy, 124–5
Uso River, 228

Valmontone, 185, 191, 193, 199, 205–12, 246
Velletri, 212
Venice, 224, 236, 239
Via Appia, see Route 7
Via Casilina, see Route 6
Via Emilia, see Route 9
Vienna, 217, 224, 233, 248
Vietinghoff, General H-G. von, 137, 139, 142, 145, 158, 166, 177, 190, 194, 197, 201, 207, 210, 213, 227, 229, 236, 238–9
Viterbo, 193, 215
Vizzini, 115
Volturno River, 131, 147, 153

Wadi Akarit, 90
Wadi Zigzaou, 91, 94
Walker, Major General F., 212
Ward, Major General O., 92–6
Wavell, General Sir A., 24, 28–30, 32, 34, 40–1, 45, 47, 251
West, Sergeant H., 117
Westphal, Lieutenant General S., 138–9, 141, 194
Weygand, General M., 14, 16
Wilder, Lieutenant N., 91
Wilder's Gap, 91, 93
Wilson, General Sir H. Maitland, 82, 152, 230
Wingate, Brigadier, later Major General O., 38–9, 48
Wolff, SS General K., 235, 239

Yalta Conference, 240
Yenangyaung, 29, 34, 42–3, 45
Yin Chaung, 42–3

Ziegler, Lieutenant General H., 83
Zigon, 30, 32

Military Formations and Units

Allied

Fifteenth Army Group, 106, 121, 131, 152, 184–6, 190, 192, 208, 212, 218–19, 222, 229–30, 233, 242, 246
Eighteenth Army Group, 82, 88, 92, 98, 144, 186, 246

British and Commonwealth

First Army, 49, 75, 82, 87, 98, 116
Eighth Army, 50–3, 55–61, 63–72, 78–81, 83–8, 90–100, 106–9, 111–16, 121–2, 131–6, 140, 144–52, 154, 157, 160, 186–9, 192–5, 198–201, 207, 210–11, 215, 218–29, 232–9, 246
Fourteenth Army, 37–8
British Expeditionary Force, 7, 10–22
Burma Army, 25–6, 29–31, 39, 47

I Corps, 11, 13, 18–19, 22
II Corps, 11–13, 18
V Corps, 131–2, 140, 150–1, 188, 226, 236–8
IX Corps, 96, 99
X Corps, 62, 93, 95, 131–3, 140–4, 149, 151, 158–60, 189, 201, 229, 232, 236
XIII Corps, 55, 58, 80, 106, 114, 133, 149, 151, 189, 195, 198–9, 201–2, 222–3, 225, 227, 229–30, 236, 238
XXX Corps, 57–8, 62, 80, 93, 106, 114–15, 119, 133, 149
Burma Corps, 36, 39–42, 45–7
I Canadian Corps, 189, 193, 198–201, 229
New Zealand Corps, 93, 95, 168, 170, 179–80, 188

1st Airborne Division, 114, 132, 139–40, 149
1st Armoured Division, 95, 98–9, 226–8
6th Armoured Division, 97, 99–100, 198, 223, 237–9
7th Armoured Division, 99–100, 144, 149
7th Australian Division, 26
9th Australian Division, 64, 69
1st Burma Division, 35, 42–4
5th Canadian Armoured Division, 202
1st Canadian Infantry Division, 134, 151, 201
51st Highland Division, 66
4th Indian Division, 99, 168, 170–1, 174, 176, 179, 188, 229
8th Indian Division, 150–1, 195, 229, 236–8
10th Indian Division, 188, 238
17th Indian Division, 26–9, 31, 36, 41, 43–5
1st Infantry Division, 10–13, 17–18, 163, 169, 178, 183
3rd Infantry Division, 12
4th Infantry Division, 99, 195–6, 198
5th Infantry Division, 13, 134, 151
44th Infantry Division, 66, 68
46th Infantry Division, 160
50th Infantry Division, 66
56th Infantry Division, 169, 183, 237
78th Infantry Division, 78, 99, 116, 119–20, 147–8, 150–1, 179, 198, 229, 237
2nd New Zealand Division, 70, 93, 95, 150–1, 170, 176, 179–80, 182, 189, 236–8
6th South African Armoured Division, 189, 215, 220, 223, 238–9

7th Armoured Brigade, 28, 30–1, 36, 41, 46–7
9th Armoured Brigade, 237
26th Armoured Brigade, 85
44th Armoured Brigade, 150
1st Burma Brigade, 35
2nd Burma Brigade, 35, 40, 45–6
1st Guards Brigade, 242
201st Guards Brigade, 99
5th Indian Brigade, 179–80
7th Indian Brigade, 179–80
13th Indian Brigade, 36, 46
16th Indian Brigade, 28, 30–1, 46
46th Indian Brigade, 28
48th Indian Brigade, 28–31, 46–7
63rd Indian Brigade, 28, 30–1, 46
3rd Infantry Brigade, 169
11th Infantry Brigade, 78–9
36th Infantry Brigade, 78
128th Infantry Brigade, 87
168th Infantry Brigade, 169
1st Parachute Brigade, 114

2/13th Frontier Force Rifles, 31
1st Gloucestershire Regiment, 31, 46
3rd Grenadier Guards, 13, 17
5th Hampshire, 87
7th Hussars, 28
1st Indian Field Artillery Regiment, 28
1st King's Shropshire Light Infantry, 22
North Irish Horse, 99
3/2nd Punjabis, 2
10th Rifle Brigade, 85
1st Royal Inniskilling Fusiliers, 32
1st Royal Sussex, 100
2nd Royal Tanks, 28
4th Royal Tanks, 14
7th Royal Tanks, 14
Strathcona's Horse, 202
Westminster Regiment of Canada, 202

Blade Force, 78
Force L, 93
Force 141, 107–8, 246
Long Range Desert Group, 91

United States

Fifth Army, 131–2, 135, 140, 142–4, 147–51, 162–3, 168, 175, 186, 189, 192–4, 196–8, 202, 205–11, 215, 218, 222–4, 226–7, 229–30, 232–4, 237–9
Seventh Army, 106, 115–19

II Corps, 74, 79, 83, 88–92, 94–6, 98, 106, 114–15, 117, 151, 158–9, 163–4, 189–90, 196, 202, 205, 211–13, 218, 223, 227, 229, 238

IV Corps, 218, 223, 238
VI Corps, 140, 143–4, 151,
    158, 160–5, 169–70,
    172, 178–9, 190–3, 199,
    206–8, 210–13, 218

82nd Airborne Division, 112,
    131–2, 137–8, 144, 149,
    153, 214
101st Airborne Division, 137
1st Armoured Division, 92,
    94, 159, 165–6, 206,
    210, 238
1st Infantry Division, 92,
3rd Infantry Division, 106,
    163, 178, 205–6, 211,
    218
9th Infantry Division, 95, 99
34th Infantry Division, 96,
    99, 166–8, 192
36th Infantry Division,
    159–60, 190, 192–3,
    199, 212, 218
45th Infantry Division, 117,
    166, 169, 177–8, 218
88th Infantry Division, 227,
    238
10th Mountain Division,
    233, 238
92nd Negro Division, 220,
    229

1st Special Service Force, 205

Others
Belgian Army, 7, 10, 12, 16
Fifth Chinese Army, 33, 45,
    48
Sixth Chinese Army, 33, 45,
    48
Dutch Army, 10
First French Army, 10, 16,
    21–2

XIX French Corps, 79, 89,
    98–9, 158
French Expeditionary Corps,
    158, 166, 189, 196–9,
    211, 218–19
II Polish Corps, 189, 194–5,
    198–201, 236–8

1st Brazilian Division, 220,
    238, 240
38th Chinese Division, 44–5
55th Chinese Division, 45
1st French Motorized
    Division, 197

12th Podolski Lancers, 199

Axis
Army Group Afrika, 87, 92

German
Army Group A, 8–11, 15–16
Army Group B, 7–8, 11, 136,
    142
Army Group C, 8, 149

Fourth Army, 15
Tenth Army, 137, 145–6,
    149, 158, 164, 166,
    185–6, 190, 196–200,
    203–7, 210, 213, 227
Fourteenth Army, 149, 166,
    178, 186, 207, 212–13
Fifth Panzer Army, 79, 87,
    100
Panzerarmee Afrika, 52–3

XIV Panzer Corps, 113, 159,
    194, 196–7

Herman Göring Panzer
    Division, 105, 112, 142,
    159, 165, 194, 205–6,
    212, 219
65th Infantry Division, 150
71st Infantry Division, 196–8
94th Infantry Division,
    196–8
162nd Infantry Division, 226
356th Infantry Division, 227
90th Light Division, 150
7th Panzer Division, 14
10th Panzer Division, 78,
    83–5, 87, 94–5
15th Panzer Division, 83, 85,
    87
16th Panzer Division, 141–3,
    147

21st Panzer Division, 83–5,
    87, 96
26th Panzer Division, 137,
    142, 150, 194, 201, 226
3rd Panzer Grenadier
    Division, 137, 142, 165
15th Panzer Grenadier
    Division, 105, 109, 112,
    115, 142, 194, 197
29th Panzer Grenadier
    Division, 113, 142, 143,
    159, 181, 194, 202–3,
    226
90th Panzer Grenadier
    Division, 150–1, 159,
    181, 194, 198, 228, 238
1st Parachute Division, 113,
    151, 179–80, 239, 251
2nd Parachute Division, 137
4th Parachute Division, 239

Italian
First Italian Army, 87, 91,
    96–7, 100
Sixth Italian Army, 105, 123

Centauro Division, 83, 85,
    92, 95
Livorno Division, 112
Napoli Division, 112

Japanese
Fifteenth Japanese Army, 26

18th Japanese Division, 32
33rd Japanese Division, 29,
    31–2, 41–2, 45
55th Japanese Division,
    29–31, 42
56th Japanese Division,
    32–45

3/214th Japanese Regiment,
    31–2